Seduced by Satan

My Trip Through Hell with a Super Predator Narcissist

Naivea Hope

Commentary by Telsha Edenburgh
"The Tea on NPD and Relationships"

3G Publishing, Inc.
Loganville, Ga 30052
www.3gpublishinginc.com
Phone: 1-888-442-9637

First published by 3G Publishing, Inc. December, 2024.

ISBN: 9781941247945

Printed in the United States of America

Introduction

Hopium – A blending of the words hope and opium. A fictional drug to help one stay hopeful when their relationship is not working out as planned, and personal expectations are being dashed one after another. This fictional drug causes an individual to try many things, including the placement of square pegs into round holes. Hopium is a brain coating substance that gives a person the ability to walk through a sea of red flags and rationalize that they are actually green.

This is the story about the time a perfect storm entered my life. A successful, lonely, middle-aged woman meets the man of her dreams – or so she thought. Unfortunately, he was a narcissist. Some people have never encountered a narcissist, but the narcissist can pick out his or her next victim within a five-minute conversation. They are like an eagle on a cliff that can spot a wandering rodent on the North American plains. There are millions of people in the world with varying degrees of narcissistic personality disorder (NPD), and this story revolves around one of them.

The purpose of this book is edutainment. I want to educate you on the realities of NPD and help you understand this disorder. I will take you on a very disturbing and real four-year journey of my intimate relationship with a cerebral super predator narcissist.

The dialog and statements in this book are true, and, where practical, are the actual spoken words taken from four years of notes, letters, text messages, and audio recordings, during my trip through mental hell. All names, locations and professions have been altered to maintain a semblance of privacy for the many other victims of this particular predator. Some of the actual letters, poems, and rants have been altered for the same reason.

After my ordeal was over, one of the many victims of this predator introduced me to Telsha Edenburgh's channel. Telsha is a popular YouTube content creator and experienced life coach who specializes in NPD. I reached out to Telsha and her content really helped me understand what had just happened to me. I also reached out to a psychologist, a trained expert in NPD, to further understand the medical terms, symptoms, and behaviors of narcissists and their victims.

My healing will be ongoing, as you will come to understand while reading this book. However, I pray this book will bring more awareness to NPD's dangerous effects on anyone that becomes embroiled in its clutches.

I dedicate this book to all the victims of NPD. I dedicate this book to the people who have healed, and to the people who continue to struggle with the aftermath of the trauma imposed on their lives because of a narcissist. May God rest upon you and bring His healing balm to comfort you and remove your pain as He is doing for me.

Naivea Hope

Table of Contents

CHAPTER ONE
JUST ANOTHER CLIENT?

Naivea sat at the desk in her home office. The whole situation was very cringeworthy to her as she fell into a trance, thinking about the last four years of her life. Her mind drifted back to the beginning, four years ago in May, when the phone rang.

"Hi, my name is Darla Staples and I'm the executive administrator for LaDron Enterprises; a multimillion-dollar company in Raleigh, North Carolina. We manufacture and sell custom T-shirts, and our sales force is in need of your expertise, so would you be willing to have a video conference with the CEO to determine whether you're a good match to train our salespeople to better close sales?"

Darla hadn't come up for breath during her spill, but Naivea was interested in what she was saying. "Sure, I'll meet with the CEO and let him or her cross-examine my skills in training salespeople," Naivea said confidently as she retrieved her biography from the computer to send to Darla once the phone conversation was over. "Oh, we already know your skills; you came highly recommended," said Darla. "Mr. LaDron just wants to have a short meet and greet to make sure your style can match the culture of our business." Naivea and Darla chatted a bit about the company's demographics and needs, and they touched on Naivea's abilities and experience. Naivea agreed to the video introduction.

Mr. LaDron seemed a bit stuffy and nonchalant, but Naivea ignored his mannerisms and focused on how she could help his sales team and make a decent profit at the same time. Within days, Naivea and the company executed a contract. The contract outlined a training program for a 25-person sales team with a blend of virtual and in-person sessions that were aimed at improving closing rates on purchase opportunities presented to potential clients.

The first thing Mr. LaDron wanted to do was introduce his sales team to Naivea to make sure they understood she was in charge, and that they had to follow her lead. The other purpose for the initial video conference with Naivea and the team was to see how she handled them; was she able to control the meeting and maintain order? The initial meeting with Naivea and the sales team was a tremendous success! The team seemed to bond with Naivea as she shared her experience of going from zero sales to closing every sales opportunity that she had for over a year. As she shared her experience, Naivea's overall business savvy also impressed Mr. LaDron. He started thinking of other ways that Naivea could help grow his sales.

Soon after the initial meeting, Naivea received a text message from Darla asking her when she would have time to get on a three-way call with Mr. LaDron and herself regarding collaborating on other business projects. Naivea agreed to a call the next day, and as Darla was mostly quiet during the call, Mr. LaDron and Naivea talked about various ways they both could increase their income through joint ventures in sales and marketing. Mr. LaDron didn't seem stuffy anymore now that the meeting with the sales team went well. He seemed like a down-to-earth businessman that was all about growing a legacy.

The next week, Naivea was busy on her treadmill and the phone rang. "Hi Naivea, this is Charles LaDron. How are you today?" Naivea was shocked as she stopped the treadmill and moved towards the bench press machine to sit down. "I'm doing great Sir, how are you?" "Oh, I was just thinking about you and the things we discussed last week, and wanted to give you a call to see how you felt about us writing a sales and marketing book together." Naivea was stunned! This millionaire was asking to partner with her on a project. "I'm sure he has connections with a lot of the well-known sales and marketing gurus," she thought. However, she didn't want to question him and make him think she didn't have the confidence to move in the circles in which he moved. "I think that would be fantastic!" Naivea exclaimed, smiling ear to ear. "Okay, let's make it happen," said Mr. LaDron. "I'll email you a schedule of my available times and days during the week and we can talk about meeting at least once a week to get started." Naivea agreed.

Mr. LaDron intrigued her, and once the call ended, she thought to herself, "Who is this man, really?" She went on social media to see what she could find. He didn't have a large social media presence, but he had Facebook and LinkedIn pages. She noticed on his LinkedIn page that he was 41 years old, and his Facebook picture made him look like he was a very flippant type of guy. Naivea thought to herself, "I'm almost five years older than he is and he has done well for himself to be so young. I will definitely be able to glean from his experience and grow my business and my brand."

June came along, and Mr. LaDron seemed really interested, not only in Naivea helping his sales team grow, but also in helping Naivea position herself as the go-to expert in sales closures all over the country. At least twice a week the two were on the phone sharing ideas and strategies about business growth. Naivea had already published a few books, but she had been working on a new sales book catered towards people and businesses that sold coaching packages. She was told by one of her mentors that if she could break into the world of helping coaches sell their packages, she would have an endless supply of business.

As Naivea was finishing up the book, she shared it with Mr. LaDron. "I like the content," he said, "but the cover you selected is very off-putting. Let me get my administrative staff to create you an exciting but professional looking cover." "Sure thing," Naivea answered, as she knew by now, based on the marketing brochures and videos that Mr. LaDron and his administrative staff created for his business, that the cover would be top-notch. In three days, Mr. LaDron presented the book cover to Naivea, and she adored it! Her book came out in mid-July and sales were incredible!

For the rest of the summer and through October, Naivea and Mr. LaDron developed a close business relationship and then a friendship. They started off always talking about business-related topics, but by October they were sharing parts of their lives. For example, they talked about their failed marriages, their children and their religious beliefs. Naivea, although she was single, abandoned any thoughts of a deeper relationship with Mr. LaDron. For one thing she was almost five years older than him. "I think he opens up to me because he looks at me like a big sister that isn't trying to get his money or get into his pants," she told herself. The other reason Naivea didn't have any aspirations for a relationship with Mr. LaDron was because she was in Denver with one child still living at home, and he was in Raleigh. Naivea never had a long-distance relationship, and the people in her life that had them at one time or another had negative results. She was satisfied that she had someone with a multimillion-dollar business that cared about her business growth, and she continued to train his sales force so that he could continue to grow.

CHAPTER TWO
COULD HE REALLY WANT ME?

October brought the chilly nights to Denver, and November brought along "coat weather." Naivea's house was large, so she placed space heaters on each floor so that she could keep the gas bills low. As she would settle down in her room at night, she found herself wishing that Mr. LaDron would call. She never called him; partly because she knew he was a busy man and she didn't want to be seen as a pest, but also because she didn't want him to think that she was interested in him beyond their current friendship. "If he thinks that I want him then he'll look at me with pity because he has access to younger prettier women all day long. I must make sure that he never thinks I want more from this relationship." Naivea was bent on convincing herself that Mr. LaDron was not the man for her so that she wouldn't spend time thinking about him romantically.

Earlier in the year, their phone calls were only during the day, but as the months passed the calls became more frequent and were at all times of the day and night. Mr. LaDron turned out to be a night owl, and he started to call Naivea at midnight Eastern time/10 p.m. Mountain time regularly. He declared that nobody was trying to get his time that late, and it was still early enough that Naivea was up and able to chat while he wasn't being constantly interrupted.

One chilly night during the first week of November, Naivea was driving home from a church meeting and Mr. LaDron called. "Hi Naivea, do you have a few minutes to talk?" Mr. LaDron hadn't called in a week, so Naivea quickly answered, "yes," as she pulled into her garage and closed the door. She didn't want to make any noise getting out of the car and opening the door to the house, so she stayed in the car and put her phone in speaker mode.

Mr. LaDron proceeded to take a deep breath and start talking. "Naivea, I really like you, and you've grown to be an important person in my life. I like your professionalism as well as your dry humor. I've been spending this time getting to know your brain and your brilliance. I like the fact that you've raised two children that are doing well, and that you stayed in your marriage as long as you could, enduring the things that you were put through. I feel that you care more about me than shows in our professional relationship. I've been married before and I have had many relationships with women. But you're different; you create and build and grow. You're amazing! I see you as a very powerful feminine woman. Your maturity, seriousness and care, along with your tenacity and spiritual values have led me to pray to the Father. That's why I haven't called you in a week. Tonight, I was released by God to ask you if you would be interested in starting a romantic relationship with me with the intent that it will lead to marriage."

Naivea was breathless! She felt like she was in a dream. Although she had attempted to train her mind not to think of Mr. LaDron in a romantic way, she knew those feelings were there. "I don't know what to say," was the first thing that came out of Naivea's mouth, followed by, "Yes, I would be interested in positioning myself to be your wife." A quick thought to remind him of the age difference jetted through her mind. But she knew how methodical and pragmatic he was, so she let that thought keep passing by. "Evidently, he's not concerned about me being so much older than him," she said to herself. She sat in the car for another two hours as Charles shared stories of his upbringing, his goals for the business, and his desire for a marriage that would last a lifetime.

Naivea was so astounded that she sat there and sucked in every word that Charles uttered, like a thirsty gazelle during the short rains of the Serengeti. "I know I've said a lot tonight, and although you said yes to a romantic relationship, I want you to sleep on it and I'll call you tomorrow evening after I finish at the office and we'll talk more, okay?" Naivea was spellbound. "Okay Charles." For the first time, she didn't feel uncomfortable calling him by his first name. As she hung up the phone she said a prayer, "*Lord, I thank you for this blessing. For years I've been taking care of everything and everybody else, from my children and parents to my friends and folks at the church. Now I'll finally have somebody that's gonna love and take care of me! Praise You!*" Life for Naivea changed on that cool November night, and from that night on she would never be the same.

CHAPTER THREE
THE THRILL OF DATING AGAIN!

Naivea usually slept till 9:30 a.m. every morning, but she was up at 7 a.m., unsure about what time Charles would call. She was pretty sure he wouldn't call at 9 a.m. Eastern time, but she didn't want to take a chance on being asleep in case he did call that early. She couldn't get much work done that day, as her mind rapidly wandered from happy thoughts of being a wife again, to sad thoughts of leaving her children and grandson to move to Raleigh, to how her business would change once they were married.

Naivea was not one to cook. Although she didn't eat fast food, she ate out regularly, and only cooked a few dishes that she happened to learn because she liked them. Her restaurant bill was five figures annually as she made sure she ate at restaurants that only served healthy food, but those restaurants were usually very expensive. "I would rather spend that time making money instead of toiling over a stove," she told her friends and family when they came over and saw an empty refrigerator. She was good at making tuna though. It was easy, nutritional and her grandson loved it. She wondered what Charles would think about her not being a great cook since they never discussed that topic.

When Charles called, it was early evening, and he was very upbeat. "What was your day like today?" Naivea smiled as she answered. "I didn't get much work done wondering how you would feel about certain aspects of my life – like the fact that I don't often cook." "Oh, I definitely like good food, and I'm used to gourmet cooking, but we'll talk about those things later," Charles brushed off her non-cooking comment. "So do you think you could love me?" he jokingly asked Naivea. "Yes, I'm sure I can and will," she answered with confidence. "So, let's do this," Charles said, as if talking about starting to build a new building.

For the next few days Charles and Naivea talked at least twice a day, once during the workday when he called to check on her, and again late at night, when they talked for at least two hours until one of them got extremely sleepy. One night Charles was in a question-and-answer mood. "Who is your favorite musical artist or group?" he asked Naivea. She didn't hesitate to answer, "You've probably never heard of them but they're a classical instrument group called 'The Piano Guys,' and they are very nontraditional." Naivea's answer was met with silence for a few seconds. "I know 'The Piano Guys,' and I really like them," Charles said in a surprised voice as he started to name his favorite songs by the group.

"Wow, I'm pleasantly surprised!" said Naivea. "Their music is not your typical music. It calms my soul and keeps me going when I'm down. We have something very special in common because the average person isn't going to like nor listen to them." Charles chuckled a little, "You'll come to realize that I am not the average person. I have many stressful days, and their music also keeps me focused and helps me bring order to my day." Naivea knew that she had met her soulmate. This obscure musical group was not on most people's radar, and the fact that Charles liked them as much as she did meant they could easily live in harmony.

Other things that the couple had in common were the fact that neither of them liked animals, they both liked science fiction movies, and they both loved sweets. Naivea knew that Charles ran a successful business, but during the first week of their courtship she learned that he owned a Mercedes-Maybach S, a Land Rover Range Rover, and a BMW X7 that he let his friends and family use when they were in town. She learned that he lived in a gated community in a six-bedroom house with a three-car garage and he had invested in a few other businesses in which he was a silent partner.

Naivea also learned that Charles moved from his home in Portland, Oregon when he was 25, and started a consulting business helping teachers deal with unmotivated high school students. That business grew, and he later started the T-shirt business when he realized that what the teachers wore to class had a profound effect on how the students acted during the day.

Another thing Naivea learned is that his three-year marriage to a woman named Rachel had been over for thirteen years, and since then he had dated a few women. He said he didn't marry any of those women because he felt that they wanted him for his money and not for who he was. His last relationship ended over three years ago. Naivea knew that Charles knew she didn't want his money. "I'm older and mature, I have assets and my own money, so he knows it's not his money that I want – it's him and his beautiful brilliant being," she professed as she lay in her bed after their nightly talks. During some of their nightly talks, Charles would ask Naivea detailed questions about her previous relationships before her marriage. He seemed very interested in the fact that she didn't have many boyfriends before her marriage, and that she was very traditional and very shy when it came to talking about sex. She proclaimed she wasn't a virgin when she got married, that she was very selective in who she had sex with, and she'd never had a one-night stand or had sex with someone that she wasn't in a long-term relationship with.

One morning, during the second week of November, at 10 a.m. Denver time, Charles called, and he seemed to be in a hurry. "I just called to let you know that I have to take a trip out to Portland to stay with my mom till the end of the year. Since dad passed away, the three of us boys have a schedule to where Clarence and Calvin take care of her January through October, and I take over in November and December because business is slow here and my administrative staff can handle things while I'm away. Her health has been deteriorating, so every year I fly out and stay till the new year to give them a break." Naivea remembered Charles telling her that he had an older brother named Clarence Jr. that was a longshoreman at the Port of Portland, and a younger brother named Calvin that was a high-school teacher for the Portland City Schools. She thought it was great that they worked as a team to take care of their aging mother, and that Charles took the time to physically go back home to help. She remembered him saying that since he couldn't spend much time out there because of the business, he contributes much more money to his mother's care, and his brothers were fine with that.

Charles left for Portland that evening, and the two talked a little less often for the rest of the year. Naivea knew that Charles would be busy with his mother at the family's Portland home, but since getting there, the conversations were shorter, and he kept proclaiming that he had to be quiet so as to not wake his mom. Naivea missed their long talks filled with laughter, but she understood that he was on a mission, and she was satisfied that he called her every few days.

Christmas season came up quickly because Naivea was in a world of bliss over her new relationship. She had been divorced for five years and only had one short relationship after the divorce that didn't work out because the gentleman had a vastly different mindset from hers. He didn't have many goals and aspirations, and he liked to watch a lot of sports on television, which Naivea thought was a waste of time for people that weren't financially independent. Long ago, her mentor taught her that if she wasn't earning $10,000 a month, she had no business watching TV, so she gave up all television to concentrate on business growth. Naivea and the gentleman parted as friends, and it had been four years since she had any relationship at all.

She felt so blessed to finally have someone she could look up to, share deep thoughts with, and love like she had never loved anyone before. She had felt abandoned by her ex-husband, Harold, because of his adultery; and when she discussed her marriage with Charles, he assured her that he wasn't like that. One day when Charles was asking Naivea about her marriage she told him that Harold started cheating six months after they got married, and that she didn't find out until five years later. "You will never be able to say that Charles LaDron betrayed you," Charles said to Naivea assuredly as she finished talking. Immediately, Naivea began to weep.

Waves of emotion came from what seemed like nowhere as she pulled the phone away from her, trying to make sure Charles didn't hear her, but that gesture didn't help; he could hear the sobbing and they both realized that the pain she felt from Harold's regular infidelity cut deep. Charles comforted Naivea, "It's okay Babe, let it out." Naivea composed herself and told Charles that she wanted to lie down, and they ended the conversation.

Charles called early in the day a week before Christmas. "I want to get you something special for Christmas. You know I've been attentive in our conversations, and I remember that you said you wear out shoes like a hot rod wears out tires, so I want to get you some of the best shoes on the planet. What size do you wear?" "Why thank you!" Naivea said as she grinned from ear to ear. "I wear a size 8." "Okay, look for your gift in three days." "What should I get you?" Naivea asked Charles quickly before they got off the phone, as she could tell he was in a hurry. "Oh, you can be creative, but if you are afraid to mess up, I'll text you a few suggestions to choose from." "I'd like that," she said with relief. Naivea hadn't really thought about exchanging gifts, and since she felt like Charles had everything, based on their conversations, she was glad that she would be able to still surprise him with one of the suggestions that he would send.

Charles' gift came on time, and Charles asked her not to open it until Christmas morning. Meanwhile, Naivea had ordered Charles an expensive bottle of cologne, which was one of the three suggestions he had sent her. His gift was due to arrive the day before Christmas, and she ordered a beautiful card to go with it.

Christmas came and Naivea slept in because she and her children had been baking desserts and playing Christmas music late into the night. When she got up it was 10 a.m., so she opened her box so that she could take a picture with the shoes on and send it to Charles. She hadn't really thought about what type of shoes he bought her, or whether they would fit, but when she opened the box, she discovered a pair of Manolo Blahnik black pumps. Naivea had never heard of this brand, so she looked them up online and discovered that these shoes cost $1,145! "Wow," she exclaimed as she stared at the shoes on the website. She put on the pumps with a nice dress. They fit like comfortable gloves on her feet. She quickly snapped a selfie and sent it to Charles as she thought to herself, "Am I going to ever get used to this kind of luxury?" Naivea was the type of person who would shop at consignment shops to save money for things she thought were more important, like taking exotic vacations with her family.

Charles finally responded to the picture with a call a couple of hours later. "Sorry for the delay Babe. Me and my brothers were opening gifts with mom." "That's okay. I want to thank you for the beautiful shoes, and I hope you liked your gift and the picture," Naivea blushed as she thought of the care and thoughtfulness that went into selecting the shoes for her. Charles lowered his voice to sound deep and sexy, "Yes, I like the picture and the cologne, but I want an extra gift tonight. I want to see you in those shoes without the dress, or any clothes." Naivea was shocked. She had never taken a nude picture before, not even in her marriage. She was silent for what Charles thought was a long time. "What? Are you going to deny your future husband a peek at his future bride?" "Oh," Naivea said in a worried voice, "I've never taken a nude picture before, but if you hide it, I'll work myself up to do it." "Don't be shy, my love, you have a beautiful body, and I won't show anyone the picture," Charles said in a reassuring voice. "I have to go now because we are about to have lunch, but I'll wait up all night for my picture," he said as he chuckled and hung up the phone.

Naivea was still a little perplexed that he would want a nude picture, but she rationalized that since he was going to be her husband and he said he would never betray her, she would take the picture. Late Christmas night, she worked up the courage, put on the new shoes, and snapped her first of many nude pictures for her man. When she texted it, he didn't respond immediately, and she got really nervous. However, within ten minutes he texted her back with hearts and smiley faces, and a text saying, "You are really beautiful inside and out! This was the best Christmas gift that I received!" Naivea was relieved that he responded, and she quickly erased the picture from her phone so nobody would see what she had done.

Chapters 1-3 Commentary
The Tea on NPD and Relationships
Telsha Edenburgh

In Chapter One, what was happening was that Charles was showing his altruistic persona, which is one of the dimensions or characteristics of a narcissist. What they like to do is observe a deficit in your life so that they can create a mask that fits the deficit.

In Naivea's situation, he became an altruistic knight in shining armor to charm her and help her with her business. His aim was to win her confidence, trust, and loyalty. Naivea thought Charles was going to be just another client, but she was actually walking into the gateway to hell.

One thing about a narcissist's cunning in the beginning is that the victim usually has no clue that this person is studying them to find out how to take control of their mind, will, and emotions. In the beginning, it looks like it's something that's heaven sent – he or she is all you ever needed, and what you've been waiting on for a long time. That's what those backwards-walking giraffes want the relationship to look like because it makes it so hard for you to turn it down. They make it hard for you to turn away from them because they are pretending to provide something that is so desperately needed in your life.

At the beginning of the relationship, the narcissist wants to be everything that you need, because they feel like you're everything that they need – until you tell them NO. If you tell them NO, that's when everything goes out the window, and you become the worst person in all of humanity; and it goes south from there.

In Chapter Two, Charles' mask is perfectly fit to his face, and he is showing off a personality that Naivea is being drawn to like a magnet. When the narcissist perfects the masks for their Supply, the Supply will not be able to tell the difference between the narcissist and the persona. The narcissist wants to keep the fact that they are wearing a mask a total secret.

In this chapter, Charles is assessing Naivea. He's doing what we call a SWOT Analysis in the business world. He is assessing Naivea's strengths and weaknesses. At the same time, he's assessing his opportunities to use her as a Supply, and he is looking for any threats that may harm him, his plan, or his reputation should she find out who he really is.

To make this assessment, the narcissist will ask lots of questions about your background and what has taken place in your life – good and bad. What they are doing is assessing how they think you will respond in the situations that they will place upon you during the relationship. For example, if the questions they ask reveal that you have a very violent past and you will break things and fight when you get angry, they will likely end the relationship before it gets started, because they are concerned that (1) you won't tolerate any abuse from them, and (2) if you later find out who they really are, you may cause severe injury to them.

The narcissist also wants to find out how much physical and emotional pain you've experienced in the past because they want to determine your threshold for pain. To accomplish this task, he or she will run small tests in between periods of bliss, just to appraise your tolerance level or any opposition that you will pose to what they want to do to you and with you.

Some of these small tests include veering off the schedule just a little bit – like being late to pick you up for dinner or changing plans at the last minute with no valid excuse – embedding subtle differences in what you all had planned, to see how you respond and to see how far they can go with you and potentially how long. In our story, Charles was asking lots of questions to open Naivea up just to see where he could go with her.

Also, in our story, the long distance was an advantage for Charles, because in this situation, distance made it very easy for him to hide his real self. Naivea didn't see him daily, weekly, or even monthly, so Charles had the liberty to do just about anything he wanted to do, and when he was on the phone or on FaceTime with Naivea, he could put his mask back on without being revealed as a hypocrite.

The long-distance relationship is something that, for most narcissists, especially if they are managing more than one Supply, works out perfectly because the distance gives them the ability to be themselves up to 90% of the time, instead of having to "code switch" more often from the mask to themselves and back. Because Naivea was so far away, Charles could put her on a schedule, knowing that she couldn't just hop in her car and come to his house at any time of the day or night.

Another narcissistic aspect to this chapter is the quick invitation into the relationship. That haste was basically to pull Naivea's emotions into himself as soon as possible. The faster he proclaimed a relationship, the faster he could win her trust and loyalty. After he found out that Naivea was useful to him, after he found out that she could work in more than one area for him, he wanted to lock her down emotionally, because to lock her down emotionally is to also gain access to all the strengths and opportunities that she had as well. Locking her down didn't just give Charles inroads to Naivea emotionally, it gave him green light access to every single part of her, because he was now in her emotional realm, which means that he was creating what we call a soul tie.

Further, Charles revealed early on that he wanted to be in a relationship with Naivea. That invitation came fairly quickly. And the reason I say "fairly quickly" is because the two of them were on two different sides of the country, which meant that it would be difficult for them to see each other on a regular basis. In my opinion, six months is a quick time frame to ask someone to be in a relationship when you know you won't be able to see them on a regular basis. This quickness is part of the emotional overhaul, of course, to gain access to her soul, her mind, her will and her emotions.

Once the narcissist gets access to your emotions, your mind is now going to be consumed with the relationship and the well-being of it. And then your mind begins to control your will—which even if you wanted to think that something was wrong or something was off—because your mind has now been consumed with this thing, and it's going to control your will to back up.

So at this point, Naivea's will is in the process of being subdued by her emotions and her mind, because now the narcissist is occupying both spaces and he's getting ready to now occupy her will, too. This is the whole game of manipulation when that invitation for the relationship was extended. Because eventually what they ultimately want to do is control your entire existence.

In Chapter Three, Charles really starts to ramp up on the love bombs. Here, what you see is love bombing at its finest. Do you remember the extravagant gift that he gave Naivea for Christmas? Not only was he love bombing, but he was future-faking as well. The love bomb and future-faking are a powerful combination that Charles was using in this particular chapter.

Love bombing and future-faking literally coat the brain with what we call mind blocking and mind blinding spirits. Unfortunately, some people think that witchcraft and spells are just about potions and things like that, when they're not. A lot of times a spell can be cast on an individual just by the repetition of words, which is literally what he was doing in this chapter. It was almost like his conversations were causing Naivea to be spellbound because of the love bombing, the future-faking, and the manipulation through the invitation into a relationship.

For example, Charles was saying that he likes good food, but he brushed by the fact that Naivea can't cook. He surely took note of her deficiency so that it could be used against her later in the relationship. As a narcissist, Charles will build up an arsenal of her shortcomings and throw them back up in her face over time, each time causing Naivea to immediately think that she's inadequate.

The love bombing and the future-faking are one thing, but also in the love bomb stage comes the sarcasm, and this is what we see starting in Chapter 3. Normally the narcissist likes to start with the sarcasm early on; so there are slight sarcastic remarks, which is what is happening in this situation. If he knows that Naivea can't cook, he'll say he likes good food. And because she had already been honest and told him she couldn't cook, now he had something to make her feel inadequate, causing her to want to make up the deficit in other areas. For example, Naivea may have decided to stay up all night working on a project for Charles because she is not a good cook and wanted to offset that weakness.

When you see the love bomb and the future-faking together, along with the sarcasm, that's a recipe for complete and total control; and for the victim, it's a road to disaster. The Supply will find themselves in a dark, lonely pit really quickly because the narcissist is getting everything. They're getting the high off the love bomb, and what the Supply feels when everything is going on, is mentally, emotionally, and spiritually draining. Take note: the future-faking and the love bombing are really part of the abuse pattern as well.

Expensive gifts, like the designer shoes, are the extents that these narcissists will go to because if you've never had those types of things, after your hurt feelings about their sarcasm subsides, they're going to go back to being that superhero, wanting to give you things that you've never had. The key is to test the vulnerability of the Supply, and how much she trusts him. A lot of times what happens is, especially in Naivea's case, when he asked for a very personal item—like the nude picture—that is to test her vulnerability and to see how much she trusts him. Asking for a nude picture is also to see how much she idolized him.

People don't understand that fact, because that's something we often miss, but he was testing her to see if she really cares for him, or to find out if he is really on that pedestal in her life. So, when that picture was given to Charles, it confirmed and validated that Naivea literally saw him like some type of God because she explained that the nude picture was something that she had never done before.

Now, with the expense of gift giving, of course, he's showing off his materialistic side because narcissists with money, especially in this case, are very materialistic. They like money, they like labels, and they like toys and things. So, most of the time, if they have money like this, they're going to woo you, love bomb you, and future-fake you with nice, expensive gifts, which is what he did, because he's a very materialistic individual. They do this also by bragging about their assets: how many investments they have and the size of their investment portfolios. In his case, he's telling Naivea about his homes, his cars, and his business, as well as how much money he's actually making. All of that is to make her feel like she really has a prize in him – to make her feel like she can never leave this person because this person has everything she would ever want.

Also, in Chapter Three, where he was taking care of his mom, he was going into basically what we call a time blocking situation. He had created a situation, which is usually a lie (a fake situation), where he was going to care for a family member. Often times, the Supply is never really able to validate the story. In this case, Naivea may not have been able to confirm that there was actually a family member being taken care of, but the narcissist will create a situation for them to be away for extended periods of time, which is what he did, in order to basically spend time doing other things, even being with another Supply. At the same time, Naivea was just supposed to believe Charles and not ask any questions, and that's the way that they do it. The Supplies they select are usually very honest individuals, and they are not expecting the narcissists to be such profound liars. Unfortunately, they are such cunning liars that the Supply has no reason to doubt these well thought out stories.

In this case, the time blocking to care for his mother between November and January is what he used to keep Naivea in a state of mystery about him. Narcissists like to be mysterious; they want people to wonder about them in a positive way. They like to play "hard to figure out" and that's the space Naivea was in during the year-end holidays.

Another point about the gifts: one other reason that a narcissist love bombs the Supply is for them to never forget him or her, and for the Supply to always have those things around. The narcissist wants you to be able to look at those gifts so that, through the gifts, the narcissist will continually maintain real estate in your mind. So, every time you look around in your house at the things that he or she purchased for you, the narcissist is going to constantly be on your mind, because the whole game in this whole situation is that he or she continues to occupy real estate in your mind long after the relationship is over.

The pair of shoes Charles gave Naivea was very expensive, and she is likely not going to just throw them out or give them to charity. In many cases, the longer the relationship lasts, the more gifts (and it could possibly be a truckload of items) there are to get rid of if the Supply was determined to discard the items. For the Supplies that decide to keep the gifts, the narcissist is still with them in their minds, as long as the gifts are still present.

CHAPTER FOUR
WHAT IS A MARRIAGE?

January came at last, and Charles returned to Raleigh. Charles and Naivea started where they left off – with daytime calls to just say hi, and long nighttime conversations to build their relationship. Charles didn't provide a timeline for their marriage as Naivea thought he would in January. What he did was challenge Naivea on what a marriage really is. "Marriage as we know it hasn't existed for long," Charles said in a lecturing voice. "The government wasn't in charge of marriage until recently. People got married when they decided to commit their lives to one another, and the marriage was consummated when they had sex.

Naivea had heard this before from some of her college friends that didn't believe in letting the state get involved in marriages. She gave it some thought but wasn't convinced about the topic either way. However, Charles was like her college friends – one of those opposed to the state being involved in marriage. He had a child before he was married, back in Portland when he was 19, and Tabitha, that child's mother, still had him tied up with a child support case even though the child was now 22 years old. In addition, when he divorced his first wife at 28, the courts gave her full custody and demanded that he pay an exorbitant amount of child support even though the ex-wife was not letting him visit the child. Charles was determined to beat the odds, and that's one of the reasons he said he was so prolific in business. He found ways to shield his money so that the courts would not rob him blind; and he was determined that when he married again the government wouldn't be involved.

Naivea had a decision to make. Either she would end the relationship with Charles because he didn't want a government marriage license, or she would research and find a way for them to be legally married without the state. She chose the latter. Naivea researched the Bible and found that in biblical times people were bound to one another, and ceremony or not, there was a marriage once the sexual act took place. The most convincing stories featured Jacob, who had to marry Leah after mistakenly having sex with her instead of Rachel, as well as the story of Tamar, King David's daughter, who couldn't marry after being raped by her half-brother Amnon because she was legally bound to her deceased husband Er.

To support this evidence, Naivea found that many people married through a covenant contract that was signed by the couple, their lawyers, and witnesses. The couple then filed that same covenant marriage contract with the clerk of the court in their state to make the contract legal and allow each spouse to receive benefits if the other passed away. She was satisfied that the marriage covenant contract route would satisfy Charles because the state would not be involved. Even though he was pleased with her research, Charles clarified he didn't want to rush things. He spoke about his past mistakes, and although he wanted their relationship to be exclusive, he also wanted to make sure the couple got to know each other very well before committing to one another in marriage. Naivea felt that she was ready for marriage, but she had to cool her heels and take that time to learn as much as she could about Charles so that she could be a good wife.

January, February and March were like a whirlwind to Naivea. She and Charles talked constantly, getting to know everything there was to know about each other. Charles asked a thousand questions and Naivea readily answered. "You seem to have a wall up, Naivea," Charles said one day while Naivea was busy washing clothes. "Why is it that you are so closed to love?" Naivea thought about it for a while. "In high school I had a long relationship with one of the guys at the school that lasted off and on all the way through high school. When it was time to graduate, he came to tell me that he chose to be with another girl because I was going away to college. He was my first love, and I cried for three days, even while I was at work after school. I finally made up my mind that I would never let anyone get that close to my heart, and I haven't. Even with all of his adultery, my husband wasn't able to break my heart like that."

Naivea hadn't really thought about the origin of her hard-heartedness, but Charles was surely brining out some deep-seeded psychological trauma. "Babe, you've got to let that wall come down. You won't be able to love me the way I need to be loved if you don't, and in turn, my love for you can't grow and develop." Naivea thought about what Charles said, and she made the decision to tear the wall down and expose her heart to Charles.

In February, Charles started sending Naivea pictures of his home. "You don't have to do that Charles," Naivea said shyly. "No, I want to. It's important for our development and growth. Besides, when you come to Raleigh, you'll feel comfortable, having seen everything already," Charles said rather authoritatively. By the end of February, the couple made plans to finally see each other in person in early April. Charles was scheduled to attend a business conference in Phoenix, Arizona on the first of April, so he booked an extra leg of the flight from Raleigh to Phoenix, then to Denver for a week, before returning to Raleigh. They found a nice hotel, not too far from Naivea's home, and she couldn't wait to see him.

When both of them were busy, they would text each other throughout the day. "Watcha doin'," asked Naivea. "Missing you," texted Charles. Each morning and night, Naivea started sending Charles love memes. She would spend time finding cute, witty, morning and night love memes, placing them into folders for future use. Then, she would send them every morning when she got up, and every evening before she went to sleep. Naivea even sent them when they talked on the phone for hours.

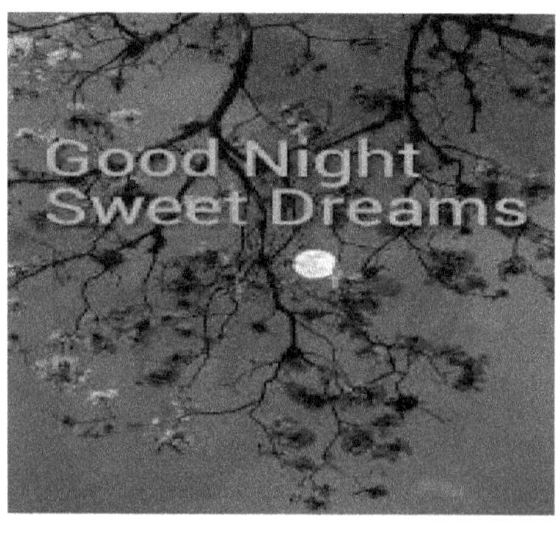

Aside from Naivea's love for their quality time on the phone together, Charles was a prolific gift giver. Not only did he buy Naivea the Manolo Blahnik shoes for Christmas, but for Valentine's Day he showered her with several gifts, including a designer purse with matching wallet, and two Wacoal sports bras because she mentioned that she didn't have separate exercise bras. Naivea was delighted with all his gifts. "You'd better get used to it," Charles said with pleasure. "I'm going to shower you with gifts until your house is running over!"

Charles wasn't really subtle about the fact that he liked Naivea to send him nude pictures of herself. He always proclaimed that the pictures kept his mind on her and away from the other women that were sometimes in his environment. Although she still felt hesitant taking the pictures, she did it whenever he asked because she wanted to please her future husband and keep his eyes on her. It took some time, but eventually she was less and less shy about taking and sending the photos.

The end of March came and Naivea was a nervous wreck. In an effort to prove her worth as a wife, she meticulously cleaned her house, had the carpet professionally cleaned, and even detailed her car. She made sure the lawn care company was prepared to cut the grass the day before Charles came so that the entire house was perfect. She kept the house tidy and even cleaned up as soon as visitors left. With every passing day, she eagerly waited for April 4th – the day he would arrive in Denver from the Phoenix conference.

On April 3rd at 4 p.m. the phone rang. Naivea knew it was Charles because she had programmed her phone with a special ringtone that was only for him. She knew the conference was going to be over that day and she was excited to hear from him. "Bad news, Babe," Charles said with a sad voice. "One of my administrative staff members broke her leg this morning in my warehouse, so I'm cutting my trip short and going back to Raleigh tonight." Naivea was devastated! "Oh, okay," she muttered as tears streamed down her face. "I'll make it up to you soon," Charles said as he quickly got off the phone.

Naivea sat there at her desk in disbelief. She had waited for this visit since that day in November when the relationship started. "When will he come now? How did she break her leg? Will she try and sue him?" All of these thoughts rushed through her mind as the tears rushed down her face. Naivea went to her bedroom and laid down. She couldn't continue to work. She fell asleep and woke up at 8 p.m., put on her pajamas, and got back in bed.

The next day was very hard for Naivea as she got up and looked all over her clean house, looked at her clean car, and looked at her fresh cut grass. "How could this happen to me?" she thought. She tried to get some work done but found herself on an emotional rollercoaster from anger to sadness to concern to prayer all day. Charles didn't even call on the day that he was supposed to see Naivea for the first time. That made her angry, and then worried; but she didn't want to call because calling might look like she was not concerned with the employee. Charles finally called on April 5th. "Hi Babe, I went to see Wendy at the hospital. Her family was there, and I took flowers. She was doing fine. I didn't ask her what happened. I didn't feel it was appropriate." "I agree. It wouldn't have been appropriate to ask any questions right then," Naivea chimed in, trying not to sound like she really felt.

"I'm going to go back to the hospital Sunday if she's still there, just to make sure her and her family know that I am a caring boss." Charles sounded like he was trying to pacify Naivea, but at the same time, he didn't mention rescheduling their visit. "I think that's a smart move," Naivea quickly recovered, hiding her feelings of abandonment. "Maybe she'll be much better by then." Charles could detect that Naivea was disturbed by the cancellation of their time together, yet he didn't mention anything about visiting. "I've gotta run so that I can do payroll before the 3 p.m. deadline." "Okay," Naivea said as she stuffed down her hurt feelings. Naivea was a little bewildered that he was being so caring and careful about Wendy and not about the fact that she had been disappointed. She wondered why he made no mention of rescheduling their visit. Eventually she rationalized it away, convincing herself, "He's trying to make sure she doesn't sue him; that's where his mind is. So many people sue for more than workers' compensation these days." Naivea went into her office and tried to get some work done.

Several days went by with no communication. Naivea kept herself busy with work while she wondered if things between her and Charles had changed. Had he met someone at the Phoenix conference and changed his mind about her? Charles finally called and they picked up where they left off with the twice daily calls. The employee didn't sue, and the office was back to normal. Naivea rationalized that Charles had been preoccupied with the injury incident and now that it was over, he was back to normal. However, he still didn't mention getting together.

May came along and although there was some talk about a visit, nothing was set in stone. Days later Charles texted Naivea, "Good morning, my grandfather passed early this morning. Please pray for my family." "So sorry," texted Naivea, "Yes, I'll pray for peace." Charles asked Naivea to send food for him and his family. Even though she had never used DoorDash, she struggled through getting an order in before the breakfast/ brunch restaurant Charles wanted to get the food from closed. Later Charles texted "The food was delicious. The family is full, and they said thank you." "My pleasure," texted Naivea, as she felt proud to show Charles that she could be a good wife. She was more than ready for marriage.

CHAPTER FIVE
MARRIAGE AT LAST!

In mid-May, Naivea received a call from one of her business associates. "Frank? It's been ages," Naivea exclaimed as she answered the phone. "Yea, it's been too long girl," Frank said with a guilty voice. "We've been so busy with these training classes all over the world. Every time I made it back to the States I was usually on the east coast, so I just neglected to call you. Sorry." "That's okay, what's the occasion this time?" Naivea asked with curiosity. Frank's voice lit up, "We'll be back on the east coast the second week of June doing some training at a company in Wake Forest, North Carolina, and we'd love for you to join us. It'll be for a week. Do you think you can swing it?" Naivea almost jumped out of her chair. "Yes, of course I can!" she bellowed. "Let me know all of the details as soon as you can so I can book a flight." "Oh, we'll pay for the flight," said Frank. "I'll send you an email with all of the particulars." "Great," said Naivea as she smiled from ear to ear. "I'll talk to you soon."

Naivea hung up the phone and shouted for joy. Not just a trip to the east coast, but a trip within thirty minutes of Charles. She couldn't wait to tell him. She waited ten minutes and opened her email. There it was – the email from Frank. The trip was the week of June 9th. Frank booked a first-class ticket, with Naivea arriving on Sunday and staying until Saturday afternoon. The training was Wednesday, Thursday and Friday, so she had Sunday, Monday and Tuesday prior to the training to spend time with Charles, and Friday evening through her departure on Saturday.

Naivea rarely called Charles, but this time she was excited out of her mind. She called after business hours. "Hi Babe, I have some good news," she said in a sexy voice. "What's the good news Babe," Charles asked with keen interest. "I have a training job in Wake Forest next month!" "Really? When?" Charles asked with excitement. "I fly in on Sunday, June 9th, and the training doesn't start until Wednesday morning, so I'll be free from Sunday through Tuesday evening, and again from Friday afternoon till Saturday evening." "That's wonderful!" shouted Charles. "I'll clear my calendar and make sure they know I won't be in the office those days. I'll be all yours!" "Excellent! I'm looking forward to our being together," Naivea said firmly, remembering their failed attempt in April. "You know when you come your life will never be the same. You're going to be my wife, so if you're not ready then we won't get together," Charles said in a stern, serious tone. Naivea took a deep breath. "I understand that there is anxiety and nervousness," Charles continued. "It's lifechanging. You have to say to yourself, 'I'm getting ready to change my life.' I'll pick you up from the airport and bring you home." Emotions overwhelmed her as she thought about finally being with Charles. Naivea continued to think about how she would react, and she had to finally ask herself, "Am I really ready?"

Naivea kept busy with work, and she prepared an outstanding presentation for the Wake Forest training. Sunday, June 9th came quickly and before she knew it, it was 3 p.m. Eastern time. Naivea was now standing at the passenger pickup curb at the Raleigh airport waiting for Charles to arrive. Although they had done FaceTime dates many times during the seven months of their relationship, this was going to be the real flesh and blood Charles she would be talking to – face-to-face.

Charles was a little late, but he arrived in his BMW X7 wearing jeans, boots, and a plaid shirt. He was truly six feet tall and had the biggest smile. Charles kissed Naivea passionately before tossing her luggage into the trunk. He held her hand as he escorted her to the passenger door and guided her into her seat. He then went around and got in the car to drive. "I'm so sorry I was late. It's so good to see you Babe, are you hungry?" Charles was noticeably nervous as he looked into Naivea's eyes. "No, I'm not hungry, are you?" Naivea asked in her nervous voice. "A little. Let's stop and get a bite to eat before rush hour gets bad. If you don't want to eat at the restaurant we can take it home," Charles said as he set the GPS to his favorite restaurant. They arrived at the restaurant and ordered a late lunch. Naivea was so excited that she hardly ate a thing. Charles ate a little more than she did, but they both had hearty to-go plates to take home.

Once they arrived at Charles' house it was dusk. He opened the door for Naivea and retrieved her luggage. The home was large and well decorated – like it had been crafted by a female interior designer. "Your home is lovely Charles, you have great taste in furniture and art," Naivea said as she walked around the main level. "Oh, thanks. I decorated it myself," Charles boasted. Charles put both their plates in the refrigerator and took Naivea's luggage upstairs. "Would you like to watch a movie, or would you like to take a nap?" Charles asked in a caring voice. "A movie is fine," Naivea said as she nervously thought about waiting to lay down.

The couple watched a movie, then Charles said, "I need to take care of a few more things in the office. Why don't you just relax right here, or you can get ready for bed." By that time Naivea was really tired, so she decided to get ready for bed. Charles showed her where the towels were, and he went into his downstairs office. Naivea showered, put on some nice sexy pajamas and got in the bed. "It's been more than four years since I've slept with anyone," she thought to herself before she drifted off to sleep. About an hour had passed before she heard the bedroom door open. Charles came in and knelt on the floor near Naivea's face and started to kiss her. He slid into the bed and undressed Naivea, then himself. After Charles was able to penetrate Naivea, the couple made love for what seemed like hours to Naivea. She was in heaven realizing her dream of having a great husband, great sex, and a great life.

In the morning, Charles got up, showered, and went into his office. He came back to check on Naivea, who was still in a trance. "Would you like to go out for breakfast Babe?" he asked. "No, thank you, I don't need food, I can live off love," Naivea said as she pulled Charles back down onto the bed. They both laughed as they got up to make the bed. As they pulled the covers up Charles said, "You bled, Naivea." She looked and there was a patch of blood the size of a jar top in the middle of the white sheets. Naivea was embarrassed, and Charles could tell. "No, don't be embarrassed. That just further solidifies our marriage. You saved yourself for me. You're family now." Charles seemed to be honored.

Naivea washed the sheets while Charles made some business calls. The couple spent the next two days joined at the hip. They went to the park, to the movies, and they ate out a few times. They even went to the grocery store and Naivea cooked

Charles her favorite salmon dish. Each night they become more and more connected as they physically shared their love for one another. Naivea was ecstatic, as her dreams of a handsome prince, who could "put it down" in the bedroom, had come true.

Wednesday morning came, and Naivea had to leave and head to Wake Forest. Charles ordered an Uber, and he kissed Naivea goodbye as she got in and was taken to the training site. She arrived to see Frank and his new business partner Mark. They had a short strategy session before going into the conference center to begin their work with the company salespeople. All day, Naivea had to fight to stay focused on the training. "I hope Frank and Mark don't notice my preoccupation," she thought.

Wednesday evening, after training, the three went out to dinner. "What have you been doing for the last few days Naivea? I know that you flew in on Sunday," Frank asked being nosy. "I've been spending time with a friend," she said with a smile. "Yea, we noticed the red mark on your neck," Mark said as the two men laughed. "What?" Naivea hadn't noticed that Charles left his mark on her neck. All she could do was laugh with them. When she got back to the hotel, Naivea called Charles, but he didn't answer. It was 7 p.m. She figured that he was catching up on work that he missed on Monday and Tuesday. By 9 p.m. Charles still hadn't called Naivea, and she became concerned. "I thought he would have at least texted me to check up on me today."

Naivea woke up out of a deep sleep as she faintly heard the phone ring with Charles' ringtone. Hi, she said weakly as she grabbed the phone. She looked at the clock and it was 11:30

p.m. "Hi Babe, sorry to call so late, it was a super busy day. How was your day?" Charles sounded rushed, as opposed to his usual soothing voice. "It was pretty good, we got a lot accomplished," Naivea was able to wake up enough to be partially coherent. "Well, I just wanted to tuck you in. Good night, Babe." Charles was gone in a flash. "I didn't even get to say good night before he hung up," Naivea realized as she hung up the phone. "That was a strange phone call," she thought, as she laid her head back down on the pillow. "I wonder what all that was about." Naivea drifted off to sleep.

Thursday Naivea woke up tired, as she had tossed and turned a little after that phone call from Charles. However, she was determined to do well with the training. "If we do well we'll be invited back, and I'll be able to spend more time with Charles," she thought. Naivea was still sending her daily morning and evening love memes to Charles, and he would eventually respond, usually with a generic hello. Naivea noticed that he wasn't being as romantic in his text responses since her arrival, but she figured that he was trying to get more done so that they could spend time together Friday evening after the training and Saturday morning. She was looking forward to going back to Raleigh Friday evening to be with him.

The training was over Friday on time at 4 p.m. It was a success, according to Frank, and the trio felt that they would be invited back again. Naivea had texted Charles to let him know that the training was over and that she could take an Uber to his house. Charles texted her back, stating that he would be in meetings until 8 p.m. Naivea was dismayed. "How could he let this happen?" she thought. "He knew the training was over at 4 p.m. Now what do I do?" Naivea said goodbye to Frank and Mark, as they got into an Uber headed back to the Raleigh airport.

Naivea decided to text Charles and ask him how he wanted to proceed with the visit. "Well, since I'm tied up with meetings till 8 p.m., why don't you check back into the hotel, and I'll come to you as soon as I'm done with these meetings. We can have a nice breakfast in the morning before I take you back to the airport." Naivea didn't relish the idea of missing out on four hours of time with Charles, but she reluctantly agreed.

Charles showed up at the hotel at 10 p.m. and he appeared to be uptight. Charles asked Naivea her overall feelings about the training, but as she told him about her experience, she noticed that he was preoccupied, so she cut her story short. "How were your meetings?" she asked quickly. "What? Oh, they were fine." Charles wasn't mentally present and Naivea could tell, and she was hurt. "I'm tired, let's go to bed now," Charles said in a rush. Naivea was a little upset at the way the visit was turning out, and Charles was in another world, but as they began to undress, their focus turned back towards each other, and they connected sexually in a glorious way.

In the morning, they ordered room service and stayed in bed till 11 a.m. having pillow talk. Since Naivea's flight out of Raleigh wasn't until 5 p.m., she didn't have to leave Wake Forest until 2 p.m., or Raleigh until 2:30 p.m. to make sure that she didn't miss the plane. She really wanted to go back to Charles' house and spend time feeling like a wife. "Can we leave here and go back to your house? We wouldn't have to leave for the airport until 2:30. Maybe we could watch a movie."

"You've just become a wife a few days ago and you're already trying to run things," Charles said with a snide voice. "I have to go meet a guy in Durham at 1 p.m. about buying a rental property, so I'm going to get up now and leave for Durham.

You can't go with me because we probably won't be done before you'd have to leave for the airport. I'll pay for an extra day so you can stay here in the room until 2 p.m. You're going to have to take an Uber from here to the Raleigh airport. If you leave at 2, you'll be there in plenty of time to make the plane."

Naivea was heartbroken! She felt like she had been kicked to the curb. Charles could see it all over her face. "Babe, you knew you were marrying a busy and successful businessman. I have to seize opportunities when they come, and this one came last night during one of my meetings. This property, if it looks right, is in the right neighborhood and has enough equity, could net us $500 per month in rental income. Don't you want to be a housewife and do training only when you want to take on a job?' Naivea couldn't refute anything that Charles just said. "Yes," she answered with an uncertain voice.

They took a shower together, hugged, and kissed goodbye. Charles took off in the Range Rover and Naivea stayed in the room, all packed up and ready to go. At 2 p.m. the Uber arrived for her ride back to the Raleigh airport. On the long ride to the airport Naivea assessed the visit. Now she was a wife, but she felt a little low on the priority list after their first three days and nights together. "He's right. He's a busy and successful businessman and this is what I signed up for. I have to learn to be a submissive wife that follows his lead," she said as she dozed off in the Uber. When Naivea arrived home, it was 6:30 p.m. in Denver, but she was exhausted and went straight to bed. She even forgot to send Charles his good night love meme.

CHAPTER SIX
BUSINESS AND FAMILY MATTERS

June, in Denver, was cool in the mornings and hot in the late afternoons. Naivea was a little disappointed with her trip to North Carolina, but she wrote it off as being an awkward but unusual first encounter. "Next time it'll be better," she said as she did her morning walk each day for the next week. Naivea had high expectations, and these expectations led to disappointment. She vowed to do all that she could to make the next visit perfect.

For the next two months, Charles was all about business. He was improving his T-shirt business and helping Naivea grow her training business. Naivea was happy for the tips, but she was more focused on becoming a wife than remaining a CEO. Charles did have a little time for romance occasionally. "I want a clear-cut goal and focus for us," he told her on one of their personal level calls. "I want a loving marriage with a wife that follows my lead, a harmonious relationship. I'm in pursuit of you, Naivea, but sometimes I don't feel like you're interested in being in a marriage. You're not doing the things that it takes to be a loving wife."

Naivea was puzzled at this revelation. "What do you mean Charles? What am I doing that makes you think I don't want to be your wife?" Charles just sighed. "First off, you seem to question my leadership often. When I lay out a plan, you always have questions and comments about it." "That's just because I want to further understand what you want and what you mean," Naivea explained. Charles changed the subject to his upcoming administrative staff meeting, then talked about how his sales team loved how Naivea instructed them in sales. He announced that sales had increased 30% since Naivea started working with his team, and she felt proud, forgetting about his concern over her lack of desire to be a wife.

The couple spoke less on the phone as summer progressed. Both were busy with work, projects, and family matters. Naivea's daughter, Melanie, had just graduated from high school and had gone straight to college for a special summer program that was a part of her scholarship. She would be going straight into her freshman year and wouldn't be coming home before fall semester started, so Naivea was busy shopping and putting things together for her dorm room. Charles had his son, Charles II and his daughter Octavia for three weeks in July.

Although the children had two different mothers: Charles II from his marriage to Rachel, and Octavia from a woman he met right after his divorce from Rachel. Charles wanted both children at the same time so that he wouldn't have to extend the time that he had children in his house. The children's mothers agreed to let the children stay with him at the same time because he paid the women extra for those three weeks. Charles seemed a bit irritated during the calls when his children were at the house, so Naivea didn't call at all. She continued to send his morning and evening love memes, and she waited for him to call her after the children had gone to bed. "That way," she thought to herself, "he'll be relaxed and ready to have alone time with me."

In early August while Naivea was doing her morning walk her phone rang. She put in her Air Pods and answered. "Hello Frank! What have you been up to?" Frank was always full of energy and a bit of a cut up. "I've been in Russia training generals, but I bet you've been having a much better time than I have," Frank said jokingly. Frank informed Naivea that they had been invited back to the company in Wake Forrest to train some new hires, and that the trip was in three weeks. "Sorry for such short notice, Naivea, but they just asked me this morning and I immediately called you. I'll be calling Mark as soon as we hang up to see if he can join us that week." "Of course, I'm in," Naivea said with great joy. She knew that Charles' children would be going back to their mothers and Melanie would be settled in on campus, so she would be free to spend as much time with Charles as she could. She could arrive on a Sunday afternoon and return the next Sunday evening on the last flight out to Denver. Since this training would be Monday through Friday, she wanted to commute back and forth to Charles' house daily.

Naivea waited until 6 p.m. to call and give Charles the news. "Hi Babe, we were invited back to do some additional training at the company in Wake Forest." "When?" Charles didn't seem excited at all. "Next to the last week of this month," Naivea said with worry in her voice. She hadn't thought about the fact that Charles may be traveling at the time. "Oh, okay. I'll be in town, but we still have to talk about how to prepare you to be a wife," Charles said sternly. "First of all, I like good food that's not cooked at a restaurant; you need to start cooking regularly. Don't take the fact that Melanie has gone off to college as an excuse to stop cooking." "Nope, I'm determined to cook and only eat out once a week, if that." Naivea assured Charles of her dedication to cook good healthy meals.

"Maybe you shouldn't come. I know as my wife you need my love, and I know you're working your way through being my helpmate, but do you think you're ready to spend a whole week with me?" "Yes, Babe," Naivea pleaded. "We need to spend time together. I need to know what you like and don't like to eat, what you like for entertainment, and how you want your house run, so that I can get on your program." Charles was pleased with that answer. "You already know what I like to do for entertainment." They both laughed and did a little planning for the trip.

Chapters 4-6 Commentary
The Tea on NPD and Relationships
Telsha Edenburgh

In Chapters Four through Six, Charles was incredibly cunning, a con artist. His smooth talk and plans for "our future" were getting Naivea excited about life again. It was no longer just mundane, day-to-day activity, but now there is something wonderful to look forward to – a second chance at marriage.

I, knowing the pattens of a narcissist, felt ahead of time that his excuses were lies. Naivea had her grass cut, had the house so clean that you could eat off the floor, she was ready for this first visit in every way. Then he said, "I got bad news." The bad news that he described was an elaborate lie, and it appears that these lies are a recurring thing for him.

Most narcissists are cunning enough to pick people that they think will believe their lies; mostly because these victims are very honest people. They select their Supplies very carefully to make sure that, at least in their minds, they are comfortable with the fact that the Supply is harmless, and even when made angry, they won't do bodily harm to the narcissist. Because of their lying nature, they live their lives in constant paranoia because of the fact that they know that they've done so many horrible things to people.

The lies are a key indicator of a narcissist. And this is my number one conclusion when people come to me and they're complaining about their exes: talking about how bad the ex was and this, that, and the third. Proclaiming that, "They did this and that to me." These birds never say anything about what they did, so I automatically suspect narcissism in them. They act as if they were perfect angels. That's a red flag.

Another thing Charles did is call Naivea a lot, and that is not normal. I said, "This guy is too nice; you are staying on the phone all night." Men do want to spend a lot of time with you when they really like you. But with a narcissist, you just know something is wrong. Your internal system goes off and it tells you. You just don't have any peace. However, in the case of men or women that are lonely, broken or have a very low self-esteem, the internal system has been hijacked by the spirits in the narcissist, and although they don't have peace, they cling to the relationship. In these chapters, we see that Naivea started having subtle discomfort, but she plowed through those feelings and warnings because she did not want her dream situation to end.

When a narcissist is always calling you or telling you that they're going to call you at a certain time, they're instituting controls right there because they don't want you to feel like you have the liberty to call them. They may not have said it out of their mouth, but their actions are conditioning you not to call them.

Because Charles learned that Naivea didn't have a lot of experience with men, he was able to do and say things that were inappropriate and make Naivea think these things were somewhat normal. The way Charles orchestrated the relationship with the lies and time blocking of Naivea was amazing to me. I said to myself, "How can he manipulate, and time block her like that," but it's easy for the narcissist to do when the victim is unsuspecting.

Some narcissists literally have a checklist of what they are looking for in a Supply. This list also contains what they will and will not deal with, along with what will cause a relationship to be dead on arrival. For example, if the potential female Supply has seven brothers, the narcissist knows that when his true nature is revealed he will potentially have seven men coming for his life for violating their sister, and that potential Supply will not be nurtured into a bonified Supply. The victims selected by the narcissist normally have a very low direct or indirect potential to end the life of the narcissist, whether the victim is very religious or does not have a support system in place that will take action once the fake relationship is revealed.

In the case of Charles and Naivea, the long distance made Charles' typical timeline for showing his true colors slower than normal. If they had been in the same vicinity, Naivea would have started to pick up on strange behavior faster than she did. This is why some narcissists only cultivate relationships that are outside of a day's driving distance from their home. And narcissists don't like boundaries. So, if you tell them 10 p.m. is your bedtime, they're calling you at 11 p.m. If you tell them you need to get up early in the morning, they want to talk to you till 3 a.m.

By Chapter Four, Naivea is engrossed in the relationship. Not only was Charles being a smooth talker during this time, while talking about what he wants to do and saying that he's going to come out to visit Naivea, what he was also doing in this situation was building up strong anticipation in Naivea concerning her finally being with him. Narcissists love to build up your anticipation and excitement concerning their lives. It's like they get high on the excitement you have regarding them. They relish the fact that the Supply has great anticipation for being with them, especially when that Supply is long distance. It makes you anxious. It makes you excited. It makes you want them more. However, if the narcissist has other Supplies, one or more of them is going to be let down.

Charles didn't come and see Naivea, and she was devastated. He built up her anticipation and let her down, and that's called a devaluation. Naivea didn't even know that she was being devalued. Not only that, but Charles also didn't say anything else about rescheduling their visit. Narcissists purposely put off rescheduling, because if they cancel, what it does is next time around, it doubles the excitement, the anxiety, and the anticipation. So, in the brain of the Supply, these actions strengthen the trauma bond. And so you know, anticipation and excitement can keep somebody hanging on for years!

I've had clients in other countries where they literally had a narcissist leading them on for one to two years before they met the narcissist. And every time they would get ready to get together, something would happen. I had one client that flew to Dubai to see this person, and the person never showed up at the place where they were supposed to meet! My client came back home, and believe it or not, they reengaged with the narcissist again! This went on for two to three years. Do you know that my client has never met this narcissist in person?

This is pure future-faking on Charles' behalf, causing the anticipation not only to grab Naivea emotionally, but it grabbed her mentally and it kept her locked into that time and space. Not only was he building anticipation and excitement to devalue her, but now he's also introduced an element that is even stronger than manipulation – it's brainwashing.

When Charles said that he didn't want to have a traditional wedding, that would have normally been a red flag. Not only was he manipulating, but there was a mechanism to his manipulation, which I would term as brainwashing. Because if you can get a person to come out of whatever their tradition is, and that's what they are accustomed to, and to literally make them think a different way, this goes beyond manipulation. Now, we're at straight brainwashing, but they have to have your emotions, and they have to have your mind in order to brainwash the Supply.

In the beginning of some of these relationships, the Supply has a wall up from previous relationship issues. When Naivea told Charles about her ex-husband and Charles told her that he would never betray her, he was trying to break through a wall that she put up based on her past marriage. What they do in situations like having walls up, a narcissist knows when you are not being completely open with them. They can tell through your body language.

Even on FaceTime, or in the phone calls, they can hear it in your voice. Because what you have to realize is the reason the narcissist can discern your walls and call you on them is because of their supernatural abilities to read you because they have demonic intel. They know when you aren't being open and honest with them about the walls coming down. Therefore, what they do is confront you about your safety mechanisms as if something was wrong with you having them, when there is nothing wrong with you having safety mechanisms. A narcissist will literally make a Supply feel like it is wrong for them to protect themselves and their feelings. They don't want you to have walls with them, which means that your relationship with the narcissist, in their eyes, should be without limits, without walls, without boundaries. When these limits are dismantled, they are actually teaching you to have no expectations of them!

In Charles' eyes, Naivea was not supposed to be mad about him not showing up for their first visit. He never turned around and said, let me offer you a different date right away. And then he turned around and went on to brainwash her about a traditional marriage and the way that most people think about marriage. Charles was disarming Naivea all the way around from start to finish. Naivea was sending Charles text messages and memes – the different things to keep the relationship going and thriving. She was actually working harder than Charles.

I want you all to remember this. When a man or woman is truly interested in you and falling in love with you, their actions can look similar to a narcissistic relationship. But the difference is you're not alarmed by the things they say and do in a real relationship. And the difference is they're not doing alarming stuff all day. A narcissist is constant. It's all day long. And they're doing it because they don't trust you. And you're doing what you're doing because you want them to trust you. You're trying to assure them that there's nothing wrong. And all day it's a constant back and forth, back and forth. That's not healthy. You need time for yourself.

So, when Naivea was sending messages and memes to keep Charles happy, she was trying to win his trust to show him that she was genuinely desirous of marriage to him. The constant attention to the relationship was part of the conditioning because Charles couldn't be there for Naivea. He had already built her anticipation. He had already built the excitement. Naivea didn't want to be let down again, so what he started doing was he started conditioning her to work harder to ensure that the next time around she was going to get what she had put all that hard work in for.

Aside from Naivea putting in time finding memes and love messages for Charles, he started adding other work to her plate! Naivea was doing all of the changing, but all Charles had to do was make a statement and Naivea would jump. You see, that's brainwashing. That's mind control. Charles told Naivea that she needed to learn how to be a wife. So, she was scrambling. "How do I be a wife?" "What do I do?" This is what they do. Charles literally had Naivea running around trying to figure out how she was supposed to be a wife.

All that Charles had said to Naivea was penetrating. It was powerful enough to cause her to start doing all of these things for him, and that's controlling an individual without telling her that. "I want you to send me a meme in the morning. I want you to send me a meme at night." No, he didn't have to tell her that. Her mind had already clicked into overtime, and she was in high gear just because of what had happened before when he didn't show up for the visit.

Naivea's mind may have fertilized the thought that Charles didn't show up for the visit because she had not yet learned how to be a proper wife. That seed he planted in her mind was immediately fertilized, and it started to produce these things that she was doing from that time forward. That's what I call mind control manipulation in its highest form.

Narcissists often have more than one diagnosis. They can be diagnosed with narcissistic personality disorder. They can also be diagnosed with Antisocial Personality Disorder, which is one of the worst ones. And they can have a Histrionic Narcissistic diagnosis. And then some of them are even borderline. Some narcissists may have all of these traits. In this section of the book, it appears that Charles may have more than one trait and be borderline on others. As he began to tell Naivea lies, he was attempting to control her with a false situation, and really, that's like false imprisonment of her mind.

Someone knowledgeable about the ways of a narcissist would have said, "Wait a minute! You are controlling me and telling me that I have to be a wife, but I have to conform to the lies that you're telling me. And then I can't have any boundaries.

So, I'm in this false world that you are creating for me, and that means that I'm being falsely imprisoned in my mind, and you are the only one with the key."

As for the nude pictures, at this point Naivea had given into the brainwashing mind control. It appears that she thought that if she didn't do this, or once she sent him nude pictures, she had to continue to do everything he said because she was scared that something may be released on her. It was as if he created a cage for Naivea and she walked into it. At that point, all he had to do was make three or four statements to her: "You need to learn how to be a wife." "You're closed off to me." "You are not following my leadership." "You're not a good listener."

Surely, everything that happened in this section of the book was to strengthen the trauma bond. Charles captured Naivea's soul. Everything that he said here is what victims that have been kidnapped or in these hate or war crimes go through, because narcissists understand that when they create a fake world or they get into the Supply's soul realm, there is no way that you are going to close the door to them. Charles believed that there was no way Naivea was going to turn back from the relationship at that point because she wanted the reward of seeing and being with him. Naivea was then conditioned to just follow his commands and not ask questions and just blindly obey him. And that's what he wanted. That's what these narcissists do.

When Naivea finally got a chance to fly out on a job near Charles' home, he was late picking her up at the airport. Some people are just late, folks. They just don't show up on time.

It's not the fact that they are narcissists, it's just a bad habit on their part. If they make a conscious effort to be on time they can overcome this bad habit. The narcissist, on the other hand, may be late on purpose to create additional anticipation. Naivea told Charles long before her arrival what time the plane was landing, but here again, he's manipulating her by being late. Charles seemed to use sex as an anesthetizer, knowing that Naivea had not been sexually active for several years and knowing that he had 1000% more experience. The physical and emotional connection was much more intense than it would have been with an honest man.

This story is turning out to be the typical sad story of a Supply being led around like a sheep headed for the slaughter. I can't wait to see what happens next.

CHAPTER SEVEN
THE FIRST HICCUP

To Naivea, August 19th took forever to arrive. She tried to keep busy with her regular clients without seeming impatient or anxious, but it was hard. Finally, the day arrived, and she was on an 8:30 a.m. plane to Raleigh. With the short layover in Atlanta, she would arrive in Raleigh after noon, allowing Charles to sleep in, as he did every Sunday. Charles didn't have a church home. He told Naivea that most of the preachers in Raleigh were prosperity pimps. He told Naivea that every Sunday morning after he got up, he did his own devotionals, looked at a pastor from Texas on television, and then met with his mentors over the phone. Naivea thought to herself, "When we are in one household, I'll take some time and find us a church that teaches and follows the Bible."

Naivea arrived at the Raleigh airport a little after noon. She texted Charles to let him know that she was deboarding the plane. Charles texted back, "Sorry Babe, I'm going to be about 30-minutes late. Had an issue at the office." Naivea was a little disappointed, but she got her bags and waited right inside the pick-up area because it was too warm outside to stand for 30 minutes. "I don't want to be sweaty when he arrives," she said to herself.

Charles arrived in 45 minutes. He smiled as he hopped out of the Range Rover and hugged and kissed Naivea. She had waited two months for his touch, and she was elated. "It's so good to see you, Babe," Naivea said, as Charles scooped up her luggage and placed it in the back of the SUV. "It's good to see you too, Babe," Charles said. For some reason Naivea felt that he wasn't as eager to see her as she was to see him, but she shrugged it off and got into the front seat as he held the door open for her. Charles began to talk. "I tried to take as much time off as I could during your stay. Unfortunately, my mom and Calvin showed up from Portland unannounced on Friday, and she's at the house, so we can't go there. What I plan to do is spend time with you at the hotel. I brought my work so that when you're in the training sessions I can work, and when you get done for the day, we can spend time together. Now, there will be some days that I have to go back to Raleigh to spend a little time with mom and Calvin, but I'll try to get back to Wake Forest as soon as I can."

This information was news to Naivea. She was again a little disappointed that she wasn't going to get a chance to play house at Charles' home. She was also a little concerned that he didn't seem to want to introduce her to his mother and younger brother, but she figured that they may want to capitalize on some of her time, so she was okay with his plan.

They arrived at the hotel in Wake Forest, and Naivea immediately thought about Frank and Mark, and how they would feel about Charles being in the room with Naivea. "We are all grown," she said to herself, trying to dismiss the feeling that Frank and Mark would judge her because she claimed to be a Christian. Naivea prayed that their room wouldn't be anywhere near Frank or Mark, so they wouldn't have to pass each other in the hall in the evenings after work.

Naivea checked in as Charles parked the SUV and got all of their bags out. She was already in the room when he texted her from the lobby with the cart. "What's our room number?" he asked. "It's 307," she texted back. Charles arrived at the room and they both unpacked the bags as Naivea talked about the trip to Raleigh. Once the bags were unpacked, Charles grabbed Naivea and started ripping off her clothes. He sat her up on the bathroom sink and proceeded to pound her; her head occasionally hitting the mirror behind her. Then he had her wrap her legs around him as he carried her to the bed, where he continued to pound her as she squirmed. "Don't run," he would say as Naivea whimpered from the pain of some of the strokes. The couple made love for hours, moving from the bed to the nightstand and back to the bed. Naivea couldn't keep from gasping and moaning from the waves of orgasms. She knew that if anyone was in the room above them or in the rooms next door, they were getting an ear full. She had never been with a man like Charles before, and it felt delicious!

Upon showering and getting dressed, they went out to a nice restaurant before they all closed, and then they returned to the room. Opening his briefcase on the hotel room desk, Charles said, "I'm going to do a little work right quick." As Naivea was standing there, she immediately noticed a set of pictures of a woman on the top of the pile of papers in Charles' briefcase. The woman was pretty, with light skin, long hair and a shapely body. "Who's that?" Naivea asked, trying not to sound shocked, angry or jealous. "Oh, that's just Freda Long," Charles answered matter-of-factly. "She's one of our top salespeople. You've seen her on the video training conferences. She modeled our newest T-shirt last week because the students are starting to show up at all of the schools for Fall Semester and we wanted to get them familiar with our brand, "Oh, okay," Naivea said, trying to act unconcerned.

She'd never noticed Freda before during the training sessions, but there were so many of Charles' employees that had their cameras turned off that she stopped paying attention to even the ones that kept their cameras on. Charles quickly gathered up the pictures of Freda and placed them in a folder at the bottom of the briefcase before he started to work on his laptop. Naivea opened her bag and started reviewing her presentation for the next morning. After a few hours, the couple watched a movie and drifted off to sleep at 11 p.m.

Naivea woke up. It was 1:30 a.m. and she noticed that Charles wasn't in bed. She sat up and looked around the room, but even though it was almost pitch black, she could see that he wasn't there. She sat quietly for a few seconds and noticed that she could hear his deep voice in the bathroom. "He's probably on a business call," she said to herself. "But it's so late," she thought with concern. Charles came back to bed at 2 a.m. Naivea was still awake, but she pretended to be asleep. "I wonder who that was?" she thought as she drifted back off to sleep.

In the morning, Naivea got off to a good start. "I'm going down to breakfast Babe, do you want me to bring you something to eat?" Naivea asked, trying to model the perfect wife. "No Babe, I'm going to make a few phone calls then go back to Raleigh for a meeting," Charles said with a businesslike voice. Naivea was a little offput that he wasn't returning the love that she was giving off. "Okay, I'll see you when you get back then?" she said as if to question whether he was going to come back that evening. Charles picked up on her inquiry. "If I make it back it'll be late because I found out last night that a private college on the west coast is interested in our shirts, and one of their reps will be in Raleigh today. I've scheduled a lunch and possible evening dinner so that I have the chance to close the deal." "Okay, that's great!" Naivea said with excitement. "That's who he was talking to last night," she thought to herself. She wasn't upset because she would be in Wake Forest for a week, and this was just the beginning of their time together.

Monday's training went well, and Naivea texted Charles afterward to get an update on his status. She wanted to find out whether she should go out to dinner with Frank and Mark or wait for him. But Charles didn't answer the text. The trio drove back to the hotel and planned to have dinner in an hour. An hour passed and Naivea still hadn't heard from Charles, so she went to dinner with Frank and Mark. After dinner they drove around Wake Forest looking at historic buildings until dusk, and then they headed back to the hotel. Naivea was getting irritated because Charles hadn't taken the time to answer her text. "I know you're a busy businessman and all, but I'm your wife and I would like the respect of a return text, at least within an hour of my reaching out," she thought to herself in anger.

Naivea went back to the hotel room and prepared for Tuesday's class. The hours rolled by without a word from Charles. At 10 p.m. she heard her phone ping. "Sorry Babe, I'll have to come back tomorrow evening. The meetings went long, and mom and Calvin wanted to go out to eat." "Okay," Naivea texted back. She was even more irritated that he hadn't called to tell her the news. She finished her class preparation and got in bed. "I need to chill, I knew that he was a busy business owner when I agreed to be his wife, so I need to be more understanding," Naivea thought to herself as she drifted off to sleep. Charles returned to the hotel on Tuesday while Naivea was still at the company. When the training team arrived at the hotel, Naivea saw the Range Rover and started to smile. Since Frank and Mark were on a different wing of the hotel, they had no idea that Charles was in the picture. Naivea arrived at the room with a smile. When she opened the door, Charles had flowers and chocolate for her! "Hi Babe!" he said with a sexy voice. "Hi back to you," Naivea said as she ran up and threw her arms around him. They talked about her day, and about the Monday meetings. "We got the deal!" Charles said with contentment. "I worked on him all day and he finally signed the contract this morning before leaving town. This client is a private college with a really steady enrollment, and they agreed to place the T-shirts on their website and in their bookstore." "Wonderful," Naivea said as she smelled the flowers and kissed Charles all over the face.

The two of them began to strip off their clothes. Charles sat on the edge of the bed and pulled Naivea close, then he told her to get on her knees and he plunged his large penis into her mouth. Naivea wasn't used to oral sex. It wasn't done in her marriage or in her earlier relationships, but she proceeded to suck as he thrust back and forth; moaning at each stroke. Eventually Charles discharged in Naivea's mouth. As she gagged, he said, "Don't waste my seed. Swallow it!" She proceeded to swallow. He then lifted her up onto the bed and placed her on top of him. She began to ride him as and he regained an erection for her to orgasm. They continued on for an hour, then famished, it was time for dinner. They showered and made their way to a restaurant.

At dinner, they laughed and joked about how Frank and Mark are so animated during the training sessions. Upon returning to the hotel, they selected another new movie to watch, and afterward, they retired for the night. Charles pulled Naivea close. "Ready to go again?" Charles wanted more sex, and although Naivea was already warn out, she complied. "I'm going to be a great wife inside and outside the bedroom," she told herself. This time Charles told Naivea to lie on her stomach. Once she rolled over, he lifted her hips up and entered her doggie style. She felt the pain as he humped forward forcefully, her head hitting the headboard that was mounted onto the wall. She screeched, so he slowed down so that he wouldn't hurt her already sore vagina anymore. After this, he turned her over and had her lie on her side. They continued to make love until both fell asleep, with Charles still inside her as they slept.

When Naivea woke up, this time at 11 p.m., once again, Charles wasn't in the room at all. "Where could he be?" she asked herself. She decided to stay awake, and once he came back to the room, she would get up and act like she was already up headed to the bathroom. It was 1:40 a.m. before she heard the door handle. She quickly got out of bed and headed to the bathroom. "Oh, you startled me," Charles said as he opened the door. "Sorry, I had to use it," Naivea said as she acted like she was half asleep. "Where were you?" she asked, this time with a very curious voice, "I went to the car to see if one of my notebooks was there. It wasn't so I must have left it at the house." Charles was lying. He'd been gone almost three hours. It hadn't taken that long to look through his car. "What's really going on? What was he really doing?" Naivea asked herself as she went to the bathroom. As she got into bed, she noticed that Charles had his jeans on but still had on his sleeveless T-shirt. His briefcase was still on the desk, which made her believe that he hadn't left the vicinity. She finally went back to sleep at 3 a.m.

The rest of the week was a little calmer and more routine for Naivea. She went to the company each day, and Charles stayed at the hotel. When she was done for the day, they spent time together talking about marriage, the T-shirt business, and merging into one household. "I want you to contribute to the marriage so that you can feel like we're a team," Charles said when Naivea arrived at the hotel Friday after work. "I plan on us moving into a larger house because based on all the clothes you brought here, you'll need your own walk-in closet!" The couple laughed. "How do you want me to contribute?" Naivea asked. "When you get back to Denver, wire me $15,000. I'll find a realtor and, once we decide on a house together, I'll put that money with some additional funds for a down payment. I'll send you pictures and videos of the final three homes that I select, especially the closets, and get your input on the final selection." They laughed again, then went out to dinner.

Saturday morning the couple slept in. It was Naivea's last two days in North Carolina, and Naivea expected them to spend the entire day together both Saturday and Sunday taking walks in the park, going to the movies, and spending time detailing plans for their eventual merging. Instead, Charles pulled out his phone and Air Pods and started watching social media videos right after breakfast. After an hour, Naivea was upset. "Charles, can we take a walk in one of the parks around here? I've gotten behind on exercise and I don't want to gain weight," Naivea said, trying not to sound upset. "Later! Can't you see that I'm busy right now?!" Naivea was aghast at the tone of his voice, so much so that she felt faint. She went back and sat on the bed, pretending to look through her phone but she was fighting back tears. "Where did that come from?" she asked herself. "What did I do to deserve that tongue lashing?"

Naivea's spirit was dashed, she was frozen and couldn't move, as she watched Charles watching video after video, almost as if she wasn't in the room. Finally, Naivea's anger came to a boiling point. "I'm going to the gym that they have in the lobby," she said very sharply. Charles looked up from his phone. "Fine, I'm going back to Raleigh." Charles got his luggage and his briefcase and walked right out! Naivea was bewildered. "What just happened here? Did he just leave me without explanation?" She began to cry.

For the rest of the day and night, Naivea stayed in the hotel room without even eating. She was so upset and confused. She didn't know what to do and she was afraid that this visit just turned out to be a disaster. Finally, she texted Charles at 10 p.m. "I'm going to catch an Uber to the airport tomorrow, so you don't need to return to the hotel." She was full of anger and pride, and she felt disrespected and confused. Charles immediately texted back. "No, you're not! I'll be back to get you at 1 p.m. tomorrow. Your flight leaves at 6 p.m., so you'll need to be at the airport at 4 p.m. We can spend a few hours together before I take you to the airport." Naivea didn't know what to say, so she didn't text him back. "Does this man really love me? What a rollercoaster ride," she thought as she cried herself to sleep.

Sunday morning Naivea woke up at 8 a.m. Her eyes were sore and red from crying, and she was hungry because she hadn't eaten since Saturday's breakfast. She was still perplexed at the way Charles had abruptly left the hotel the day before. "What was he angry about? All I wanted was some time. All I wanted was to be made a priority." Naivea began to cry again. She eventually dried her face and went downstairs to get something to eat right before breakfast ended for the day. Instead of eating downstairs, she brought the food to the room and picked over it, eating just enough to make her stomach stop growling.

After eating, she laid back down on the bed to think. "Was this all a mistake? Charles said he loves me, but he sure showed a different side of himself yesterday. Is he bi-polar and didn't tell me? Does he have a mean streak?" Naivea fell asleep again, as she was still tired from the tossing and turning that she did overnight. When she woke up it was 12:30 p.m. She jumped on her computer and started doing some research to see if there was anything online that would reveal anything new about Charles. However, Charles had no real social media presence. He had a bio on LinkedIn and a very generic Facebook page with nothing out of the ordinary. She even paid on a site that said they had lots of information about people, but there was nothing on that site that she didn't already know.

Naivea researched until 1 p.m. She was numb. She didn't want to find anything negative, but she felt that she should look because of the way he acted the day before, and the way he disappeared the previous night. She turned off the computer and just stared out into space, saddened that this visit, that she had waited nearly two months for, went so sideways. Charles arrived at 2:30 p.m. To Naivea's amazement, he practically acted like nothing happened! "Hi. What'd you do yesterday," he said as he entered the room and hugged Naivea. She noticed that he didn't call her "Babe" and he didn't kiss her. "Nothing," she said rather stoically. "I went to the house to see mom and Calvin off," Charles quickly chimed in when he saw that Naivea wasn't in a talkative mood. "We went to my aunt's house and had a big dinner before they went to the airport." Charles talked as if his Saturday departure was pre-planned. Naivea said nothing. She just looked at him as if he was a stranger. "Come here Babe, what's wrong?" Charles said in his deep, sexy voice. "You left me here yesterday after I asked for some time with you. All I asked for was to take a walk in the park, but you wanted to watch videos, and you yelled at me." Naivea started to cry again.

"I'm so sorry Babe," Charles said as he pulled Naivea close. "I apologize for treating you that way yesterday. Mom kept texting me, wanting me to come back, and I was ignoring her but then she started blowing up my phone while I was trying to watch a business video. I shouldn't have taken it out on you." Charles started to kiss Naivea. He didn't seem to understand that he had put his mother before his new wife, and she was trying to make him realize the gravity of her hurt, but he was pulling off her clothes, and soon they were in bed making love.

Naivea looked at the clock, "Oh, Charles, it's 3:45! We'd better leave so we can get to the airport before I miss my flight. "I don't think I want to let you go," Charles said as he sat up on the side of the bed. Naivea then realized that in her depressed state, she hadn't packed. Her clothes were in the drawers and in the closet. Her toiletries were all over the bathroom, and she had two bags to pack. "I have to pack these bags," she said as she rushed into the bathroom to wash up. When she came out with her toiletry bag to get her clothes back on, Charles was still sitting on the bed. He hadn't gotten up to help her get her things together as she had envisioned in her mind. She looked at him, then started carefully packing the carry-on bag to make sure that it didn't contain any large liquids. Charles put on his clothes and sat in the chair at the desk while Naivea rushed around the hotel room grabbing her things and tossing them into the two pieces of luggage. She didn't have time to get mad because he wasn't helping her –it was time to go!

During the one-hour drive to the airport the couple did very little talking. Charles turned on R&B and rap music as they drove. Naivea hated those songs and wondered why he wasn't playing "The Piano Guys" or some other jazz instead of "that unholy music." She thought back on her other visit and realized that he'd told her that his jazz drives were in the Maybach S. She thought to herself, "I know he told me that he likes the Piano Guys as much as I do, and he knows I hate rap, so why is he playing this stuff?" To add insult to injury, once they neared the airport, Charles turned off the music. "I know this trip was a little rough and, again, I apologize. Don't forget to wire the money tomorrow so I can start looking for a home for us. I can't wait till we are able to get a house. Then we can have a wedding reception here and in Denver." Naivea was still in her feelings.

She had calmed down some when they bonded while making love before they left the hotel, but she was salty that Charles didn't help her pack, and now they were rushing so she wouldn't miss her plane. She thought to herself, "for better or for worse, I pray that this is the worst it gets." When they arrived at the airport Charles was still moving as if they had all the time in the world. He took Naivea's two bags out slowly, placed them on the curb and gave her a hug. "Call me when you are in your house safe and sound, Babe," Charles said as he rounded the SUV to get in the driver's seat without giving Naivea a kiss. Naivea answered with a weak voice, "Okay, I will."

When Naivea reached the gate, the plane had already started boarding. "Thank God, I didn't miss it. I don't know what I would have done if I did; this is the last plane out today." She breathed a sigh of relief. When she boarded the plane and lifted up her carry-on bag to place it in the overhead bin, she realized that the front zipper was open. "Oh, no!" she panicked because that's where she kept her portable luggage scale. She placed the bag on her seat and reached into the open pocket. The little scale was gone. Evidently it had fallen out sometime between leaving the hotel and getting on the plane. "If Charles would have helped me pack, I wouldn't have had to rush and this wouldn't have happened," Naivea lamented. This second visit ended like the first one: with Naivea feeling devalued in the end.

As she walked into her empty home, she remembered the way she felt when she got home in June after having to get an Uber to the airport. "Well, at least he didn't Uber me this time," she tried to shake the feeling that this relationship was getting off to a bad start. She texted Charles when she got into the house, "I'm home." Charles quickly responded with the heart and lips emoji. Naivea sent his nightly love meme, but instead of laying down in her depression, as she did after the last visit, she felt the urge to go online again and look up anything she could find about Charles. "Is he for real? He is so unpredictable, and I want to see if there's anything online that will help me understand him," she said as she sifted through the internet for three hours looking for clues as to why this man was so different from anyone she's ever known.

Naivea found nothing new. His business information was generic and she didn't find any articles that helped her figure him out. After three unfruitful hours, she closed her computer and prayed that the Lord would reveal the problems in their relationship and how she could correct them.

Chapter 7 Commentary
The Tea on NPD and Relationships
Telsha Edenburgh

Chapter Seven, page 1, was basically a devalue with another late arrival to create anxiety. Narcissists do this to basically build anticipation, and the anticipation will turn into anxiety when it literally doesn't pan out the way that it's supposed to be. It's another way that they abuse your emotions and also lie about what they've been up to. In addition, when church is mentioned, here it shows that he was not accountable to anyone! He didn't want to be exposed, so he didn't have a church home even though he claimed to be a Christian.

Charles told Naivea that his mother and brother had come into town. Without warning, he was blocking her from getting more "wife practice" at his home so that he could deny that she was improving, so his future-faking lie could last longer.

When I look at the hotel arrival, it's an administration of what I like to call the sex antidote. What narcissists do a lot of times—when there are problems or disagreements, or perhaps things that you may not particularly like about what they're doing—they like to use sex as a way to detour you from having your own opinion, or not having something to say about something that they've done that you didn't like. More than likely by the time they finished having sex, Naivea had forgotten all about the fact that she wasn't going to be able to stay at Charles' house. That was his plan: sex her up so that she is spellbound and happy.

And of course, I couldn't miss the triangulation with Miss Freda. So, Freda was a person that was also being used to triangulate Naivea. Triangulation is when the narcissist provokes jealousy in a Supply by mentioning other men or women in their environment. For example, a male narcissist mentioning the office secretary to his wife or girlfriend any time she gets upset is a strategy they use. It could be a subtle threat for the Supply to be quiet and line up or other options will be pursued.

The narcissists will do things to make you intentionally question them. And what they're trying to do when they do things like this is to get an emotional rise out of you, to see what they can get done emotionally. Also, in Chapter Seven, I noticed there was a lot of time blocking going on. Charles disappeared from the hotel room in the middle of the night. Narcissists like to time block. They make up a reason to not be available so that they can account for the time they're not going to be with you. For example, not texting back in time could be disrespectful to a degree, but mostly that's because the Supply has fallen into the devalue category and the narcissist has gotten comfortable and just doesn't feel like they need to put forth that much effort anymore.

Now, later in Chapter Seven, there was more of what I noted as the positive intermittent reinforcement. Positive intermittent reinforcement occurs when a narcissist does something kind after several acts of abuse toward the Supply. In addition to the positive intermittent reinforcement, there was the overdrive with the sex. I mean, just more of the overload of sex to keep

Naivea quiet and not saying anything about what he was doing. It's basically supposed to be a pacifier for her.

After having a night of wild sex, Charles devalues Naivea again by not paying her any attention the next morning. Charles' mask slipped when he yelled at Naivea, saying, "Don't you see I'm doing something?" His yelling at her left her confused and it was an indication that his mask was slipping. Also, this may have been an argument created to get an emotional response out of Naivea. Then he leaves the hotel with no explanation when she stated that she would go to the gym. In other words, when she decided, "I don't want to sit here and watch you ignore me, I'll find something else to do," he couldn't let her outdo or upstage his devaluation tactic. His departure was a devalue, leaving her to wonder what happened.

Charles continued the future-faking with Naivea, making all these plans to merge their households to become one. That is an important thing for him to do at that moment because it needs to keep Naivea hoping and wishing and on the path of being abused by him. Without question, that future-faking brings the Supply back into perspective of the relationship.

Near the end of Chapter Seven, Naivea's comparison of the relationship with a roller coaster ride was interesting, and it's very key too, because this is where the institution of the trauma bonding is taking place in this saga. What typically makes or causes the trauma bond to start are the highs and lows of the relationship. Up until this point, there had been a lot of highs, but now at this point his mask slipped and now the relationship dipped to a low point. What has to happen, in order to reinforce the trauma bond, there has to be more highs and lows, which is what Charles was creating in this scenario. As these highs then lows were created, he was then backing it all up with the future-faking, talking about the wedding again to bring Naivea back into a positive perspective and to continue to push the relationship and make it a priority now.

What I also noted in the last portion of Chapter Seven was that depression and anxiety start to set in for Naivea. That's what happens with the Supply once the mask slips. That's when the Supply ends up trying to decide whether you're going to go or whether you're going to stay. Is this real or is it not? That's what was happening at the end of Chapter Seven.

CHAPTER EIGHT
THE WORLD IS UPENDED

The next day, Naivea awoke to a text that Charles had sent two hours earlier. The text contained the wiring instructions for the $15,000. The odd thing that Naivea noticed about the instructions was that the company, Collegiate Tees, listed the bank account holder as someone by the name of Ida LaDron. Before going to the bank to wire the funds, Naivea called Charles. "Hi Babe, who is Ida LaDron?" "That's my aunt," Charles said with a surprised voice. "Don't you remember me telling you that I have my accounts in my aunt's name because Tabitha has that child support case against me, and since she won't prove that that boy is mine, I can't let her know how much money I make because the government will be after it. My properties are also in my aunt's name because she's a banker and she keeps good track of all of my assets. When we get into one household, I'm going transfer that responsibility to you."

Naivea did remember Charles telling her about Tabitha, but she didn't remember him mentioning that his bank accounts and properties were in his aunt's name. "Okay, I see," Naivea said. She didn't argue with Charles concerning the fact that he never told her about Aunt Ida – by now she had learned that every time she disagreed with Charles, he took it as an attack on his leadership skills. Once before, when she told him that she didn't remember him giving her some information, he told her that she was having memory issues and she should buy some Gingko Biloba supplements. Since she knew he was obviously a good leader she chose not to disagree with him on most things.

Naivea began to wonder if Charles' aunt was really trustworthy. After all, this money would be "their money" soon. Before she left to go to the bank, she researched Ida LaDron on the Internet. She found very little about Ida, namely that she was seven years older than Charles and that she was heavily involved in her community. Per the information Naivea found online, Ida lived in Durham, North Carolina and worked as an administrator at a local bank. Naivea thought to herself, "This aunt is barely older than Charles." But Naivea had an uncle that was only 3-years older than her, and she had a friend that had an aunt that was the same age as the friend, so she thought nothing of it, and went to the bank to wire the funds for the down payment on their dream home.

Fall came quickly in Denver. It got cold quickly. Naivea's contract with Charles' T-shirt company was due to end at the end of December, so she had four more sessions with this team. She wanted to see if she saw this Freda Long on any of the monthly video classes. Freda was on the video sessions, but she never showed her face. She pulled her roster of company trainees and found that Freda lived in Denver! "Oh, she lives here!" Naivea said with relief. Because Naivea realized that Freda wasn't one of the Raleigh sales team members, she no longer saw her as a potential threat and dismissed her and the pictures that she saw in Charles' briefcase, realizing that this woman was as far away from Charles as she was.

One day in late September Naivea received a call from Darla, Charles' administrative assistant. "Naivea, your contract is up at the end of the year," Darla said in a rather disparaging tone. "I'll be sending you a letter to that effect, and I'm letting you know that your access to the company training platform will be terminated immediately after the last session." "That's fine," Naivea said, trying to sound businesslike and unmoved by Darla's tone. Naivea and Darla interacted occasionally because Darla had to coordinate the sales team training dates and keep up with the paperwork showing each trainee's progress and whether their sales had increased. Naivea had done a great job training Charles' sales team, and she knew, based on conversations with Charles, that their sales figures were much higher.

During the summer, Naivea felt a shift in her interactions with Darla. It felt like Darla was jealous of her success, but she kept their conversations short and cordial, thinking that Darla just wanted to oversee something; and she was trying to wield authority over the training project from her home office in Seattle. Sometime that previous Spring, Naivea asked Charles why he selected an administrative assistant all the way across the country. He told her that he went on a nationwide search for someone that was an excellent administrative assistant, and one of his close friends recommended Darla. Charles had the utmost confidence in Darla. "She follows orders without asking a bunch of questions," he told Naivea in one of their summer conversations. "She also lets me know when one of the sales team members is off track in their sales, and she gives the bookkeeper all of the sales numbers to formulate the reports for the CPA. I have to make sure my taxes are done correctly," Naivea recalled Charles stating when they discussed how the business runs.

Still, Naivea felt something was off. "Charles, have you had a personal or sexual relationship with Darla?" Naivea was bold enough to ask because she really wanted to know why Darla's attitude toward her changed. "Of course not," Charles said, sounding like the idea was disgusting. "She just works for me. She reminds me of Lurch on 'The Addams Family.' "You rang?" Charles said, and both he and Naivea started laughing uncontrollably at the recollection of the Lurch character on the 1960's show that ran on the TV Land network.

With time running out on the contract to train Charles' sales team, Naivea knew that his team was ready to win the world, and she felt that Charles would praise her for their accomplishments. Charles, in fact, did praise Naivea, and bought her a beautiful and expensive watch for her birthday, and for Christmas he bought her a very expensive set of designer luggage.

As a matter of fact, after the August fiasco, Charles and Naivea did a "reset" of their relationship and things significantly improved. They decided to talk business before 5 p.m. Denver time each day and save their nights for relationship building. Charles sent Naivea videos about how successful businessmen operate, so that she could understand how they have ups and downs that effect their families. He also sent her videos about how wealthy people operate in a vastly different manner than poor and middle class people. Since Naivea was considered middle class and Charles was a millionaire, he wanted Naivea to learn how to move like the wife of a millionaire, and she enjoyed every lesson.

Throughout the winter, Charles sent Naivea a series of home pictures for her review. She gave her opinions about some of these mansions, but Charles said he wanted to take more time to find their dream home. Meanwhile, Naivea continued sending Charles nude pictures of herself all over the house, as he swore that those pictures kept him honed in on Naivea and away from the arms of other women. Naivea longed for the day that the couple would be in one household. "All of my worries about other women coming on to my husband will be gone," she thought constantly day and night.

However, just like he said about taking his time to find their dream home, Charles talked about taking their time to get to know each other better, before they merged households, so that their relationship would, as he would always say, "flow like a mighty river." "You are my Moon, and that means you are my everything," Charles told Naivea one night in September, and from then on, that was his term of endearment for her.

In October, Charles left for Portland, again, to take care of his mother and give his brothers their break. This was Naivea's second fall season with Charles having to be stealth on the phone so that his mother wouldn't wake up or fuss. Their chats during the day, although they were only about ten minutes long, became non-existent. Their chats at night were longer but they were every few nights instead of every night. Naivea wanted Charles to come and spend time with her in Denver before going back to Raleigh, and he agreed. "Since your birthday is coming up, I'll try to steal away from here for a few days to celebrate with you. I won't be able to stay for a whole week, but I'll keep you posted, Babe." Naivea was overjoyed, and she immediately started planning for his visit.

November 9th, in the wee hours of the morning, Naivea had a nightmare. She woke up sweating and her heart was beating extremely fast. She got up and got a glass of water as she went over the dream in her head. She drifted off to sleep again at 7:37 a.m. as she pondered what it all meant. At 9:30 a.m. she awoke to the sound of a siren going down her street. "Wow, I overslept," she said as she sat up in bed. But before she started her day, she wanted to reach out to Charles and tell him about her dream.

Actual Text Stream:

(Naivea) Last night I dreamed that I couldn't find you, then I went down this dark cold street and heard noise and saw lights at this house. I went to the front door and could see in the window. You were in there with a lot of strange people (they looked like circus performers). I knocked on the door and you came to the door but you wouldn't let me in nor would you come out. That jolted me, probably because I have been feeling a little curious about some of the things you have told me. Maybe when you get some time we can discuss.

(Charles' response) Crazy dream but they fit you.

(Naivea) I've always had them. I've seen many things that have come true.

(Charles) Except it's your life that's the circus.

(Naivea) A grand three ring one, and I'm about to exit, stage left!

(Charles) Well why the heck am I in the house with them?

(Naivea) I have no idea. I can't interpret that one. It hasn't been revealed to me. I need to clear my head of all the noise and get some fresh air. That's what I meant by exit stage left and by going off the grid for a while. Somehow, I feel trapped, with my back against the wall, and I feel like I'm running blind about to hit a wall.

I usually get someone to interpret or tell me what they think, but I'm reluctant to share the dream with anyone because although most people seem happy for me being in this relationship there are those that may internally be fearful of it because you live in NC. I don't want anyone to have reason to think anything other than what I have said. As a matter of fact, I have stopped talking about the relationship to the few people that I have shared it with in the first place. When Jamie (the colleague that got married today) started dating Donald, she got the third degree from her close friends because they care about her and were skeptical because he had already been married twice before. They finally laid off her.

Although Naivea wasn't expecting a long back-and-forth after her last text, Charles never responded to her final text in the stream. Later that night he called, and Naivea felt that he was concerned that she was backing away from the relationship because of her dream.

"Hi, my Moon, how are you feeling?" Charles said in his low, sexy voice, this time as if he was on a mission to woo Naivea back from the trauma of the dream. "I'm doing okay," Naivea's response was low and dry. "Whatever this is, we need to tackle it together. You know by now that I'm a great leader and I'll come through for you. People put their lives in my hands," Charles exclaimed as he seemed to be building a case for Naivea to shake the nightmare and move forward with their marriage. "There are other women in my life but not romantically, and I don't have any problems with any of my exes," Charles said after a long silence on behalf of Naivea. She remembered that he had mentioned before that he had good relationships with his ex-wife and girlfriends. "Why would he keep mentioning this?" she thought as she felt her neck heat up.

After another awkward pause, Charles continued sternly, "I need you to remember that I'm a busy, successful businessman and I'm not going to be able to cater to you. I need honor and respect – I demand it from you and everyone around me." Naivea was still numb from the nightmare. She nodded her head and said, "Understood," as she prepared to let him know that she needed to get off the phone and prepare for her 8 p.m. client. Before she went to bed, Naivea sent her usual goodnight love meme:

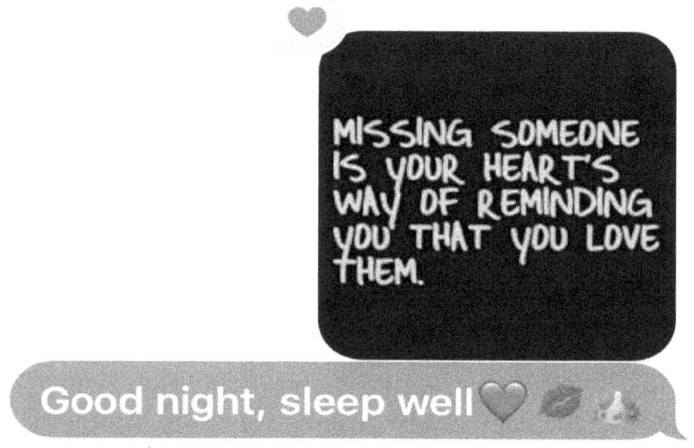

But to her surprise, instead of responding with the typical wish for a good night, Charles sent a very romantic text:

Thinking of you🩶

No mountain, nor sea, no thing of this world could keep us apart, because this is not my world .... you are.

"He's making an effort," she grinned as she put the phone away for the night.

In mid-November, Charles called with news, "Hi Babe, guess what?" "What?" Naivea asked with wonder. "Earlier this month I bought a house in Olympia, Washington. I wanted to get my mom out of the old house in Portland; our neighborhood has gone to the dogs. I wanted to keep the house, rent it out, and use the income to support mom. The house in Olympia is in a very nice, quiet neighborhood with a low crime rate. I took mom up to see her new house and she absolutely refused to move. It took all I had to get her to even go into the house – actually it was Calvin, her favorite child, that got her to get out of the car and go in. She didn't have any real issues with the house, she just doesn't want to leave the home she's been in almost 40 years."

"I understand that, Babe," Naivea said as she thought about how older people don't like change. "One of the reasons I bought this house is because it already had $50,000 in equity built in. So, instead of renting out our Portland house I'm going to fix up the Olympia house and rent it out for income. "Sounds like a plan," Naivea opined as she swelled with pride at having a husband that could outright buy a house like that.

Charles was a very busy man after buying the Olympia home, he was between staying at the empty home on an airbed, back at his mom's home in Portland, and at another aunt's house in Tacoma. When he wasn't at the Portland home, Charles and Naivea had much more time together. They started regularly having FaceTime dates. They even dressed up and had dinner on their respective tables. Afterwards, they would play music and talk about the song, or play "get to know you" type games, that ask questions like, "What's your love language?" or "Do you love or hate your birthday?"

One night Charles called and found Naivea in a flustered state. "What's wrong Naivea?" Charles seemed ready to jump into problem solver mode. "I'm concerned about my parents. They keep having financial issues," she said in a high-pitched rant. Earlier in the relationship she had explained to Charles that although her parents provided a decent life for her and her sister, they had not sufficiently prepared for their older years, and because her sister was financially irresponsible, Naivea had the burden of making sure her parents were going to be all right as they approached their mid-seventies.

"Don't worry about a thing Babe, I'm going to take care of your parents, and if we need to move them into a house in Raleigh when we get together, then that's what we'll do. You're my wife and I'm committed to making sure you don't have to work, and your parents are taken care of. I need you to understand that I'll do right by you and honor you." Charles' words were music to Naivea's ears! She felt a heavy burden lift from her shoulders, and she smiled as she gained a renewed longing for the day when they would be in one household. "Thank you, Babe, I love you!" Naivea said as her countenance settled down to a peaceful state. "I love you too Babe," Charles said in a comforting voice. This was the first time that Charles actually told Naivea that he loved her, and she went to bed holding on to that conversation like a child with a beloved teddy bear.

Soon it was ten days before Naivea's birthday and Charles hadn't mentioned coming to see her since October. As she did in April when Charles was supposed to come before, she had the house clean and smelling great. She had gone to the grocery store and purchased the ingredients for all of the foods and desserts she knew Charles liked. She even got her car detailed again so that when she picked him up from the airport she could show up in style.

That night Naivea waited for Charles to call. "Hi Babe, how was your day?" Charles started off with his regular greeting. Naivea executed her birthday inquiry, "It was busy. I was preparing for my birthday visit. I've been cleaning up and buying groceries to make sure I can show you my cooking skills," she said with excitement. "About that," Charles said with a sorrowful voice, "of all times, Calvin decided to get married that weekend, and since he's going on a week-long honeymoon and Clarence is going on vacation right after the wedding, I'm going to be stuck here alone with mom. Sorry, Babe, I'll have to make it up to you soon."

Naivea was speechless. She had just been denied a visit again for the second time in seven months. "You have to understand I have people depending on me," Charles said as he knew she was devastated. "I'll come as soon as I can, or I'll fly you to Raleigh as soon as I get back home." Naivea could hardly choke the words out among her tears, "Okay. I have to go now," she said as they ended the call. All of the life was sucked out of Naivea, and she went straight to bed in tears, thinking about the words from a video she had seen a few days before, "Expectations are premeditated resentments."

Charles was still in Portland in January, when the news of a serious viral outbreak rocked the nation. Within two months, businesses and churches were ordered to close, and people were instructed to stay home. "What do you think all this means, Charles?" Naivea asked as she listened to news story after news story claiming that people all over the world were dying of this strange virus. "They are locking the country down because they think it will stop this virus, and because of that, I have to stay here in Portland." Although his brothers were there in Portland, Charles decided to stay a while until the virus scare went away because he was concerned about his own health due to health problems that he'd discussed with Naivea earlier in the relationship. Naivea really wanted to be with Charles during this scary and uncertain time, but she knew that it was best for everyone to stay put until this virus was brought under control.

The months went by, and things got worse. World travel was brought almost to a complete halt. Businesses scrambled to find ways to make money online, and it became more and more of a burden to leave the house and do simple errands like grocery shopping, due to the long lines caused by the social distancing requirement. Naivea focused on daily survival. She had clients that she serviced online, yet she had to cancel six live training jobs because of the travel ban. She concentrated on getting those six clients to pivot and have her perform the sales training online. Three of them agreed but the other three canceled the training all together, fearing that their businesses wouldn't be able to take advantage of the sales force training due to the viral outbreak.

March came, and now Naivea was concerned about her finances. She had savings, but she thought to herself, "I can't wait until Charles and I are together in one household. I won't have to worry about all this." Charles called that night with comforting words for Naivea. "At the end of the day Naivea, you have to see my honor to God – no games, no trickery. My job is to love you. You will be the queen over everything I have, and I will be your lord. You belong to me, and I belong to you." The lord part sounded a little strange to Naivea, but she remembered that in the Bible, Sarah called Abraham lord, so she overlooked it.

In early April, as the virus raged on, Charles decided to find ways to increase sales because business was declining. He called Naivea with great news. "Hi Babe," he said with glee, "I just signed a contract for the T-shirts to be marketed on a wildly popular radio show on a station out of Miami, Florida. I found out about the host, Pamela Isaacs, from one of the high school principals that moved from Miami to Raleigh. This guy suggested that our business would skyrocket if we would advertise on Pamela's show, which caters to the college world.

I listened to her show for an entire week and decided that it would be a good business move to be a sponsor on her show. The radio station that we're talking about doesn't pay any of the hosts a salary, they only receive commissions when they have high listenership, and they have to get sponsors for their shows. They have to be great entertainers because they get paid based on listenership and sponsorship. All the college kids in Florida listen to Pamela Pie—that's her stage name because she loves pie.

Her show is entertaining and educational, and her audience fits with what we want to do with the business. Darla and I drew up a sponsorship agreement with Pamela and she accepted. As of this coming Monday, she'll be advertising the T-shirts on her show, and I'll track the show sales by giving her the product code PIE. I'm also creating a link for her website, and she can use that link to make money as she helps us grow. I plan to share my secrets and experience when it comes to winning high school and college student's hearts with her, and I believe that her audience is going to grow as she starts to talk about these wonderful shirts, so it'll be a win-win collaboration. Charles finally came up for air. He was really hyped, and Naivea had only seen him that excited a hand full of times. "That's wonderful news, Charles," Naivea belted out, trying to match his excitement.

The two talked for a few more minutes and Charles was off to wrap up some work. For some reason, Naivea didn't feel comfortable with this new business partnership. Maybe it was the fact that Charles was so excited about it. She decided to do a little research on this Pamela Pie. She searched the internet and discovered that Charles was right, this woman was an icon in the Miami area. She had the top show on the radio station, and her social media pages proved that she was well loved and respected by high school and college students alike. "What does she look like?" Naivea searched and finally found a few pictures of Pamela.

"Wow, she looks like Olive Oil from Popeye," Naivea laughed out loud. Pamela was around 5'8" tall, was only around 130 pounds soaking wet, and had a face full of freckles. I won't have to worry about her at all," Naivea's jealous side had begun to emerge. Darla was also light skinned, but she looked more like Olive Oil in the face than Pamela did. Darla was homely and Pamela was unattractive by what Naivea knew by now were Charles' standards. The only one that was really pretty was Freda, and since Freda lived about 20 miles from Naivea, she felt comfortable that the women in Charles' inner circle were not a threat to their marriage.

As business declined for Naivea, she also decided to look for other streams of income as the virus didn't seem to be letting up, and businesses were still on lockdown. Melanie was still at school, and because of the lockdowns, the college offered a summer program in which the foreign students could stay on campus and take two extra classes because they couldn't fly home to their respective countries. These classes were then opened to all students to prevent the appearance of favoritism to the foreign students. Melanie begged Naivea to let her stay and take these extra classes. "Mom, it'll put me ahead of the game when it comes to getting an internship my sophomore and junior year," Melanie pleaded. Naivea's funds were tight, so Charles sent $1,000 to the college so that Melanie could be a part of this special summer program.

Naivea's house contained a basement level that she sometimes used for training, with a back room for storage. She got the idea to make the basement into a full apartment, because it already contained a separate entrance. "Dad always told me to buy a house with a basement, and now it's about to pay off," she said as she started to gather the paperwork needed to refinance her home. "If I get my equity out, I can use the rental income to pay the loan back and pay off the house much quicker," she said as she performed the calculations to make sure that this was a wise decision. She discovered that rent prices in her area were hundreds of dollars above what her new mortgage would be upon refinancing, so she went ahead with her plans.

The refinance process was very quick. The mortgage broker told Naivea, "Wow, you came with all of the necessary paperwork, nobody does that! We'll have you processed in no time." While Naivea waited on the underwriters to approve her refinance, she gathered up reputable contractors to build out the one-bedroom basement apartment. Within a month, the funds were approved, and Naivea had done such a great job of selecting contractors, furniture and appliances that she realized that she would have $35,000 left over after paying for the basement to be completed.

"You did an excellent job managing your refinance, Babe," Charles said to Naivea when the job was finished and she sent him pictures of the newly renovated basement. "What do you plan to do with the remainder of the funds that you have?" Naivea was proud of her financial plan. "I'm going to invest most of the funds so that I can get a decent rate of return, and I'm going to keep $12,000 in my savings account for emergencies. Also, I'm going to keep $3,000 here at the house. My washer and dryer are old, and so is my refrigerator. If they go out, I won't have to borrow to replace them." Naivea had it all worked out.

"I have an idea," Charles said as his mind went into calculation mode. "Instead of investing the $20,000 with an investment broker putting it at risk, why don't you invest in the expansion of our T-shirt company? As I mentioned last month, we plan to expand the business by placing a warehouse on the west coast, and we are already picking up new business online like crazy. Shipping the packages from Raleigh is getting to be more expensive, and because of this virus, package delivery has become more hit and miss, causing our customers to get upset. With a production center in Washington State, we can service the west coast and the mountain states better. If you invest the $20,000 with our business, I will give you a 40% return, because you are the CEO's wife!"

Naivea had mixed feelings about Charles' proposal. Although she was happy that he was thinking of them as a couple and planning for their future as a team, she was uneasy about giving him the money – not because he was a bad money manager, but because she had already given him $15,000 to find them a new larger home in Raleigh, and he hadn't said anything about the home in several months.

Naivea was still thinking about that second visit when things took a disastrous turn. She decided to do some more digging online, not just to see if anything else surfaced about Charles, but Naivea wanted to see what info she could find on the two women in his life that dominated his time: Darla, the administrative assistant, and Ida, his aunt with the purse strings. She spent an hour looking for information about Ida. There was one article online about Ida's charitable and community activities, but Naivea didn't find any other social media pages for her. Darla had a Facebook page, but it was pretty dry and generic.

However, another business page showed that Charles was a part of one of Darla's side businesses. "Um, he never mentioned that before," Naivea thought. Due to her lack of social media findings, Naivea felt more assured that these women weren't a threat to their relationship, either time or money wise. She thought about the $15,000 that she had already wired Charles, and the $20,000 that she was thinking about sending him. "Well, it's the virus shutdown that's put the new house on hold," she rationalized. She then decided to go ahead and send Charles the investment funds because, "nobody else can deliver a 40% return, and, after all, I am the CEO's wife."

It was late August and the basement was finally done. Naivea and her property manager were ready to decorate the basement. "Make sure you decorate it in a feminine way so that a man won't want to live there. I don't want any men, young or old, to live in your house," Charles told Naivea in a very protective voice. "But whoever moves down there won't have any access to the upstairs," she reminded him, emphasizing that point because he had not yet been to see the house. "I know that," Charles fussed. "I just don't think it's a good idea for a man to be there. You can find a nice lady to stay there, and you'll feel much safer." Charles insisted.

Naivea visited many craft shops, department stores and discount stores, and finally the basement apartment was beautiful and ready to have its first tenant. The property manager took pictures and placed them on the MLS, and the apartment rented in one day! Now Naivea could use the money from her clients to grow her savings and pay other expenses. The mortgage was taken care of, for at least a year. The tenant was a very nice young lady, and Naivea prayed for her to stay there as long as possible because she was quiet and didn't have a lot of company.

"I need to expand my security system," Naivea thought one morning after thinking about the fact that she only had a doorbell camera. She figured that since the tenant was parking in the driveway and using her side of the garage for storage instead of parking, she wanted to make sure the woman's car was safe. When she talked to Charles about it, he suggested that she replace her current system and get a high-tech system like the one at his house. Charles had security cameras all around the outside of his house, as well as inside the house in several rooms. All of these cameras were tied into his cellphone, and he could watch each camera day and night.

He told Naivea that since he kept money and guns in the house, he wanted to make sure that he could see what was going on, even when he wasn't there. "My children are there sometimes when I'm not, and I want to make sure they aren't getting into mischief," he told Naivea. Naivea researched the system that Charles was suggesting, but it was a little expensive and it looked too complicated, so she just added cameras to her current system, so that she could see the driveway and the backyard, making both her and the tenant feel safer.

When she told Charles that she was just going to add cameras to her current security system instead of buying the one that he told her about, he was livid and began yelling at Naivea. "Here again you are disrespecting my leadership. You are a horrible wife! You can't even follow directions!" Naivea was upset, but she handled her surprise and anger by explaining that she didn't have the money for the new system because she gave him the extra money from the refinance. So he calmed down and changed the subject.

September came, and on this Saturday morning, Naivea was preparing her wardrobe for the cold weather when her phone rang. "Hi, my name is Angela Baker. Charles LaDron gave me your number to see if you could give me a few quick pointers on how to close sales. We worked together at the bank in Portland back in the day, and I'm gonna work for the T-shirt company selling the shirts here in Chapel Hill, and the surrounding areas on the college campuses."

Angela had said a mouthful, but Naivea felt intruded upon by this overbearing, ghetto sounding woman on the other end of the phone. Before Naivea could get a word out, Angela continued, "I know you've been giving classes and that they're almost over, but I invested $200,000 in his business two years ago. I had hit the lottery a year after moving to Chapel Hill to work for my sister's dental practice, and I quit and started being a businesswoman. I thought I would have some extra income from my returns on the money I let him borrow, but he said it's coming, and that you would train me to sell the T-shirts while the company grows."

Now Naivea was irritated. Not only was this woman a motor mouth, but she was appalled that Charles had let such a creature invest that much money into the business without giving her a return after this long. "Okay Angela, what days and hours are you available to have sessions with me on Zoom?" "Well, since I'll be working on meeting the decision makers soon, I will be available Monday through Friday for the first two weeks so that I can try and catch up with the rest of the class." Naivea thought to herself, "There's no way I want to hear your annoying voice five days a week woman!"

"Okay, Angela, let's shoot for an hour on Mondays and Thursdays at 7 p.m. Eastern time. Does that work for you?" "Sure does," said Angela as she slurped down the last of some kind of drink in Naivea's ear. "Okay, I'll send you a link and we can get started this coming Monday." Naivea hung up the phone. "Who is this woman?" she thought. She didn't want to have anything to do with Angela, but she wanted to find ways to show Charles that she was a good wife, even while they were still living separately. When Charles called that night, he thanked Naivea for being so nice to Angela. "She said you were so sweet and patient with her," he told Naivea so proudly. Naivea just rolled her eyes and said, "She was interesting, but I'll turn her into a pro in no time."

For the rest of that year while the virus went up and down all over the country, Charles remained between Portland and Olympia. He told Naivea that it was working out well because his sales team and his administrative staff in Raleigh were doing well, and he was building the business on the west coast. Charles sent Naivea several expensive gifts for her birthday, including more designer purses and spa equipment so that she could keep her skin smooth and body tight.

The couple talked more frequently during the holiday season, with Charles learning more about Naivea's life as a child, her marriage, her family members and her children. Naivea asked questions too, but usually Charles wasn't as detailed in his answers, and Naivea chalked that up to the fact that men are much less verbally expressive.

Most evenings after working with her clients, Naivea would sit on the couch dreaming about her hopes for the new year, praying that it would be the year they would not only be joined spiritually but also physically into one household. "But now it's time for me to sober up and prepare for the two biggest dinners of the year," Naivea would remember as she shook herself from her daydreams so that she could keep up with all of the preparation needed to make the holidays special.

Thanksgiving came and went, everyone stuffed their faces, sat and talked, then ate again, as usual. Some of her friends and family members were afraid of the virus and wouldn't even come out of the house, while others were determined not to let the virus stop them from normal life. Thanksgiving dinner was spent with her children, parents and some other relatives having lively conversations about the state of healthcare in the States, the inequality of the lockdowns, and the liveliest conversation was "to take or not to take the vaccine."

December blew through with a quickness, and the Christmas holidays were upon Naivea. A few days before Christmas, Naivea received a package from Charles. It was her Christmas gift. She smiled as she opened it, as he had instructed her not to wait till Christmas day if it arrived earlier. The gift was, again, very expensive – it was a Mont Blanc pen and pencil set. Naivea had seen some of these on Charles' office desk.

She wasn't much of a name-brand person, so she looked up this brand and realized that it was used by presidents and many wealthy people. She said to herself as she opened the bag and the boxes, "I don't want to ever lose these, so I'll keep them at home." When she pulled everything out of the bag, she noticed that there was a small yellow sticky note stuck to the bottom of the case which held the pen. She took the note off of the case. "For Ida."

Based on the note, the pen was originally for Charles' Aunt Ida. "Wow, am I getting something his aunt didn't want?" Naivea stayed in her feelings all day. She texted Charles to let him know that she received the package, but unlike most times, she didn't send him a picture of her holding the gift. Charles called later that evening. "If you don't want the gift, you can send it back," he said very matter-of-factly. "Why would you say that?" Naivea fired back. "Because you didn't have much to say but thank you in your text. You didn't say how you love the set, and you didn't send me a picture with you holding it like you normally do." It was clear that Charles was in his feelings.

Naivea quickly took a picture of the set and sent it to him. "I really like it, and I'll cherish it forever," she said in a patronizing voice. "By the way, there was a yellow sticky note on the bottom of the case the pen was in that said, 'For Ida'" Naivea was being downright snarky when she mentioned the sticky note. She felt like this gift may have been a hand me down. "Oh, I was wondering where that note went. I bought Ida and all of my administrative staff Mont Blanc pens for Christmas and I separated them out with the sticky notes. You can just throw that out." Charles was obviously angry with Naivea for bringing up the sticky note, but he also wanted her to know that he had spent a lot of money on his administrative staff and had given the sales team large bonuses.

All that did was make Naivea feel like she wasn't special because she got the same gift that his employees received. "I'll throw it out, thank you so much for the pen and pencil set. I will use it, and I'll make sure I don't let anyone walk away with either of them," Naivea said trying to keep the peace but still feeling rather insignificant. The couple talked a little about Christmas plans and then got off the phone. Naivea tried to shake the feeling of being undervalued by Charles for the rest of the night.

Overall, Naivea had a decent Christmas under the circumstances. Once again, the brave friends and family members gathered at her house for Christmas dinner, music, and to exchange gifts. Naivea was reluctant to show off the pen set that Charles sent her for fear that her relatives would start asking questions about why this mystery man hadn't come to Denver yet. She only showed the gift to Melanie, and they prayed that the new year would bring Charles to Denver and eventually have Naivea moving to the east coast.

The first quarter of the year flew by like a bullet train. Naivea picked up two large training contracts as businesses attempted to recover from the prior year's health crisis. She was still not doing a lot of travel, as most work was still via video training classes, but one of the companies had her fly to Boston in February and again in March for live training. Both Charles and Naivea seemed to be getting too busy for any quality time together. This fact made Naivea long for a visit from Charles. "Can you just come to Denver for a weekend?" Naivea whined one night when she was frustrated and lonely.

The tenant in the basement, although she was quiet, had found a boyfriend, and when he arrived to visit the woman, Naivea would make sure she immediately headed upstairs. She dreaded being in her living room or office while the boyfriend was there, fearing that she would hear them having sex. "If I can't have it, I don't want to hear it!" Naivea frequently thought to herself. She didn't hate on couples that were together, but she didn't want to frustrate herself by stirring up her sexual feelings while Charles was not around.

"Honey, I really don't want to go over this again. I'm not comfortable traveling right now, except by car between mom's and the rental property. I have a whole lot of people depending on me for their livelihood, and I can't afford to get sick from this virus. I told you that I've had some medical challenges before, and this virus really wreaks havoc on people that have pre-existing conditions." Charles had just shut down Naivea's hopes of seeing him soon. She would have to wait until he felt comfortable getting on a plane. He knew that she wasn't afraid, but she didn't want to make him feel like she didn't care about his health, so she decided not to bring it up again.

Then in April the news came. A text from Charles came in. "I got the virus. Not going to the hospital but having a doctor come here to the Olympia house. I've taken all the natural remedies that I have, and they haven't worked. Please pray for me." Naivea was horrified. As much as Charles had tried to downplay his past medical issues, she knew that they could exacerbate the effects of the virus on his body. "*Dear God, please heal my husband and let him recover quickly from this virus.*" Naivea got down on her knees, right there in the kitchen, after she read the text.

For the next six days Naivea didn't hear from Charles, she was terrified, but she realized she had no way to contact him. She didn't know his mother's or brothers' telephone numbers, and she didn't want to call the office in Raleigh because she wasn't even sure that he told them about him catching the virus. Naivea got on her knees every night for hours and prayed. "I have to learn now how to be a praying wife," she said each night as she cried out to the Lord and also physically cried.

By the seventh day, Naivea was out of her mind. She decided to text Darla. "Maybe she knows something," Naivea rationalized, since Darla was in Seattle and not with the rest of the team in Raleigh. Naivea reached out by text. "Hi Darla, I have a question for you," she reluctantly pressed send on her phone. Darla responded about five minutes later, "What's your question?" "Have you heard from Mr. LaDron?" Darla never answered. Naivea had no other way to find out what was going on with Charles. She decided to just let go and think about life without him. She took comfort in worship songs and tried to keep focused on her work.

On the eighth day, while she was cooking dinner, her phone rang, and it was Charles' special ringtone. She put down the cooking spoon and rushed to the phone. "Hi Charles, how are you?" she said with panicky delight. "Not too good, but I'm alive. How are you?" Charles said, sounding like a 100-year-old man. "Much better now that I've heard from you," Naivea said with glee. But then Charles had smoke for Naivea.

"Why'd you call Darla asking about me?" Naivea was fearful that she made a mistake in calling Darla but, remembering that she never mentioned the virus to Darla, she recovered. "I hadn't heard from you in seven 7 days and you hadn't given me any of your relative's telephone numbers. I was panicking because I didn't know how you were." Naivea spoke firmly but with much concern. "I tried to share that information with you before, but you didn't seem interested. I have to go now because I'm getting weak again."

Charles was off the phone in a flash. “At least I know he’s alive and getting better,” Naivea said to herself. She felt strange about how their conversation had gone. She never remembered having a conversation that involved getting his mom or his brothers’ contact information, even though she had given him Melanie and Harold, Jr.’s contact information in case he hadn’t heard from her.

For the next few weeks Charles called often and was very pleasant. He told Naivea that he was 80% better after a week. However, by the end of May, he seemed to be back to the old Charles. He was more adamant about staying put in Washington because he’d heard about people who’d contracted the virus getting better for a while and then getting much worse because they didn’t let themselves fully recover. In the meantime, he was very pleased with the way Pamela Pie was increasing the T-shirt sales.

“She’s tearing it up!” Charles told Naivea in June. “Sales from her daily radio show are almost as much as my top salesman in Raleigh.” Naivea was happy that sales were increasing instead of going down during this national health dilemma. “I wonder if he’ll give Angela some of that money for investing that $200,000,” she thought, but would never utter a word to Charles about it because she was pretty sure Angela wasn’t supposed to tell her about that.

One Thursday morning in late August, as she sat at her desk working, Naivea heard the doorbell ring. “Who could that be?” she said to herself, imagining Charles giving her a surprise visit. She would often think of him showing up at her door or coming in and sitting down on the pew next to her at church one Sunday. But this time it was FedEx with a package. Naivea wasn't expecting a delivery. The package required a signature, so she signed for it, closed the door, and took the package back to her desk. It was from a law firm, which made Naivea nervous. She hurried and opened it because whether it was good news or bad news, she couldn't stand the suspense any longer. She screamed out loud, "Praise the Lord!" as she read the first paragraph of the cover letter.

Before Naivea started her business, she'd worked for ten years at a company that sold corporate training packages to medium and large corporations. This was a multi-million-dollar company that only recruited the top salespeople from around the world, and to keep them, they promised a hefty salary and a percentage of the annual net sales. Before she left the company, she heard rumors that the accounting had not been done correctly, and that the salespeople weren't actually receiving the proper amount of revenue-sharing they were promised. Naivea heard that there was a lawsuit, but she soon forgot about the whole matter as each year passed while she grew her business.

The letter that she received was to inform her that all appeals for that lawsuit had been exhausted and the company was ordered to pay her and the other salespeople $35,000 plus the interest that accrued from the judgement to the final appeal. The check was even in the envelope! Naivea was so excited that she started dancing around her office. "Wow! $57,000! I can't wait to tell Charles," she said, as she settled back down to try and get some work done.

That night after finishing up a workshop presentation Naivea called Charles. "Hi Babe, how are you today?" she said with an energetic but sexy voice. "Okay, how about you?" Charles seemed to be irritated, which made Naivea's countenance drop. "What's wrong?" She asked with concern. "Just a rough day," Charles breathed a deep breath. Naivea felt that he didn't want to talk, but she also felt that the news of the settlement would give him something to rejoice with her about. "My old job sent me $57,000 to settle the lawsuit that I mentioned a while ago. I had all but forgotten about it, but we all received a settlement including the interest all the way up until the company exhausted all of their appeals!" Naivea waited for Charles' response.

"That's great Babe. What are you going to do with the money?" Charles pepped up just a little bit. It sounded more like curiosity than rejoicing to Naivea, but she thought to herself, "At least he's not sounding irritated anymore. "I'm going to invest it. I think I'll get some more precious metals and find another sound investment for the rest; you know I don't play in the stock market," she reminded him. "Why don't you invest more in our company? You can help me open up the Atlanta market since there are so many colleges there that I'm sure will love our shirts. I plan to have a small office there with an area to receive shirts in bulk and pay someone to deliver them to all of the colleges in person. You'll get more of a return on your money than you would with another company because this is partly your company."

Naivea felt honored that Charles was including her as part owner. She felt like soon they would be together, and her investment would turn into her being able to work at home or not work at all because she would be helping the business grow. By the end of that week, Naivea sent a certified check for $30,000 to Charles to help open the Atlanta office and hire one salesperson there to work exclusively with the colleges in the area. She put part of the other $27,000 in savings, paid off her credit cards, and bought precious metals.

September and October flew by, but Naivea and Charles' relationship sputtered. Charles was not consistent with the calls and still was not ready to travel back to Raleigh. Naivea was getting discouraged, but she made a deal with herself: "I'll just deal with all that comes along, because when he is ready to fly back to Raleigh, he'll come here and we'll reconnect, then we can work towards me moving to Raleigh. I'll put the house up for rent and use the profit to live on and maybe train people virtually while spending most of my time as a housewife!"

She made a pact that she would be pleasant, even when Charles was mean on the phone, which he had been a lot lately. Naivea realized that she had become used to being on a roller coaster ride in her marriage to Charles. One day she could be on top of the clouds, with Charles telling her to plan a cruse for them in the Spring; and the next day could be a steep swift dive, with Charles berating her about not being ready to be his live-in wife for some obscure reason.

November came and Charles treated Naivea to a new recording studio for her office so that she could start creating online sales training videos. She received a professional microphone, a new computer, special lighting lamps, a green screen with a wall mount, and several other items that she hadn't ever seen before. Once she started unpacking the items, she realized that they were used items from Charles' home office. "Evidently he got himself new equipment," Naieva said to herself as she remembered seeing a few new items in his home office during one of their FaceTime calls. Nevertheless, she thanked Charles for the wonderful birthday gift, but what she really wanted was for them to be together. "Soon Naivea," Charles said in a soothing voice. "Let me wrap up a few things here and I'll be heading back to Raleigh, and I'll make a stop in Denver for a few days." Naivea couldn't wait!

The new year brought excitement and anticipation for Naivea. Charles said he would fly out in February, then it turned to March, then April. Charles said that he was run down and started to have health issues again. "I have to stay here and see a specialist before I go home, my Moon. I am weak and I have bouts of dizziness," Charles explained reluctantly, not wanting his shining armor to show any dents." I'm praying for you always," was Naivea's response as she tried to show concern through her disappointment. She prayed for Charles day and night and dreamed of him having a clean report from the doctor. She wanted him to stay with her for two weeks in Denver so that she could nurse him back to health. In the meantime, Naivea kept herself busy expanding her garden and taking a few cooking classes.

In early May, on a Saturday morning, Naivea's phone rang. "Hi Babe, I'm back home!" Naivea was barely awake, but now she was in shock and didn't know what to say. "Did you hear me?" Charles asked with an exasperating voice. "Yes." That's all Naivea could get to come out of her mouth as she broke out in tears. All of her anticipation of Charles coming to Denver to meet her parents and friends, to meet her children, as Melanie would be home for spring break soon and Harold Jr. was looking forward to meeting Charles. Naivea fought back the tears, not daring to ask why Charles didn't keep his word about visiting her.

"I'll see you soon, but I needed to get back to Raleigh as soon as possible and take care of some business that was falling apart. It looks like one of the salespeople has decided to start his own T-shirt company and is soliciting some of the schools that we have contracts with. I will meet with our lawyers first thing Monday morning because all of the salespeople had to sign a non-compete agreement, and I just pulled his to take to the lawyer's office." As Charles waited for some sign that Naivea was still on the phone, she was not saying a word. "Well, I guess you don't care that I needed to get home to save our business, so I'll just get off the phone." With that, Charles hung up the phone, and Naivea cried even harder.

"How could he not understand how I feel? I've been waiting months for a visit, and he just flies right over Denver without even letting me know." She was distraught and went back to bed. Naivea stayed in the bed all day, hoping that Charles would call back and apologize, but he never did.

Chapter 8 Commentary
The Tea on NPD and Relationships
Telsha Edenburgh

In Chapter Eight, the first thing I noticed was the institution of triangulation with Aunt Ida. Charles was likely subtly making Naivea jealous of the fact that he had his aunt in charge of his finances, which is a show of her prominence in his life.

The biggest thing to note about the narcissist is that they often have several Supplies in proximity to each other. They often act is if these people are "just co-workers" or "just church members," but in reality they are telling them the same thing about the other Supply. They will cloak the Supplies' reason for being in their lives so that they can keep them as a Supply so you will never suspect that they are romantically involved with this individual.

Next, we see the manipulative gift giving to cloud Naivea's mind and secure the $15,000 that he had asked her for – you remember, the down payment on the home they were supposed to purchase together. This tactic was of course more of the future-faking. But this time on a larger scale because at this point, he's talking about a mansion because he wants her to have a bigger walk-in closet because of all of the clothes Naivea has told him about.

Also, after the devaluation during their last encounter, he again reeled her back in with promises and gifts. She cooled all the way off and he sent a "relationship reset" video to reel her back in. He also decided to let up some on the time blocking. He continued to frame her mind with videos about how high value men operate, so that she would think his behavior was normal.

In addition, Charles would continue to stress getting to know each other better before combining the households. This is AFTER he already declared that they were married, which was a trick because he had her thinking that once they were "married" they would combine households. Naieva felt that, based on his actions, they had already passed the "getting to know you" stage, but he had tricked her. He expected her to hang on loyally though, because they had already gotten so far and had already created the physical bond.

I think it's important to note near the beginning of Chapter Eight that Naivea's dream was actually a spiritual one. It was supposed to be a spiritual warning. The dream had different parts and pieces – moving pieces. But to me it served as a warning when I looked at the details. The dream had Charles perplexed, and he may have been trying to stop Naivea from thinking about or pondering on that dream because the dark entities in him knew that she was on to something.

Mentioning other women that he had not been romantically involved with is what narcissists typically do when they are triangulating and also what they do when they want to keep Supplies around even if they've moved on to new ones. They do this by cloaking them under another identity.

Charles sent the text message back to Naivea, and Naivea saw it as Charles trying to make an effort. But literally, when narcissists appear to be making an effort, trying to be better in the situation, or trying to behave more appropriately, this is them just instituting more emotional manipulation to get what they want from the Supply.

Next, Charles made a promise to take care of Naivea's parents, which is huge because Naieva was preparing to take care of them and was persuaded to depend on Charles to do it. Narcissists will make these promises to keep the Supply locked on. He knew that he could keep Naivea locked on as Supply because he knew that her parents' well-being was very important to her.

Now we actually get into more of the devaluation, where Charles again built anticipation for a visit – this time for Naivea's birthday. And all of the anticipation had been built up only to turn around and tell her that he couldn't make it – after she'd made all types of preparations to be with him. This is devaluation, but also, too, it's reinforcement of the trauma bond because the anticipation and the letdown, the highs and lows, define a trauma bond.

Charles definitely used the virus outbreak to control this entire scenario. It was to his advantage that everyone was told to shelter in place. And that is huge for a narcissist because during that outbreak, he had a huge reason to not engage in a lot of, what he might deem, unnecessary travel. So, the pandemic would have really made his job a lot easier if he was juggling several different Supplies.

Up to this point, Charles is basically introducing Naivea to more of his world and also painting himself to be this high-profile millionaire with all of these social connections. And this is done to keep the Supply locked on and to keep the Supply from questioning anything that he does. And so Naivea was basically playing right into it because she felt privileged to be with a person that had so much going on.

Now we get to Pamela Pie. She had a top radio station in Miami. So, this is more of Charles' positive, intermittent reinforcement. But even more than that, it's establishing his character. And narcissists like to paint an image of themselves that they are greater than anyone else. And that's what he's really doing in that section. He's managing his image, managing the perception of others about him; and to a narcissist, their image and what people think about them is everything.

It's important to note that when business started to decline and Naivea started to have financial problems at her home, even though Charles was a "self-made millionaire," from what we could see, he was actually not willing to help her. He would buy Naivea gifts, but he wasn't willing to step in to be the husband that he had claimed to be to Naivea; helping her to alleviate some of her bills so that she could maintain her household until they got into one household. So, he was willing to send $1,000 to the school for Melanie, her daughter, but there's no mention of anything he was actually willing to give to Naivea. Narcissists are very selfish and self-serving individuals. They spend money to make themselves look good, not to help others, even Supplies. It's all about what's in it for them.

In fact, right after Naivea had a slight recovery in her finances, Charles was praising her about how she did such an excellent job managing her refinance to get money to keep her going. But he wasn't willing to invest anything. Instead, what he was doing, was wanting to get more money from her.

After he had already asked her for the $15,000, he began presenting a proposal to get part of the equity money that she took out to convert her basement, which is more of that parasitic relationship where narcissists are just takers. I think it's important for us to note here that the minuscule gifts that he was giving Naivea were only small trinkets compared to what he was asking for from her to build up his business. He knew that his proposals had to include Naivea in them in order for her to feel that these plans were to make their marriage better.

It's interesting to note that Charles wants to make sure that Naivea doesn't have a man moving into the basement apartment, no matter what age. Narcissists are very jealous individuals, and although they may have multiple Supplies, they want those same Supplies to be totally loyal to them alone.

Charles was back to gift giving again here. I think it was very interesting to highlight that Charles gave Naivea the same exact gift that he gave to his employees. That right there was a complete devaluation, and basically taking her from wife status down to staff status. That act is also a part of the emotional roller coaster and the emotional manipulation that narcissists like to enact upon their Supplies.

Here we also see Naieva longing for Charles to visit her. However, he made it very clear that he was not comfortable traveling, which indicated that she was not a priority to him. That's important because when the Supply feels like they're no longer a priority, they will work harder to become the priority again. Once the narcissists' mask slips, they go to a place of just not really caring, and they just move how they want to move because the Supply has usually lost their will to fight for anything. Here, the identity that Naivea had was being stripped from her. Not only that, the identity of her being the wife, her being the main person in his life, was also being stripped from her. This was happening, slowly but surely, because of his unwillingness to bend and accommodate her wishes, even during the pandemic.

Another big development in this section is that Charles ghosted Naivea or discarded her. Charles said he got the virus in April and then disappeared off the planet, and Naivea didn't hear from him for several days. She was more than worried, but this is something that narcissists do. I don't really see this act as a ghosting. I really see this as a discard. So, she's just basically waiting for him to reappear on the scene. And they will do this often to pull the Supply in even more.

When Charles finally called, Naivea was again devalued because he fussed at her, and then got off the phone abruptly. We see for sure now that her mind is not her own, because, as opposed to being angry or hurt, she was just happy that he was alive. This is an example of the reinforcement of the trauma bond. He also said that he'd tried to share his family contact information with Naivea, but she didn't remember it. She didn't argue with him here, because he had already shamed her about her memory earlier.

Later we see more money coming into Naivea's life. Naivea told Charles about the $57,000 settlement, and although he was having a bad day, he pepped up when he heard that this Supply received more money. That's because he was trying to figure out how he was going to emotionally manipulate her to get his hands on some of that money too. Narcissists typically go up and down in their emotions. You see them having those down moments because they're managing so much evil and deception in their lives; they're depressed by nature.

Naivea happily gave Charles a certified check for $30,000 from the $57,000 legal settlement. This is more of the emotional manipulation. Not only that, it's also direct financial abuse. And yes, he treated her to a brand new recording studio full of his used equipment for her office so she could do her sales and training videos. But that was nothing compared to the $30,000 check that she had handed over to him; not to mention the $15,000 that he received from her for the house, and the $20,000 to invest in the business earlier. So, this is a direct example of financial abuse. And narcissists love to financially abuse their Supplies.

During this time in the relationship, Naieva made a deal with herself in her mind, and her keeping up this deal prolonged Charles' hold over her. She etched into her mind that soon she and Charles would be living in one household, and all of these troubles and mishaps would be over. She used this "deal" to buffer the roller coaster ride of a relationship she was on.

The anticipation Naivea felt about Charles coming out to Denver, her desire to take care of Charles and for him to meet her parents, fell in the toilet because there was likely never a desire on the part of Charles to meet Naivea's family. He was again making her wait, building up anticipation only to let her down AGAIN. His excuse was lame, and when she was silent, he used SIGN language again—[Shame, Insult, Guilt and the Need to be right]—telling her she didn't care about saving the business, when in fact, there may not have even been a real crisis.

Being traumatized so many times can launch a Supply into a state of depression, anxiety, and loss of all self-esteem. His showing up to see her is no longer important to him; and that usually happens before a narcissist discards a Supply.

CHAPTER NINE
IS THERE HOPE?

Charles called on Monday evening. As if nothing had happened, he started to talk. "Hi Babe. The meeting with the attorneys went well today. They assured me that we have grounds to terminate the traitor, and they drafted a letter for me to send out to all of our customers to which he was assigned, making sure that they know not to deal with him anymore." Charles stopped and waited for a response from Naivea. "That's good," Naivea was still very hurt that Charles not only flew straight home but didn't tell her of his intentions in advance. She felt like she wasn't a priority in his life, and over the weekend she had been praying to the Lord about what to say to him about her feelings.

"Is that all you have to say?" Charles bellowed as if pressing Naivea to be happy about their current relationship status. "Charles, I am hurt," she started out. "For over a year I've been waiting for us to get back together and rebuild our relationship, but you flew right over Denver after telling me that you were going to come and spend time with me. That makes me feel like I'm not a priority in your life, and your wife should be a priority over business." Naivea was even surprised that she got that sentence out. She felt a burden being lifted from her shoulders because she realized in her prayer time that she had been operating in the fear of losing Charles. Now she felt that she must let him know what was on her heart so she could find out what was really on his.

"I am so sorry for not treating you like a priority Babe," Charles began. "I'm trying to run a multi-million-dollar company, and I have over 20 employees and salespeople and their families that depend on me for their livelihood. You have to understand that I can't cater to you!" Naivea expected the conversation to be a little more caring, but when Charles stopped talking, she felt her anger arise. "I'm not asking you to cater to me, just to keep your word or let me know when you have to change your plans." She wanted to add that it was only common courtesy, but she knew that statement would set him off.

"Well, business changes rapidly and I have to turn on a dime on a regular basis," Charles said as he doubled down on his actions, refusing to apologize for not coming to Denver. After that comment, Charles changed the subject to how well Pamela Pie was doing with sales from her Miami radio show. "By the way, Pamela's show is very witty and entertaining and with my help, she has added a little more education to her entertainment, which has grown her audience and T-shirt sales. Her listenership has increased over 30% since we signed her on, and our Florida sales are pretty solid."

Naivea decided to suck it up and start engaging Charles in conversation. "That's excellent! What time does her show air? And do people only listen on the radio or can they also stream it on their computers?" Naivea was trying to make conversation, but she also wanted to start paying attention to what Pamela was doing to increase sales. "Maybe I can use some of her techniques to get some attention," Naivea thought with a touch of jealousy. Their conversation was short as it was getting late on the east coast, but it ended positively as far as Charles felt. Naivea, on the other hand, was still feeling hurt and a little angry. She prayed that her attitude would improve soon.

That Wednesday, Naivea received an email from the National Association of Sales Trainers, informing her that she was voted one of the top 50 sales trainers in the country, and that there would be an awards ceremony in Dallas, Texas to honor her and the others. They would receive a plaque and an all-expense paid vacation for two to anywhere within the continental United States. This news made Naivea feel a lot better. She had been working so hard to keep busy and create new ways to help people learn to be good at sales, and now it was paying off.

Instead of calling Charles, Naivea texted him the news. Charles texted back, "Wow, that's great news Babe, you're number one of the 50 people. I'm coming with you to the ceremony. I wouldn't miss it for the world!" Now Naivea was delighted. She would get to see Charles in two weeks, because the awards banquet was the Saturday before Memorial Day. Naivea sent Charles the invitation that she received from the Association, so that he could make his flight arrangements. She also asked if they could stay in Dallas a few days and make it a mini vacation. Charles agreed.

A week later, Naivea received devastating news again. She was in the shower and missed the phone, but when she got out, she listened to the message from Charles. "Hay Babe, sorry to disappoint you again but I just found out that I need to be at a big T-shirt convention in Atlanta that same Saturday. Lots of big schools and companies that purchase T-shirts will be there. Darla is flying out to help with our booth and I plan to get several more contracts that day. I promise, I'll fly you out to Raleigh for a week in June." Naivea was disgusted. She sat down on the bed and cried tears of frustration. "Why does everything keep getting in the way of us getting together? Why can't he send some of those people I trained; he doesn't have to be the one to go!"

Naivea was so upset that she canceled her lunch appointment with her best friend Sophia. She couldn't bear to tell Sophia that Charles was standing her up again. Sophia and Naivea met at church 30 years ago and had been best friends ever since. Sophia wanted the best for Naivea because she knew how hard Naivea tried to make her first marriage work. Sophia and her husband George looked out for Naivea and neither of them had a good feeling about Charles, especially Sophia. "You deserve better than him," Sophia would constantly tell Naivea when she would hear that Charles was letting Naivea down.

Naivea didn't talk to Charles until after the awards ceremony was over. She came back from Dallas happy about the award but disappointed that her husband was not there to see her receive it. She was feeling depressed, and she started having anxiety attacks, thinking that Charles was never serious about them being in one household. She finally wrote Charles a long note and sent it by text.

Actual text:

It has been almost three weeks since our last conversation when you said that you were not coming to the awards ceremony so that you could go to a convention that any one of your well-trained [by me] employees could have handled, and after saying you wouldn't miss it for the world. I don't feel that I will ever be a priority in your life – not the number one priority, just a priority.

I believe that it is time to untangle this relationship. I would really love to know why you have kept this "thing" going for so long since men control relationships. I have been in love with you for a long time, forgiving your crass comments and interruptions when I am speaking, helping you think of advertising slogans even when I have a ton of work to do, trying to be the perfect helpmeet for you, as you truly deserve. I am only angry at myself for letting my heart rule over my head and trying to believe that all the things you said were true and all the things I went through were going to end in a beautiful marriage.

I am not equipped to deal with this. I don't know where to put this. Please, get back with me at your earliest convenience and let me know your plan to untangle this relationship so that it will not further negatively affect my health. Naivea

After she sent the text, Naivea felt a little like taking it back. "What if he says that he doesn't want me anymore? How will I cope with that?" Charles called Naivea a few minutes later. "I read your text. I wish I had known how much that award ceremony meant to you," Charles started out in his attempt to win Naivea's heart back. "I really want to learn how to balance my business life and my romantic life. I've never been a big romantic, but I'll start making a bigger effort because I know I've been slacking with our relationship." Naivea started to feel a little better.

"I said I would fly you out in June, so send me some flights for the second week in June. Pamela Pie is coming to Raleigh the first week of June to spend some time with some relatives she has here, and while she's here we'll go over some plans to expand her show to Atlanta radio." Naivea didn't know what to say. On the one hand she was happy that she would finally get to see Charles after so long. On the other hand, she was a bit upset that Pamela Pie would see Charles before she would. "Okay, I'll look up some flights and send them to you later tonight," she said as she contemplated her feelings about the whole conversation.

That night, Naivea sent the flight information and Charles sent her money to book the ticket. That next week Charles sent Naivea promotional pictures of Pamela standing next to his Maybach-S for their Atlanta Campaign. Pamela seemed to be relishing in the luxury of the three cars in Charles' three garage beys. Naivea wondered if Pamela had been inside Charles' home, but she never asked. Even though Pamela came to Raleigh with her siblings to attend a family reunion, she wondered how much time Pamela spent with Charles. Naivea referred back to the pact that she made with herself. "Once we start seeing each other more often and merge into one household, all will be well, and I will have priority and the ability to see what the women around him are all about."

It was time for Naivea's flight to Raleigh. Her flight left at 6 a.m. so that she could have as much time with Charles as possible. She was met at the airport with a big kiss and the couple held hands all the way back to Charles' house. Charles seemed a little on the anxious side, and Naivea was concerned that he was nervous about something. It had been three years since she came to the house the first time, and Charles was eager to show her the improvements that he had made since returning a month ago.

The first two days were bliss for Naivea, as they moved like a married couple. They made love all through the night, then slept late; and when they did get up, Naivea cooked a hearty breakfast. They went to a nice restaurant for dinner the first night, and Naivea cooked the second night. However, by the third day, there was trouble in paradise. Charles became upset that Naivea left several dishes drying on the kitchen counter overnight. Naivea had cooked a large dinner and a homemade dessert. She didn't want to leave the kitchen a mess, so she washed all of the dishes. It was late, and since there wasn't enough room to place them all in the dish rack near the sink, she got a towel and laid the larger pots and pans on the towel to dry overnight. "I don't want to make a racket putting all of these dishes away tonight because Charles has gone upstairs already," Naivea said to herself as she turned out the kitchen light to go upstairs.

On that third morning, Charles got up early and went downstairs. When Naivea woke up she went downstairs to find Charles working at his desk. "Good morning," Naivea gave Charles a kiss on the cheek, but he retracted. "What's wrong?" Naivea asked bewildered. "You left all of those dishes all over the kitchen like this is some kind of junk house. You may keep your house looking like that, but that's not my world! My house is always immaculate, and dishes aren't scattered all over the kitchen!" Naivea was about to pass out! She had no idea that drying the dishes on the counters overnight would be such a big deal.

That's what she had done even when she was a child, and her family had big dinners. All of the girls pitched in and washed the dishes and laid them on towels to dry. Charles hadn't even looked up at her when he was blurting out his rant, but her utter silence made him turn around in his swivel chair and look at her. He could see the dismay in her face. “I’m sorry for being so forward, Babe. You know how I am, and I like things clean. I know it was late when you finished up, but I would have preferred it if you would have put the dishes away. When you move in permanently you can rearrange the kitchen any way you want, and I’ll be fine with it.” Charles was trying not to scare Naivea into wanting to go home early. Naivea was still very hurt, but she straightened up her face and cracked a smile. “Okay, Babe. I’ll put everything away right now, and I’ll never do that again.”

The rest of the week flew by quickly for Naivea and it was time to go. As before, she booked the last flight out to Denver so that she could spend as much time with Charles as she could. During their last day, Charles spent a lot of time on the phone. “I need to get with my mentors today; they are helping me to plan for our joining.” Naivea had no problem with that. After lunch she started taking her clothes out of the closet. “Pretty soon you won’t have to do that,” Charles said when he came upstairs from his office. Naivea smiled and the couple made passionate love one more time before Naivea had to leave.

Charles got a phone call a few hours before having to leave for the airport. He got out of bed and went downstairs. When he came back, he had news. “I’ve got to go to an emergency meeting. One of the companies that we source the shirts from is trying to raise the prices and my representative needs to nip this in the bud in the morning, so I need to meet him this evening so that we can decide what to say to them. I’ll call you an Uber. I know you want me to take you, but this is important; our profits will fall quite significantly if they try to raise the price. We have to pull the contract out and review it before we receive another bill from them."

A disappointed Naivea got up, showered and prepared her luggage to go home while Charles darted in and out of the room checking on her, kissing her on the neck and face each time he came in. Once he got off the phone, he pulled her down on the living room sofa into his lap. "I hope you had a good week. We'll start spending more time together. Your next visit will be soon because we were apart so long. Give me your phone so I can show you how to share your location with me. I want to make sure you're safe when you are riding in the Uber, and I want to cover you while you are anywhere because you are my wife, and just because we aren't together every day doesn't mean I can't try to keep you safe." Naivea smiled as she unlocked her phone so that Charles could set her phone up to indefinitely share her location with him.

The Uber arrived and Charles took her luggage to the car, kissed her passionately and shut the door as she got in. She blew a kiss at him, and he smiled as he turned and went back into his house. Naivea slept most of the way home on the plane. When she was awake, she was dreaming of being in Charles' home full time. She tried to memorize every detail of every room, and she contemplated how she would fit all of her clothes into the limited closet space that was there. When she arrived home this time, unlike the other two times, she had a smile on her face as she got ready for bed and fell fast asleep.

For the next few weeks Charles and Naivea spoke at least once a day, but their conversations were more about how the T-shirt business was going and less about making plans to be in one household. The Saturday after Independence Day, Charles called around noon. "I had a rough week, and I need to see you, my Moon. Please book a flight for the last week in this month if you don't have any training classes to teach." Naivea was euphoric. "Even if I did have training classes, I'd cancel them first thing Monday morning to come and be with my husband, you are my priority!" Charles laughed with pride, and the couple talked about their love for each other. "I'm going to get you a very nice ring, but you have to stay within the $20,000 range." Naivea's eyes bucked. She had never thought of getting a wedding ring that costs that much. When she was married before, the entire ring set was less than $1,000. "But I have to remember, I'm married to a multimillionaire," she said to herself as she smiled during their entire conversation.

Time flew and Naivea was back in Raleigh. Charles picked her up from the airport and they went shopping for shoes for Charles, and Naivea got a nice blouse to complement some slacks that she brought with her for a nice dinner date. When they arrived at the house and Naivea started unpacking her bag, she noticed several pairs of footies in one of the drawers next to the bed. When Charles saw her looking at them, he quickly explained. "Those belong to Octavia. She loves to leave things over here." Naivea remembered that Charles' children spend time with him during the summer. "She must be 17 by now," Naivea calculated her age based on their conversation from four years earlier. "Yes, and she has a lot of mouth, I wish I had more influence on her upbringing, but I do what I can now, "Charles said as he shook his head. "Teenagers!"

The rest of the week was up and down for Naivea. It was too hot in Raleigh for many outdoor activities before 7 p.m. In the evenings they went to dinner or spent some time out on Charles' back porch. Most of the time during the day, they were watching movies, talking business or listening to Pamela Pie's radio show. Naivea thought it was very interesting that Charles wanted her to suck him while listening to Pamela's live radio show. She wondered if he got a rise out of listening during sex because Pamela would mention the T-shirts several times during the show; sex and money made him happy. "It's the kinky in him," she thought to herself as she crouched on her knees while Pamela did her thing on the Miami radio station.

Charles was an exceptional lover. Naivea had been with a few men before she was married, but neither those young men nor her ex-husband Harold had done the things that Charles did. She found herself explaining to him again and again, "I can't compare that to anyone else because I've never done that before. She was addicted to his voice, his intellect, and the way he made her feel in bed. As the day passed by, she grew more focused on being with him permanently.

Once again, time flew, and it was time for Naivea to go back to Denver. "The last day is always the hardest," Naivea said to herself as she started to gather her belongings a few hours before they had to leave for the airport. Charles was downstairs in his office on a call with his mentors, so she decided to see how she could further show him that she was ready to be a housewife. She looked around the bedroom. "Nope, I've cleaned up everything here, and the other bedrooms haven't been used." Naivea spotted the dirty clothes basket and pulled the top off. "Bingo!" The basket was full of dirty clothes. "I have time to wash and dry all of his clothes before I go," she said to herself with a very mission-minded attitude. As she pulled the clothes out of the basket, she stopped dead in her tracks near the bottom. There she slowly pulled out a pair of red lace panties and a red and black lace bra. She held up the bra and turned it around. She held up the panties and turned them inside out. There was dried discharge in them, so she was careful not to touch the crotch area. She laid them down on the floor separately from Charles' clothes.

"These don't look like a 17-year-olds underwear. Why would they be in Charles' room anyway?" Naivea sat there for a moment not knowing what to do. "Should I say something? What should I say?" Naivea put all of the clothes back in the basket, put the top back on and went downstairs, trying not to look upset. Charles was in his office but wasn't on the phone. "Babe, I was going to wash clothes before I go. There are some women's underwear in the basket, what do you want me to do with those?" Naivea was trying her best not to show any emotion. "That's Octavia's stuff. You can leave all that in the basket. I'll get it later. I don't want you doing any work, it's your last day." Charles pulled her over onto the swivel chair with him and she sat there as he designed the latest T-shirt.

When she did get up and go back upstairs, she checked the other bedrooms to see if there were dirty clothes baskets in them, and there were none. "I guess the kids have to put their stuff in his basket, because it's the only one in the house." Naivea still felt bothered, but she figured that she was just being a jealous emotional female. "And even if he were messing around, I have no way to prove it," she thought.

It was finally time to go to the airport. Charles put Naivea's bag into the Range Rover and they took off. "I'm glad you didn't get all upset about Octavia's clothes in my room," Charles complemented Naivea as if he thought she was maturing into a good wife. "You could have approached it in a very nasty way, thinking those were some other woman's things." Naivea had thought of that possibility, but she just smiled as they drove. "I trust you Babe, I know that you love me and trust me, and I trust you. Where there's no trust there's no relationship." She had heard that once when she was listening to a relationship coach on YouTube, and she knew it was true from her previous marriage and other marriages that she'd seen over the years. The trip back home was somber. She longed to shut down her operations in Denver, pack up her belongings and be with her man. But he wasn't ready yet. She got home, opened the mail, returned some emails and went to bed.

August seemed to drag along for Naivea. She wanted to start scaling back her training classes and start planning for a move, but Charles seemed to downplay or even avoid the subject most of the time she brought it up. Naivea decided not to mention the move anymore until the end of the year. Most of their conversations were pleasant, and some were romantic. Charles still regularly asked Naivea to send him nude pictures and videos of her prancing all over the house, and she complied, hoping that, as he often told her, the pictures kept his eyes on her and off of other women.

One day in late August, Naivea's ex-husband Harold texted her. He was at their old house preparing it for sale, and he found a handbag that was hers. He wanted to know if she wanted it, and she texted back "no thank you." Then they had a long text exchange in which he apologized profusely for his adultery and all that he put her through. Naivea, in turn, apologized for not being a proper wife and being more committed to growing her training business. Harold then told Naivea that she had been a good wife and mother. The text stream was a sort of closure for Naivea. Even though she no longer had romantic feelings for

Harold, she was happy that they were able to clear the air and apologize for each of their parts in the failure of the marriage.

When Charles called later that evening, Naivea told him about the beautiful exchange and closure that had taken place earlier that day. Even though it had been eight years since the divorce, Naivea felt a chapter finally closing so that she could start the new chapter wiser and more equipped to be a wife. To Naivea's dismay, Charles flipped out. "He didn't mean what he said! He was just telling you what he knew you wanted to hear. You were a horrible wife. You can't brag on any wifely qualities! If you were such a good wife, why is Harold married with a new younger wife that's meeting all his needs while you're alone?" Naivea was speechless! Charles' words were very angry and hurtful.

Immediately, Charles tried to clean up the last part of his rant about her being alone. "You're not alone, but you're by yourself," Charles said, as if that was going to make everything else he had just said all better. They both knew that he was trying to make sure that she wouldn't ask him what he meant by her being alone. She was surely going to make a comment concerning their marriage and the fact that she is alone because he hasn't made the arrangements to join their households.

As Naivea tried to absorb what she had just heard, she thought to herself, "I should have NEVER said anything to him about this." "I have to go Charles; I have to get up early for a meeting." She quickly got off the phone and went to bed exhausted and angry, as Charles was silent, knowing that he'd royally messed up. As Naivea laid down, she thought of the Scripture, "Love covers a multitude of sins." She also thought about her father telling her as a young woman that in relationships you'll never get 100% of what you want; you'll be lucky to get someone that meets 80% of your emotional needs. You have to get that other percentage from friends and family. Naivea had a few friends that she would share with once the couple was living in one household; friends that would encourage her if Charles hurt her feelings. She always thought that since the business was sometimes so stressful this was what any wife of a CEO had to deal with, and she knew she was tough enough to handle it.

Chapter 9 Commentary
The Tea on NPD and Relationships
Telsha Edenburgh

In Chapter Nine, Charles continues with devaluation. Sometimes devaluation can take on many different forms. But in this case, it was the form of neglect, which is oftentimes how narcissists dish out their devaluation. Neglect and insults are their main weapons. After the big blow-up about him flying over Denver, Charles called Naivea as if nothing had happened. It's normal for narcissists to cause a fight and when they don't want to fight anymore, abandon the issues and act like they don't exist.

Clearly, Naivea was being devalued. The priority that she should have taken as his wife was clearly taking a second seat to the first love of his life, which was his business, which was attached to his image. Narcissists will do anything to protect that golden image that they've portrayed to the world, which is clearly what Charles was doing at that moment.

When Naivea stood up to Charles, to get back at her, he changed the subject to talk about how one of his other business ventures was having success. This tactic produced more triangulation with Pamela Pie because of the success that she was having. Increasing her listenership on the radio, and thus his revenue, was now Charles' new focus. Pamela Pie was beginning to become a priority even over Naivea, and talking endlessly about Pamela was supposedly to make Naivea back down and realize that if she didn't bow down to Charles, then there were others that would.

Charles canceled on Naivea again after he had promised to meet her for the big association banquet. Again, this is actually a devaluation, but it's also jealousy starting to rear its ugly head. Charles appeared to be jealous of Naivea winning a prestigious award, because no one is supposed to get accolades but the narcissist. He probably didn't want to go and celebrate with Naivea, so he likely lied in the beginning, acting like it was so wonderful, only to disappoint her once again. With the narcissist, the disappointments are supposed to break the Supply down enough to the point they start to not expect anything but disappointment from the narcissist. It's called conditioning.

After the great few days of positive intermittent reinforcement that Charles and Naivea had in June when she finally made it to Raleigh, he had to destroy the bliss with the whole dishes situation, throwing her right back into the devaluation stage. Many Narcissists thrive on the breakup and make up cycle, using it to control the Supply and as a way to create a reason to have "make-up" sex. Make-up sex is like a spell on the Supply; they've been brought down by the fighting and devaluation, then the overpowering make-up sex is like heroin to them. Naivea has been overpowered in her flesh by Charles' sexual prowess, and the make-up sex helps to keep her from breaking up with him, even throughout the consistent devaluation episodes.

During this June encounter, Charles devalues Naivea by having her take an Uber to the airport after the powerful make-up sex episode – keeping her on the roller coaster ride even as she leaves for home. This was another incident of sex control and positive intermittent reinforcement. There was more of the future-faking in this section, with Charles talking of them spending more time together. His claims that he was going to make more time for her had, by that time, stopped garnering a lot of anticipation on Naivea's part. She had settled on just getting in where she fit in.

Wow! The red lace panties and black bra. Panties with a discharge at that. Clearly, Charles was cheating, but he lied and said those were his teenaged daughter's clothes. Naivea didn't believe him, but since she had no proof that he was lying, she didn't cause a fight. Her mantra that "once they are in one household all her troubles would be gone" had become a stronghold over her mind. She was no longer thinking clearly, logically, or objectively about anything to do with Charles.

Naivea had a very important conversation with her ex-husband, and there was some closure and peace made. Charles was clearly jealous of Naivea's closure and used that opportunity to devalue her even more because of the things that he had noticed about her as a wife. His response to her communication with her ex-husband was more mental anguish and torment through the mechanism of devaluation and manipulation. It's awful.

CHAPTER TEN
WHAT'S REALLY GOING ON?

September in Denver was a little cooler than normal, and Naivea took out all of her winter clothes. She packed up a lot of her old clothes to give to charity. "I know there's not enough room in the closets at Charles' house for all of this, and since it doesn't get as cold in Raleigh, I won't even need all of these clothes.

October was a slow month also, but Naivea kept working on becoming a housewife; making sure her cooking skills were improving and scaling her business to be more online and less in person. One day in late October as Naivea was cooking, she looked up at the clock and saw that it was time for Pamela Pie's show. She decided to stream it on her computer and finally listen to how Pamela delivered her message to her audience. "She's a salesperson just like me, only she sells the end product and I want to hear what she does to make the audience consistently buy Charles' shirts."

As Naivea turned up the volume she heard Pamela tell her audience, "Hey guys, for the next three days I'll be out of the studio, bringing you the show from a remote location. I don't have all of my bells and whistles with me, but the show's gonna be just as dope as it always is." Naivea kept listening. The topic for the day was how to win scholarships even if it's last minute, and Naivea wasn't the least bit interested in the topic because Melanie's tuition was already covered.

However, as she listened, something else caught her ear. There was something she thought she heard in the background, behind Pamela's blaring voice. Naivea turned the pots on to simmer and turned up the volume on her computer. She totally drowned out Pamela's voice and listened to the background noise. Then she gasped! Naivea had heard that noise many times before. It sounded like the noise that Charles' printer made! Charles had a state-of-the-art color printer that made a very distinct sound every few minutes when it rotated the ink to make sure that the color copies came out perfect. This was not an ordinary noise; it was more like a bird trying to break out of its shell at hatching time. Naivea listened carefully. She remembered the rhythm of the machine, and it was the very same rhythm. "Could this be a coincidence?" she thought to herself. But she knew it probably wasn't. "What is Pamela doing in Raleigh?"

Naivea felt sick to her stomach all day. That night she waited for Charles to call, but he didn't. She decided to text him at 12:30 a.m. Eastern Time.

Actual Text:

"Good night my Love. I didn't make it to bed at 11:30 like I meant to. It's one of those days/nights where my spirit is troubled, so I would appreciate your prayers as I do the same. Nothing to do with my training classes though. Sleep well."

Instead of Charles calling her or at least trying to find out what was wrong, he responded, "Good night and sweet dreams. Your spirit is in trouble a lot – I pray you address that spiritually."

At that point, Naivea was almost sure Pamela was with him at his house, and she was on edge all night. The next day she called but got the voice mail. She sent several text messages in addition to her morning love meme. Charles finally responded with a video that he wanted her to watch that might improve her online presence. "No romance, just business," Naivea said in a huff.

Later, she listened to Pamela's show and, again, heard the printer noise in the background. After the show, Charles called and asked her about her online platform and how she planned to enhance it. There was no "Babe" and no romance. "Charles, do you have guests at the house?" "No, why would you ask me that?" he said with obvious shock at the question. "Because you've been talking to me like I'm a business client not a wife," She was as firm as she chose to be without outright asking him was Pamela there. "No, I've just been in business mode a lot lately, and I want to make sure that your online platform is done correctly."

Charles didn't stay on the phone long. It was as if someone was there listening to him talk. Naivea was devastated but she couldn't prove that Pamela was there. After three days of being out of her studio, Pamela returned to her regular bells and whistles, but Naivea, even though she felt that Pamela wasn't Charles' type, couldn't shake the feeling that something was going on. She reverted back to her pact: I'll just jeep quiet and keep working toward being in one household and once I'm there I'll be able to relax and not be suspicious.

November came and so did the opportunity for Naivea to speak at a two-day event in Atlanta. The organization was paying for her airfare, hotel and meals during the entire event. She quickly accepted the invitation and created a presentation for the event. When she told Charles, he was excited and said that he would come and support her. However, when she mentioned that several of her colleagues would be there also, he changed his mind. "You're making a big deal out of introducing me to your friends and all I wanted to do is support you during your presentation. I was going to stay in the room and work while you speak and mingle with your colleagues. I wasn't planning on being in the auditorium for the entire weekend, and since you're talking about introductions, I'll just stay home!" Charles spouted.

Once again, Charles backpaddled on attending an event to support his wife. "But how is supporting me staying in the room and working?" Naivea asked sincerely. "I'm not arguing about it, I said I'll stay home." Naivea was sliding down the roller coaster again. She wrote Charles a long letter about how he seemed not to want to be with her in public. But she knew that wasn't true because they were together in public many times when she went to Raleigh stores and restaurants. She decided not to text him the letter, as she had done many times before when she was hurt. Charles got to the point where he wouldn't even read them anyway.

Charles asked Naivea to let him know when she was leaving Atlanta to go home, so when she was being driven to the airport by the host company that morning, she called from the car. "I'm headed to the airport; I'll see you soon!" Naivea acted as if she was going to come to Raleigh instead of going home to Denver. "Well come on! See what it would take for you to divert to Raleigh for a few days. I'll pay for it." Naivea couldn't believe it. They fought over him not wanting to support her at this conference and now he was asking her to change her flight and come see him. She wasn't interested in bringing up that fact though, she wanted to see her husband.

Naivea changed the flight to go to Raleigh, spend five days with Charles and return to Denver. However, this time, instead of staying at the house, Charles got Naivea a room at an up-scale hotel in the Five Points community of Raleigh. "Charles Jr. is at the house with a few of his friends for the week and I really want to see you, so we'll stay at the hotel," Charles told Naivea on the phone. "This trip was last minute, and I have meetings all day, so I'm going to have to Uber you to the hotel." That's fine, Babe," Naivea said as she walked through the colossal Atlanta airport trying to find her new gate.

She arrived in Raleigh and called an Uber, which took her to the hotel. She'd made reservations while at the Atlanta airport, so she checked into the room at 4 p.m. and waited for Charles. Naivea waited, and waited, and waited. She finally got dressed for bed and dozed off. At some point, she heard a faint knock at the door. She got up, put the mint on the nightstand in her mouth, and went to the door.

It was Charles and it was 11:30 p.m. "Hi Babe, sorry I'm so late," Charles said as he grabbed her up like a stuffed animal. Within no time they were rolling in the sheets as Charles released all of the stress from his day on Naivea's welcoming body. When he would orgasm, she noticed that he would never say her name, he would cry out, "Oh Babe, oh Babe." Naivea said to herself, "One day, I'm going to get around to asking him why he never says my name when we make love. I think that would really turn me on even more. "

The couple stayed in bed the next day until noon, then they went to find lunch and some clothes for Naivea because she only brought enough clothes for the conference. The first two days were bliss, but the third day was a nightmare for Naivea. Early in the morning Charles was checking T-shirt sales numbers for the first half of the month. "We did very well," Charles said as he came out of the bathroom. "That's wonderful," Naivea followed up, proud of the company growth. Charles was on and off the phone for the next hour, then he started acting as if Naivea had done something wrong. "What's wrong Charles?" she asked as he sat in the chair across the room. "Why are you always so disagreeable?" Charles yelled. "What did I do?" Naivea was thoroughly baffled. "You figure it out!" he yelled. Naivea was dizzy and confused. They had only been up for a couple of hours, they hadn't even had breakfast, and now Charles was literally yelling at her for something she didn't know that she did and that he couldn't tell her that she did. "I haven't done anything!" she said as she teared up. She then thought to herself, "When are we going to have a week together where there's not some type of blow up!"

Naivea and Charles went to lunch but there wasn't much communication. When they got back to the hotel room Charles sat in the chair on the other side of the room and played in his phone, and Naivea sat up on the bed and stared into space. After two hours she realized that they weren't going to the movies as previously planned, so she started to write a letter to vent her frustrations:

Actual Letter:

Today is our third day together. It seems like there's something about the third day. It's currently 10:25 p.m. EST and I am in a suburb of Raleigh, North Carolina.

Today I was accused of being disagreeable 4, 5, or 6 times, and there was an attitude that was noticed at the point where he was dismissive about me. Hair being up or down, then went to wait for me in the car while I had the towels changed out.

Once returning from the restaurant this conversation started about why I am always disagreeable and we can't get along for more than a day. I couldn't think of what I had done, and he couldn't either.

I have no idea what I did to be disagreeable and I told him three things that may have been an issue, and he said that was nitpicking but couldn't tell me any. He said those were not the things I did, then he said it was my responsibility to figure out what I did. Me trying to figure out what I did is like Nebucudnezer telling the wise men that they had to tell him the dream then the interpretation.

Then, when talking about how we can't get along, he brought up an incident from three years ago, after he said he wasn't going to bring up that old stuff anymore, but he has been doing it anyway. He never mentioned that old stuff in June or July when we had two good visits.

Then he said this, "Because of all the stuff you did in the past, I am always waiting for the other shoe to drop!" This statement let me know that I will never live that stuff down and that I will never be trusted by him. It let me know that the goal post will always move.

So, I am not his wife because he has a back door open because he says that I have a negative spirit that he is waiting for me to get rid of.

He has the negative spirit too. I came here with joy and up till this morning things were fine. He is the one that got upset and he doesn't even know why. He is always negative and skeptical about people and things that happen. He wants me to tell him what's going on in my life but then comes back and throws it up in my face as being chaos.

He said it is okay to interrupt me in mid-sentence because the husband gets the last word. I looked that up and it is considered rude by everybody's standards.

He says I am going to bring all my chaos here to Raleigh because I have a negative spirit. Get rid of the negative spirit he says, but then he is very negative also.

Once the conversation got to trying to remember what happened earlier in the day, before we went to the restaurant, and he couldn't even come up with one of the 4, 5 or 6 things that he said I did that were disagreeable, he went to sleep from 4:45 to 6:45, then got up and got on his phone. He has not said a word. I have no water, he did not take me to the movies, he has not tried to be the leader and solve the issue. I guess I am just one of those women that is not a priority.

Naivea was so mad that she got out of the bed and slept on the closet floor. The next morning Charles lectured her about getting out of the marriage bed. "If you get out of the marriage bed that leaves room for me to leave it and go to someone else," he explained. Naivea didn't have much to say except she still didn't understand what happened the day before.

Charles was a different person the next day. They went out to eat and he took her shopping, and actually shopped for clothes and shoes with her. Naivea wanted to get a small purse since she didn't bring one on the trip to Atlanta, only her bookbag. Charles said, "I have some designer purses at the house that I use as employee gifts. I'd rather you take one of those than buy one of these cheap ones. Naivea agreed, "What do they look like?" "Octavia is at the house about to order the boys some food by Uber Eats, so I'll get her to take pictures of them and you can select the one you want." Charles showed Naivea pictures of four purses and she selected one.

That day was getting better. But by the end of the day, Charles told Naivea that he had to go back to the house. "I have a big meeting tomorrow, so I'm not going to stay the night with you tonight." "When will you be back? Tomorrow is my last day, and I want to spend time with you and go see the movie." Naivea whined. "The meeting is an hour away and it may be long. I'll try to make it back as soon as I can, and I'll bring your purse." Charles left and Naivea was flying down the roller coaster again.

The next day Naivea knew she wouldn't hear from Charles for a while. She found a movie theater close to the hotel and looked at the movie times. The hotel let her have a late check out, but she had to be out of the room by 1 p.m. By 4 p.m. she had not heard from Charles, and she had been sitting in the lobby with her bags for three hours. At 4:30 Charles texted and said he would be there soon, so she looked at going to the 5:30 movie. Her plane was supposed to leave at 10:50 p.m., so she calculated that the last movie they could watch, and safely get to the airport, was the 7 p.m. movie. "As long as he's here by 6:30, we can still make the movie."

Charles didn't show up until 6:45 and Naivea was livid. She tried to hide her anger, and she rationalized that missing part of the movie would be okay. Charles gave her the purse, and she transferred her personal items from her bookbag to the purse as they loaded up the Range Rover with her luggage. It turned out that the movie was so close to the hotel that they made it to the 7 p.m. movie with time to even get popcorn. As they walked from the parking lot to the theater entrance, Charles walked a little ahead of Naivea, and she wondered why he wouldn't hold her hand. A young woman was walking towards the parking lot and commented, "You two make a great couple." Naivea smiled at her and thanked her.

The movie was good, and now Naivea's time with Charles was almost up. She received another shocker when they were leaving the theater. "I'm going to order you an Uber to meet us here at the theater and take you to the airport because I have another meeting this evening," Charles said in a voice that assured Naivea that he didn't want to hear any opposition. Naivea kept her feelings to herself. They sat in the SUV for a while with little conversation. When the Uber arrived, Charles jumped out and got Naivea's luggage out of the trunk. He walked back to the Uber and placed the luggage in that car as Naivea slowly got her bookbag, the new purse and her coat out of Charles' vehicle. As she walked back to the Uber, Charles gave her a half-hearted kiss and said, "Safe travels, I'll be watching you on the location sharing app." "Okay," was all Naivea could muster as she got in the back seat of the Uber.

All the way to the airport, Naivea questioned their relationship. "Does he really love me? Is this the way other CEOs treat their wives? Is he being faithful to me?" Once again, she reverted to the self-made pact. "Soon I'll be here in Raleigh for good and we'll be able to get along much better.

Chapter 10 Commentary
The Tea on NPD and Relationships
Telsha Edenburgh

As I read Chapter Ten, I feel that it's an important and pivotal Chapter. I thought about how this man was literally, I won't call him a psychopath, but he's definitely a sociopath. I say that because a sociopath doesn't have a heart, and you can't have a heart to treat someone like Charles was treating Naivea. The difference between a sociopath and a psychopath is that the sociopath tries to make horrible behavior look like it's acceptable, whereas a psychopath doesn't care what it looks like. Charles is a skilled sociopath – he's a manipulator and a grand liar. It shows in the messages that he texted back to Naivea that first night and in their conversation when he called her.

Naivea is in denial when she hears the peculiar noise of Charles' printer because she has been so brainwashed that she is willing to ignore the fact that he is not being faithful to her. Pamela Pie is probably at Charles' house, and Naivea is suppressing that fact. His thorough takeover of Naivea's mind shows me that he is a mastermind at socially engineering people.

Narcissists will tell lies without a conscience. Their skill level depends on where they are in the spectrum. Sometimes you can see them get nervous about it. Sometimes they won't. But lying is the name of the game for Charles and for most narcissists, male or female.

Charles is basically hell bent on having his way, because that's what the whole relationship is about, him having his way. The selfishness of this individual and the uncaring behavior is breathtaking. He cares nothing for Naivea's mental health because she expressed to him that she was troubled spiritually, and he clapped back at her with insults and gaslighting.

When Naivea left the Atlanta meeting, she was joking with Charles, subtly letting him know that she could show up at his doorstep at any time. I recall that Charles lives in a gated community, and he probably picked that community to make sure that he had control over who came to his home and when they came.

Since Charles wanted to keep the "marriage" going, he allowed Naivea to divert to Raleigh from Atlanta. He didn't want her to go back to the Midwest still angry that he reneged on coming to Atlanta to support her. His actions are still a form of manipulation; he wants to keep a tight grip on Naivea.

Then, my mind drifted over to the fact that he put her up at a hotel, so now I'm suspicious. Is his son really at the house with his friends or is it someone else. We've already established that this man is a skillful liar, so it wouldn't surprise me if he has one Supply at the house and has Naivea at the hotel.

And then Charles left this woman at the hotel overnight, then the next day for hours after checkout time. Not only is that embarrassing, but it could be dangerous because if the hotel felt she was in the lobby too long they could have asked her to stand outside with all her luggage. Charles said he would be at a meeting about an hour away. Why didn't he reschedule that meeting. This man is cruel!

By this point in the story, Charles' behavior depicts that of a person who has no empathy. He's not your low-range or mid-range narcissist, Charles is a cerebral narcissist. Not only is he a cerebral one, but he vacillates to the somatic as well, because he's very sexual. So that makes it even worse. That makes it even worse because he not only pulls on the mind, but he pulls on the body, too. As women, we get caught up in our emotions through the body. These birds have to get our mind first. But then once they get the body, women feel like we've given everything.

I feel so strongly about what should be said about this chapter because people need to see in this context right here, what happens in the mind of a sociopath, and how they behave. This is sociopathic behavior that's skilled in social engineering, that can build webs and destroy lives!

CHAPTER ELEVEN
THE BEGINNING OF THE END

December was cold, literally and physically. Charles seemed irritated more than half the times that he called. In mid-December the phone rang at 8:30 a.m. Naivea was startled, because her phone automatically stays on Do Not Disturb until 9 a.m., except for calls from her parents and Charles. She reached over to the nightstand to grab the phone. It was Charles. "Good morning, Babe," she managed to get her first words out without it being obvious that she was coming out of a deep coma. "Good morning my Moon, let me ask you a question," Charles was very direct and evidently on a fact-finding mission.

Before Naivea could agree to the question, Charles went on. "What do you see as my flaws?" It took no time for a list to pop up in Naivea's head, but she wanted to formulate and communicate the most important two. "When I'm explaining a scenario or a story to you, you jump to conclusions and formulate a diagnosis in your mind that's not true or partially true even before I finish telling you the story. When you do that, it makes me feel like you don't want to take the time to listen to me. I know I go into great detail sometimes, but so do you when you are explaining things that you're passionate about." "That's fair," said Charles. It was evident that he was writing down her answer.

"Also," Naivea continued, "frequently, you cut me off when I'm talking and trying to explain something or define something, and by the time you're done talking I've lost my train of thought." Charles seemed to ponder that answer for a minute. At first, Naivea thought that Charles was trying to find ways to be more sensitive in the relationship. But soon it became clear that was not his intent. "You need to call me and ask me for what you want, without nagging!" Charles said in a nasty tone. For Naivea, nagging was a trigger word because she was always very careful to make sure that when she approached Charles with anything, she made her requests without whining or nagging; and she was offended that he would imply that she had failed in that area. Naivea didn't say a word because she knew that Charles wasn't finished.

Charles continued, "And you say you want to support me as a wife who lives in the same house, but I haven't been asking you to support me lately because I don't find your support to be genuine." Naivea was outdone. She felt as if a rug had been pulled from under her feet. She started thinking of all the times that she had stopped what she was doing to help Charles do research or to proofread documents that he had written, checking for errors. She began to feel unappreciated, yet she continued to remain silent. "You need to get yourself together because we're not joining households until you become a proper wife!"

With that, Charles hung up the phone. Naivea was DEVASTATED. Her day hadn't even started, and she had just been read the riot act by the man she loved. "What's going on?" she thought, as she got out of bed to get some water. Her throat had totally dried up during the exchange. Naivea went about her day in a daze, she felt like the roller coaster was going down much more often than it was going up, and she felt like she may need to get off this ride. She remembered a day earlier in the year during a spat when she hinted that she was having health issues from the stress of trying to live in two worlds. Charles was very matter of fact then also. "Would you rather grow old alone and force your children to take care of you in your old age, or would you rather us grow old gracefully together?" he asked her bluntly.

Naivea remembers how offended she was with that question. It was as if she was being given an ultimatum to do whatever Charles wanted or die alone. She remembers answering him, "Of course I'd like to grow old gracefully with you." She also remembers thinking that she was definitely operating in the fear of losing him.

The couple's next two phone calls were pleasant, and there was not a continuation of the beat down that Naivea felt she received in the first call. However, the pleasantries didn't last long. Charles called again a few days later and was irritated and evasive. "I'm not going to take unnecessary risks. I want to be with a woman who wants to be a wife. I want peace." Again, Naivea had no idea where that statement came from and she was offended, thinking that Charles was telling her that she was not wife material and was chaotic.

"I want a wife that desires to cook, clean, sew, iron, garden; one that loves me, forgives me, and wants to give herself to me; and for those things to be consistent, because often times it's not consistent with you, Naivea. I'm a husband who knows he needs a wife, and right now you aren't fulfilling the part." Naivea was silent as tears began to stream down her face. Charles continued, "I think that you're growing impatient with the fact that I don't want to take a bunch of unnecessary risks. I have too much at stake to jump into something that you really don't want, or that you really do want, but you're faking your newfound love of cooking. I don't want to find out that I was set up in terms of your doing what housewives do when you really don't want to do those things." As far as Naivea was concerned, Charles was off his rocker somewhere out in left field. As she wiped her tears and her nose, she wondered had he gotten into some drugs or something.

As if he hadn't said enough, Charles muttered on, "I keep saying to myself, 'Why don't I be patient until she knows with no uncertain terms that she is a wife that knows that she needs a husband and wants me as that husband.' We've been getting you ready for that wifehood, but it feels like you are impatient. I'm not doing this stuff until you are a wife because a man that finds a wife, not…not a man who finds a woman or someone he can have sex with…. Finds a good thing. The guy that will marry you is the guy that realizes you are a wife. You don't put a ring on a woman's finger hoping that miraculously she is going to turn into a wife."

Naivea felt like she was in a nightmare and the levels of terror kept getting deeper and deeper. After a long silence, she was able to speak. "Charles, I know that when you met me I wasn't in wife mode, but I have been cooking and doing wifely things for a couple of years now, and I'll continue to cook and clean because these simple things are what any man would want in a wife, and anybody that's an adult wants to be able to take care of their own household, and that's why cooking, cleaning, gardening and the rest of the things you mentioned become something engrained in a person and in me. I'll do these things from now on whether you are around or not! I am not being impatient. I'll continue to do what I am doing. I am not trying to dictate marriage to you. You just said you are not going to marry me until I am a wife, and I'll assume by that statement that you mean we won't be joining households until I've crossed some finish line that you've concocted, but my issue is: it seems like the finish line keeps moving farther and farther away!" Naivea felt her neck getting hot again. She had gone from surprised and hurt to flaming mad, and now she wanted nothing more than to get off the phone with Charles.

Charles realized that Naivea was fired up, so he led the conversation to a conclusion. "Naivea, I want you to be at peace with me. I need you to be sure that you want to be my wife. I've got to go now but please understand that I'm just trying to be careful with my heart and your heart." The phone call ended on that note, but Naivea's heart was hurting and confused. It seemed like their relationship was on a wild ride and she didn't know where it was going.

The couple didn't talk for another week. Charles wrote Naivea stating that he no longer wanted to participate in the Christmas pagan rituals of buying gifts because the celebration had been turned into a commercial boon for department stores and people were going into debt trying to please others. Naivea agreed, as she had felt that way for years. They talked a few times before Christmas, on Christmas and a few days later. On December 29th Naivea asked Charles what he was going to do for New Year's Eve. She always went to her church that evening to bring the new year in with the church members, but this year, she wanted to be with Charles, and since they were still not together, she asked could they do a FaceTime date like they had done in the past. Charles agreed, and Naivea was set to dress up and have a small dinner ready for that night.

New Year's Eve came and Naivea was waiting to hear from Charles all day. She kept busy cleaning the house and talking to her relatives. She texted Charles at 6 p.m. Eastern time but he didn't respond. Charles finally called at 7 p.m. Eastern. "Hi, my Moon," he said with a cheerful voice. "I'm headed to Chapel Hill to meet with Angela Baker and her team for dinner. They claim I've been so good to them that they want to present me with an award. I'm not going to stay long but I wanted to see how your day is going." Naivea could tell that it was raining hard. "Be careful Babe, I hear the rain," she said. Naivea didn't know how to feel about the fact that Charles was going to a work-related event shortly before they were supposed to have a FaceTime date to bring in the new year. "Tell Angela I said hi," Naivea said with a gleeful voice, trying to hide her concern for the time.

The couple talked all the way until Charles arrived at the restaurant. Charles said he would be back home by 10:30 p.m., and since the drive was only 40 minutes each way, he had plenty of time for dinner and a presentation, so she didn't fret. At 11 p.m. Naivea's phone alarm went off to remind her of the time. She got dressed in a sexy dress and heels, made up her face with a little make-up and set her tripod up in her family room to get ready for their date. At 11:30 she texted Charles, "You home yet?" There was no answer. Naivea started to get angry and felt like Charles was not going to make the date. At 11:58 p.m. Charles called. "Sorry, I'm running late Babe. Traffic is a mess out here. Happy New Year! I'll talk to you soon." Naivea heard the phone click. "Did he just hang up?" She was furious!

She sent a New Year's meme at midnight, and she called Charles at 1 a.m. and at 1:50 a.m., but there was no response.

Finally, after dozing off around 2:30 a.m., she woke up and looked at her phone to find a text from Charles that came in at 2:28 a.m. "Sorry my Moon, I got home out of that traffic and fell right to sleep on the sofa. I tried to get home, but the party goers took over the highway. I'll make it up to you Babe." Naivea just rolled over and went to sleep. In the morning, as she lay in bed, she thought to herself, "Is our marriage always going to be full of disappointments?"

Later on, during New Year's Day, Naivea texted Charles at 1:54 p.m. and again at 7:04 p.m. with no responses. She was wondering what was going on. Finally, Charles texted her at 7:35 p.m., "It's been a rough January 1st, but I'm okay." "I'm praying for you Babe." Naivea texted back, as she had feared something was wrong. "I appreciate it," Charles answered. The next day they had a few loving exchanges via text. Naivea told Charles that she was performing her wifely routine of cooking and cleaning, and Charles responded, "Loving you is my nightly routine."

Loving you is my nightly routine

Tue, Jan 3 at 12:43 AM

But a little after midnight Mountain time, while Naivea was asleep, Charles called, and the call was severely alarming. "Naivea, we need to talk," Charles' voice was high pitched and angry. "I realize that we clash often, and that you don't like listening to me and following my leadership." Naivea was shaken. "What in the world brought this on?" Charles continued, "You say you want to be in one household, but you've been independent for so long that I think the thought of someone else controlling your life scares you. You mean the world to me Babe, but I feel like you get an attitude about our relationship moving too slow, then an anger comes over you. I don't feel that you prioritize me enough in your life, and especially not above your life."

Now Naivea was really mad. She again thought of all the times she put herself aside to do what Charles was asking her to do. "Just this past Friday I missed a meeting with the banker;" listening to him lecture me while I sat outside in the car at the bank; afraid, he would yell if I told him I had to go into the bank! A wave of worry and fear swept over Naivea, but she kept quiet. Charles continued, "Every time we talk, you never ask me how I'm doing, how's my stress level or my health. We always get straight into your day and your problems and stuff." Naivea still didn't know what to think about this rant, but she knew she needed to pray.

"You don't make it a habit to support me; you used to be supportive, and there was some consistency, but now you've been stop-and-start for a while. And you don't share. There is nothing you said this week or last week that makes me feel prioritized; not even in the whole month of December, and I don't want to do these low points in this new year. There is a better leader for you out there than me. I'm not good for you. I need to avoid the stuff we went through in the past. I'm done with arguing, fighting and fussing. I'm taking a stand against the chaos. I'm just not good for you and I need you to understand that." Naivea couldn't breathe. She was not prepared for what Charles was saying.

Then Charles wound up the one-sided conversation with, "So why don't we sleep on it and talk about it tomorrow because apparently you aren't connecting with what I'm saying." He hung up. By now Naivea was sitting up on the side of the bed with her heart racing like she had just run the 100-meter dash. "Did he just all but end our marriage?" Naivea began to cry bitterly, thinking of all the hopes and dreams she had of being Mrs. LaDron, the housewife.

Naivea didn't sleep the rest of the night, but at 6 a.m. her fatigue got to her and she slept till noon. She didn't do any work that day, even though most people were going back to work, as it was the end of the winter holidays. She ate very little that 3rd day of January, and she stayed in bed most of the day without answering any calls. As she lay in bed, she thought back over their entire relationship and how it had not been normal by any standards that she had ever seen. She thought about how she had been on a roller coaster ride as Charles was loving and showered her with gifts, then he would become rude and sometimes downright hostile. She remembered thinking to herself that his behavior must be normal for wealthy business owners, and then she thought about all of the documentaries she'd watched about wealthy business owners and how all of their marriages ended in divorce.

Charles called at 7:15 p.m. Naivea was almost afraid to answer, but whatever he had to say needed to be said so that she wouldn't be in limbo about where their marriage was headed. This time Charles' voice was calmer and more reflective. "Naivea, I've been through a lot with women, especially manipulation, chaos, and anger; all this stuff women claim they don't put you through.

When women think they have the upper hand, they are disrespectful, vengeful and hateful. They also smell blood and think the man is weak. These women become mean and angrey, and think men are vulnerable. But men are fighting back. As a leader, I get angry when the women act this way, but I wonder where the humanity is in them." "This sounds like a misogynistic rant to me," Naivea thought as she sat down at her kitchen table to listen carefully.

"I talked to my mentor, and he says that I need to get these things out of my life because you'll need more of my help as we become one household. So, I need this time –six months. If you're not available in that time it'll be my loss and whoever's gain." Charles stopped talking; and it was as if he was waiting on Naivea to answer him concerning putting their marriage on hold, but she didn't say a word.

"You are an incredible woman! It's my hope that the time apart equals me being able to benefit for the rest of my life. I love you and I know that my love for you has grown, but I have a lot going on in my life right now, and I can't make you a priority with so many other things competing." Naivea's ears perked up. "What things does he need to get out of his life? What are these things that are competing with our marriage?"

Charles went on. "I feel like if we take the time, with your permission, we'll both be in a better position to make this marriage wonderful and everlasting. I know there's no guarantee because any man may snatch you up within this time. Look at it as if I were going to jail for six months until I can do right by you. I'm asking you to wait six months." Naivea's mind was all over the place now. "Is he going to jail? What did he do?"

Charles felt that Naivea was thinking the worst. "No, I'm not going to jail. I really believe in my heart that you'll do right by me and wait for me. I have to believe that. I believe you'll be there and be willing to drop everything and come be by my side when all this gets straightened out and I get all this stuff off my plate. I believe you will love me or have the possibility or ability to love me like I've never been loved. I feel like, the things you worry about or have a concern with, when you understand the depth of my love – in time, I'm hoping that those things will go away. I've watched you. You've given yourself to me. Naivea, I know how much you love me, I'm fully aware. But there is a dark side to you, and that's the thing that bothers me. So in six months, I'll be able to prioritize you better and do right by you better and take your issues on, carry them for you, and not have the weight of what I'm dealing with right now – my plate stays so full." Naivea still did not understand what Charles meant by getting things off his plate; so, she continued to listen intently, and Charles kept explaining.

"I've been battling some things in the past, women being one of them. Also, where to take the business and how to deal with my children as they become adults. A lot of these things I've been wanting to talk to you about, but we always seem to put out your fires and address your issues. Plus, I really don't think you're stable enough to handle the severity of my issues, as I am stable enough to handle yours." Charles knew that Naivea had honed in on his statement about battling with women, so he went on to address that topic.

"When I say I've been battling some things with women, I mean the women that care about me. I've been trying to figure out how to place these women. I know that Freda, Darla, Pamela and other people have been concerns of yours, and I am addressing them. I don't know if you listened to Pamela's show today, but one of the reasons that she was sounding so sad is because I told her there will never be an 'US' because I am not interested in her. Every now and then, during our interactions, and when she came to Raleigh last June, there would be these advances. There are women that you don't know that are after me, and I also need to check this flirting with the women that you do know." Now Naivea's ears started burning, "What and who is he talking about?" she thought.

"A successful businessman is often offered sex. I don't want sex, and I'm not telling you that I've been having sex with a bunch of women or that I want a bunch of women. What I'm saying to you is, I'm trying to distance myself from everybody because I have to reevaluate Charles at 45 years old. In that evaluation, as a sidebar, I'm saying I think you want to be in a relationship with me; I truly believe that in my heart. But it doesn't stop the fact that I need to clear my slate, my life, my head. All the stuff I'm doing with Pamela, and now trying to get celebrities to come on her show weekly. I can't do this anymore! I can't and I won't do it! I'm done with it! She has always had somebody, and it wasn't until her business started to explode with the T-shirt sales that those men started stepping away and she started to push her sights onto me." "Oh" Naivea thought, "So Pamela IS an issue!" She continued to listen to Charles.

"I think the best way to sum it up is that I'm worn out. I don't see Pamela in my ten-year plan, and I have to move on and find other ways to promote the business. For right now, I really need the next six months. I want to end our intimate, personal relationship – I want to end it. I'm asking you, and I'm ending it because I have to focus on me. It's not about these other pieces and it's not about me having sex with anybody, far from it. It's about me getting rid of anybody who even thinks they have the possibility or a shot at being with me. I don't want to be with anybody right now. I want to prioritize me! I'm an empty nester now, and I want to get my kids right, get my assets right and my homestead right. There is so much that I want to do, and it can't get done the way my life is currently moving.

I'm praying that it only takes me six months, so I can prioritize my life and get all of the chaos out of my life. AND THAT INCLUDES EVERYBODY. That's why I asked you if you thought you could take over Darla's responsibilities! She's got to go too! I'm getting this stuff out of my life – out of my way. It's finally coming to a head. I have to get off the phone now, I'll call you a little later."

Naivea was in total shock as she said, "Okay." After she hung up the phone, a call came in from one of Naivea's clients that had a pressing question. She started to just let it ring, but she instinctively answered. The call was short, and after she finished giving the client the information she needed, she had to think about whether she sounded strange to the woman. "What did I just say to her?" Naivea couldn't even remember what she said. She prayed that she gave the woman the right advice. Naivea laid down on the bed as her head swirled around as if she had a hangover from a night of drinking.

"What just happened? Did he just break up with me? No, he said let's take a break for six months. Why? What's really going on?" As she pondered the last conversation, Charles called back.

Naivea wanted to clarify what Charles had said in their last conversation. She also wanted him to know that she would support him as he got his life in order, "Our relationship is totally different than anything else I've ever been involved with and anything I've ever seen," she thought she'd start off on a positive note. "It sounds like you are saying that you want a divorce, and I am saying whatever it's going to take to help you get where you need to be, I'm down with it. Evidently there are some things that you expected me to do along the way that I didn't do. Evidently those things didn't have anything to do with me having my own business already, nor with me being long distance, so I failed at that. I will admit failure, because I don't know what those are.

Many times, I feel that I misunderstood what you were asking for or what you needed, based on your reaction after the fact, so I also failed at being able to read you." Naivea felt that she needed to humble herself and admit that she wasn't meeting Charles' expectations. She wasn't sure if he was attempting to slowly end the marriage or if he genuinely felt overwhelmed and wanted to take a sabbatical to fix his life, so on her part she wanted him to start out with an understanding of how she felt.

"Thank you for saying those things," Charles said as he started out on another rant. "Let me further explain where the six month's separation comes from. I had a talk with my mentor and, as we often do, we talk about you. He told me that you are looking for support from me in being the wife that I want you to be. He asked me how I've been showing you what I want, and I wasn't able to properly articulate it to him. He said that I need to support you, but I can't right now because my life is so convoluted. I need time to work with my kids, the business and my assets. My innerworkings with the women involved in my business have become too familiar, and familiarity breeds contempt, so I need to get focused on this and cleaning off my table. That's where the time out came from."

Naivea still didn't understand it and didn't like it. "But what can I do?" she thought to herself. "I can tell him that it's over and walk away, or I can wait six months and see what happens." Naivea chose to hold on for six more months. She had already been waiting four years for their union to solidify itself, what was six more months? As she contemplated waiting another half year, Charles began talking again. "WE will make that move into one home, we will be a family, we will define what that looks like, we will get it done, we will have cars, bank accounts, we will work together. The biggest issue we have is I've been waiting on you to get yourself together and now both of us will have the time we need to get it together." Naivea wasn't clear on what it was she needed to get together, but she didn't say anything or ask any questions.

Charles began again, "I'm expanding the conversation from earlier by making it clear that instead of saying 'let's not be together,' I'm saying to you, 'maybe it's friends or something like that.' The bottom line is this: let me prepare myself for this marriage, because I'm not prepared for it, and preparing for it means the house will be ready, everything will be ready, lets walk down the aisle if you're ready for that, and let's go from there." Charles expounded, "But for now, I'm not coming to you for comfort. I'm praying that we are just preparing ourselves for a fruitful union, we'll have plenty of time for intimacy. "I'm not trying to use up your body or put you in some holding pattern, that's why I said if you don't want to wait you don't have to. I'll work on me, and I'll get a lot of my stuff ready to go because there is a lot that I have to remove from my plate, and to be with a woman like you, I'm going to have to get a lot of stuff out of the way."

With that, Naivea felt that she was ready to support her man and, in the end, she would be the wife that he wanted and needed. "Thank you for explaining it and no I'm not going anywhere, so I'll continue to prepare myself and do what I need to do to make sure that I have myself together," Naivea said with confidence. It was now going on 11 p.m. and the couple said good night and ended the call. Naivea had mixed feelings. She was afraid because anything could happen in six months. She was also happy that Charles said that once his plate was clear they would have a formal wedding ceremony. She went to sleep thinking of how she would keep herself busy for another six months, and how she could become a better support for Charles during that time.

Chapter 11 Commentary
The Tea on NPD and Relationships
Telsha Edenburgh

At the beginning of Chapter Eleven, Charles did a bait and switch. He asked Naivea what he could do better or differently to improve himself and the relationship, and when she gave an honest answer, he lit into her like a hot knife on butter.

Narcissists use this bait and switch tactic often because they want to figure out what you see in them, specifically what about them annoys you. Once they find out your issues with them, they use that information to torment you. With the negative things that you tell them you see, they end up doing that exact thing to torment you. Naivea told Charles that he jumps to conclusions before she finishes her story, basically interrupting her before she is done talking, he doesn't listen to her sometimes, and he frequently cuts her off. He took that information and did exactly what she asked him not to do and then turned around and used it against her and told her that this is why he needed a six-month break. That was cold blooded.

When Charles got that information, he put Naivea in a double bond. And what a double bond means is, "damned if you do and you damned if you don't." So, it didn't matter who she was, he was going to come after her if she told him the truth, and he was going to come after her if she didn't say anything.

His conversation in this chapter is a circular conversation, he's talking but not making sense to Naivea. It sounds a little like he's losing it too. A circular conversation is supposed to make a Supply frustrated because the conversation isn't going anywhere. These backwards walking giraffes want you to pay attention to them, but these conversations are so random. But it's a manipulation tactic that they use to control the conversation, because the person that's asking the questions is the one that's controlling the conversation.

The nefarious part that I want to discuss, the part that got me early on was how he treated her for New Year's Eve. She got dressed up for a FaceTime date. She was looking forward to spending that time with him and he made her miss her church watch night because he didn't show up for the date and probably knew in advance that he wouldn't. He called her two minutes before midnight and was off the phone in seconds, saying he was in traffic and headed to an employee event. This devalue was so sad to me because she ended up bringing in the new year by herself, dressed up with no place to go. What this episode really did was to show the depth and magnitude of his sociopathic nature. This dude is a devil dressed up, walking.

The entire chapter was a devalue, preparing Naivea for the discard. And he did a discard, but he turned it around. And this is what got me, he turned around with the future-faking, saying that he would be ready in six months, and acting like he wanted Naivea to wait for him. He made it all about him.

Charles dressed up the conversation by saying that he realized that he was taking a risk letting Naivea go, but in reality, he knew that she didn't have anyone else in her environment romantically, and I believe he knew that she would wait on him because she had been waiting so long already. Telling Naivea that it would be his loss and some other person's gain was supposed to make her feel better about herself and feel sorry for the fact that he had to defuse the relationship to get himself together. Charles used this time to create a future-faking devalue, while he was low-key discarding Naivea, he still talked about them having a future once he was ready.

It's interesting to note that in all of the previous chapters, Charles badgered Naivea about not being ready to be a wife. Now he has to come out and admit that he doesn't have his ducks in a row. Here, you can tell Charles is cerebral because of the way he worded the devalue/discard. The things he said made Naivea think that he was doing it to preserve the relationship when all he was doing was discarding her.

Really, when you look deeply into this chapter it wasn't a discard, it was a shelving of Naivea! It was a shelving because he knew that she could still be useful to his selfish behind. His devalue was worded in a way that made sure that Naivea wouldn't just automatically up and cut the relationship off and then go find somebody else. He used his words very carefully to keep her in his web. What he did in the devalue is ensure preservation of the relationship and then make her be happy to sit there and wait!

That was nothing but pure manipulation. There was no love in it. There was no future in it. It wasn't even a hard discard. And then he turned around at the end and Naivea was happy to wait until he got it together. She was actually sitting there trying to figure out what she was going to do to occupy herself during those six months while this fool gets it together, or to wait to see if he even got it together.

But it was unbelievable. I mean, I just sat there. And I read, and I was like, this negro is crazy. I saw the sociopath in him last chapter. This right here is definite, true, genuine sociopathic behavior. Sociopath, straight up. Okay!

CHAPTER TWELVE
FULL DISCLOSURE

Charles and Naivea didn't talk on January 4th, they had such deep conversations on the 3rd that they both needed some time to reflect. Charles called on January 5th with a devastating revelation. "Naivea, I need to let you know something. I'm trying to clean my slate so that I can wrap my life around you. Right now, I can't because I'm pulled in so many different directions. A lot of the women that I've dealt with in the past are coming back into my life and they were starting to try and reconnect on an emotional and intimate level. I realize now that I have to learn how to juggle that, how to check that.

Full disclosure: I have slept with some of the women in my inner circle in the past, or we had some level of intimacy before. This is what I mean by getting rid of things and getting things off my plate. In most cases, we were able to maintain some level of friendship or business relationship afterwards, but you should know this, or they shouldn't be in my life. For example, I could have known somebody two decades ago and we dealt with one another in a sexual way, but because I'm not dealing with them sexually now, I don't want you to feel threatened or bothered or concerned. This time for me is for a plethora of reasons, so I really don't want to wrap it around sexuality because that's probably one of a dozen."

Naivea tried to swallow but the knot in her throat wouldn't move. She tried to wrap her brain around what Charles said, and she finally got a few words out. "I would be unrealistic if I thought you were a monk from the time of your divorce until you met me. I'm not concerned about women from two decades ago, it's more about these women that are in your inner circle. Pamela, Darla, and I know for a fact that Freda is gunning for you." Charles stopped Naivea before she could continue. "No, no, no! I addressed that with Freda, and Freda and my friendship is over. I don't care if Freda continues to sell the T-shirts, but she won't be dealing with me ever.

That is one of the biggest things I had to address because we did have a sexual relationship. That is one of the people I went to high school with, and some things transpired. My mentor told me to immediately cut ties with her so that you and I could have a fresh start. As far as the other women in my inner circle, I'm not interested in those people and I'm not looking to invest in those people. But it sounds like you're more focused on the drama with the women than the pledge of the marriage."

Naivea had mixed feelings about this part of the conversation. On the one hand she was happy to know that the relationship with Freda was over, that Charles has solid mentors and that he is not interested in these women in his inner circle. On the other hand, she didn't like the fact that he seemed to be trying to cut her off at the pass as she fished for more details about which other inner circle women he had slept with. Charles continued. "I feel like you're trying to make it a juicy thing like who did you sleep with and when, but I don't want to get into it, I'm trying to make the relationship with you work, and that's the bottom line."

Naivea wanted details but she knew it would only make matters worse. She spoke up, "I'm not looking for details. If these people aren't going to be around, if you're working towards getting them out of your life, then I'm good with it." "That's exactly what I'm doing. I know the jealousness of women and I don't like it, but I know that, so I need to make our marriage work without these women around, I don't want to give any of that jealousy or cattiness an opportunity. I need to make a few calls before the business day ends, let's talk later," Charles said as he wound down the conversation.

Naivea's mind was already racing when they were talking, but now it was moving at warp speed. She often wrote when she was angry or had any type of negative emotions, so she wrote a letter to Charles. She never intended to give it to him, it was for her to let off steam:

The Actual Letter:

My concerns were valid. Now, for me, the scenario moves from, "she wants what I have" to "she has had a taste [or a full serving] of what I have and desperately wants to possess it."

The question now is **who** are we talking about and **what** was the timing of the relationships. These answers will clear up a lot for my mental health trauma and help me to not be blindsided. For a while, I have suspected that there was more than a business relationship and friendship with some of these women, and I have stressed about it when I was triggered, causing me to write the nasty letters to you, especially the one I wrote after the Dallas awards ceremony. From that point on, I truly felt that you didn't want to be seen with me, which made me strongly conclude that you were sleeping with others; but I kept all this bottled up inside. If my suspicions were true, then I will not feel that my overactive imagination was getting the best of me. [you've said my suspicions were demonic]

I have also had dreams, and based on my past experiences with dreams, your revelation has been validated. The dream I had long ago that I was walking down a street in the northeast in the cold looking for you, and I heard loud voices at a house and went to the door and could see you inside with a lot of circus type people, but you wouldn't let me in. Remember that?

The major question that looms is this: when you decided to sleep with them did you also explain to them, or had you previously explained to them that once you enter them you all were married? Who did you sleep with **after** our marriage was consummated?

Darla – you spent a year and a half in the northwest, often being very vague about where you were staying. Even prior to that you were going up there in December and staying several weeks and saying you were with your mother. Were you with Darla? Also, the sheer awkwardness that she and I experienced when interacting with one another. I don't know if that's because she knows that we are together or because she fears it. I have often thought that she believes that the worst thing she ever did is connect the two of us.

Freda – you went to high school with Freda for at least a few years. Every time I see a picture of Freda she is posing as if to impress you, and in my interactions with her she seems to have that goal. You've admitted to sleeping with Freda, but did you also do it since we've been together?

Angela – she was never suspected, but now that you've revealed that you slept with some of them in the past, I remember talking to Angela about her finances, and she revealed that she had invested thousands in the T-shirt business and had not seen a return on her money. My thought goes now to whether that was a time that you were sleeping with her. If so, she may look at that as money manipulation. But the biggest thing is less than a week ago you said you went to dinner with Angela and her team. Did you really go to dinner or were you at her home. Is that why you called me two minutes before midnight – because you wanted to bring the new year in with her? Then did you sleep at her house, is that why you didn't return my calls after midnight?

Pamela – the new kid on the block. You helped her expand her radio reach and she hangs on your every word. Is there more than a business or platonic relationship going on with Pamela? She was so excited when she flew to Raleigh in June – did you sleep with her then? Was she in Raleigh again, at your house again in October when she said she was broadcasting from a remote location?

Women bond with the men they sleep with, and they develop an emotional connection that is harder to break the longer the sexual relationship took place.

The more times you slept with any of the women, the more prone they are to being hurt by the fact that you are disconnecting. If these women have an evil heart, they will retaliate.

I believe that the saying, **"Hell hath no fury like a woman scorned,"** goes for women retaliating against men for breaking their hearts, and I now have to buffer myself against what may come to you or even to me based on how hurt any of these women are when you disconnect from them.

After January 5th, the two didn't talk much at all. There was the occasional text, but Naivea wanted Charles to have the full six months to get things in order, so she was determined not to call. She answered his texts when he contacted her, but she didn't even initiate any texts herself. She also felt that she needed to evaluate herself and their relationship.

On January 10th Charles called. Naivea expressed her concern that the women in his circle were going to have a problem disconnecting from Charles. Charles didn't really respond to her concerns. He started the conversation with thanks to Naivea. "Thank you for letting me sift through all of this, it's a lot on me, and I needed this time. I also prayed about it, and if you don't want to wait, Naivea, you don't have to, I can't ask you to wait on me. I know time is of the essence, I know that a beautiful woman like yourself, you have suitors, and if they knew what I know they'd be in line. But I know I have a lot of stuff that I have to deal with, and as a man I have to learn how to take care of me."

Naivea worked up the boldness to ask a question that had been burning in her head for a while. "Charles, I know Pamela came to Raleigh for a family gathering in June of last year, but was Pamela at your house in October?" Charles took a quick second. "No, she wasn't here in October," Charles said matter-of-factly. Naivea said, "Okay," and proceeded to change the topic, but Charles continued on the subject of Pamela. "I don't know where she was, I thought she was traveling as well, but that wasn't my business to ask, but she wasn't with me." Naivea said, "Okay," again and proceeded to update Charles on the fact that she had been doing a lot of writing, praying and reading. But Charles stopped her from continuing. "Well, I don't want to skip over it. Tell me why you asked. I know you didn't accuse me of being with her, but you had some kinda' hunch or intuition or curiosity or something, so do you mind telling me where that question came from?" Naivea didn't want to tell Charles the truth about the sound of his copy machine rotating the color cartridges. For one thing it sounded corny, and for another, he would know that she was very focused in on him and his dealings with other women.

Naivea told him A reason but not THE reason. "At one point or another she was not in her recording studio and the background sounded different." Naivea stopped there. Charles explained, "No, her studio was going through some renovations, and she was just in another part of the building." Naivea felt that he was not telling the truth, but she had no proof. "For all I know, Pamela has a similar printer in her building," Naivea rationalized away her intuition.

As usual, Charles dominated the conversation once they were done discussing Pamela. "What is best for me is to really distance myself, and this is why I said I really needed this time because there are several people that need to be removed, and Pamela is the main one. I also need to heal and recognize my faults, my flaws and the things that I did, but also make sure that these people heal. What happens in situations like this is I create the distance then they sometimes start offering me more sex and more of themselves to the point where I have to curse them out. But I can only do that after I've found ways and systems to protect myself. I've dealt with suicide attempts, women throwing themselves out of cars, hurting themselves, etc., and I've had to deal with that drama. Then, when I go to see about them, they try to give me sex." Naivea was confused. "How many times has he dealt with this before, and how long ago?" she thought to herself.

Charles went on. "I would love to have a wife to be able to be with me during this tough time. I know you can't be there for me because you're dealing with your own stuff that other people did to you. In a perfect world I would love to be able to go to my wife and say, 'this is what I'm dealing with' and she loves me through that, we get through that and live happily ever after. My relationship with you is wanting to take care of you, for you to be treated like my Queen. I don't want you working, having bills, or doing manly things. I don't want you doing anything but being the beautiful woman that you are." Naivea was taking it all in.

"I'm making incredible headway. I'm going to get the results from distancing myself, I know exactly what I want. That's why I say, if you need to leave, Naivea, then leave. This is something I have to do, and it is worth the risk of losing you, because I NEED MY SANITY BACK!!" Charles almost screamed when he said that, and it was clear that he was way out of sorts. "Please don't talk about me not waiting on you anymore," Naivea told Charles in a comforting voice. "Okay, I won't ever say it again," Charles repented.

"It's hard for me to deal with distancing myself from you though. It's like going into the wilderness without contacting you, but that's only metaphorically because I can barely make it through the day without thinking about you." Charles stopped and was silent. Naivea took the opportunity to share her heart. "I appreciate you for making a hard stop and first of all putting yourself first." Charles jumped back into the conversation, "I'm doing it because I'm going to love you like you've never been loved before. I want to have the ability to love you, to shower you, to treat you like you've never been loved or treated before. Just laughter and fun and smiles, because you're a good woman and I believe that. But I can't right now, I'm being pulled in so many different directions. This is my last chance for love, so when you talk about spending the rest of your life with somebody, it's got to be that ONE PERSON.

Remember the time when I told you that I would never do wrong by you?" Naivea spoke up, "Yes, you said that I will never be able to say that Charles LaDron betrayed me. I remember it like it was yesterday because I wept on the phone because Harold had betrayed me so many times with other women." Charles started to explain. "Those words came from my spirit because the human being that I have grown to love put her heart into my hand and with it being in my possession, I have the ability to hurt it or treat it well before I give it back, so I made that declaration to you that I would treat you well." Naivea didn't quite understand all that Charles was saying about giving her heart back, but he sounded so sincere and was bearing his heart to her, so she didn't ask any questions.

"I am good for you, Naivea, I thoroughly believe it, and I realize that what you need and what I can give are finally lining up, if certain things happen. If I can remove people and circumstances and issues out of my life then not only can I do right by you, but I can help you learn how to deal with a busy businessman as your husband. I'm trying the best I can to express that you are my Moon." Naivea was delighted at his words. She was basking in his deep bass voice and absorbing the love that he was expressing. "Thanks for expressing your love, Babe, I want you to know that I understand and I look forward to freedom and transition for both of us because I'm working on being the best wife that I can be, and you don't have to worry about me leaving because it's not like I have anybody in my life that could take your place," Naivea said as they said goodnight.

Calls and texts became scarce after January 18th, and Naivea concentrated on learning new meal recipes and scaling her business down to make sure she would have enough time to cook meals and clean house every day. She wanted to reach out, but she just waited for the text messages of memes and videos that Charles wanted her to watch. Most of the videos he sent were about relationship building.

A few days later, Naivea received a text from Charles that surprised her, "Just got back from the west coast. The flight was terrible. I didn't want to tell you I was going, as my prayers while there were not answered." Naivea wanted to know what the trip was about, but she refrained from asking any questions as she responded, "Okay, thank God you're safe. I'm sorry about the trip turnout. God is faithful and He will work things out for your good and His glory. I really believe that." She included the praising hands emoji. Charles responded, "It's working – I'm so grateful. And thank you for your prayers."

Naivea was feeling a bit lonely, and she was questioning the validity of the relationship. She had overheard a conversation between two women in the bathroom at her church, where one of them said to the other, "Girl, that man knows what he wants, and he knows after three months of dating that woman whether he wants to marry her or not. After that, he's just playing around filling his time." That comment disturbed Naivea. She had been with Charles for over four years, and although the relationship was long distance, she felt that he should have been making moves to bring them together long before now.

That next day, Naivea received a call from a former health coach named La'Nita. Naivea hadn't heard from La'Nita in four years, and it was so strange that she called because when Naivea was doing laundry the day before, after church, she'd thought about La'Nita. Naivea and La'Nita talked for two hours. Both discussed their current relationships, as La'Nita had gone through a divorce two years earlier, left Colorado, moved to Tennessee and was in a new relationship.

During La'Nita's discussion of how she made it through the trauma of a very nasty divorce and the difficulty of having to start over with nothing, there was one thing that stuck out to Naivea in the conversation, and she wrote it down. La'Nita said, "Girl, one prayer got me through all of this, and that prayer was, '*Lord, please remove anything and anybody from my life that is hindering your call on my life and what you have for me.*'"

When Naivea wrote it down she taped it up on her desk so that every time she sat there, she would pray that prayer.

Chapter 12 Commentary
The Tea on NPD and Relationships
Telsha Edenburgh

Chapter Twelve is a summary description of how Charles, the narcissist, treats Naivea and how he's switching up, and he's going back and forth. First, he's saying we need to end the relationship, then we need to just take a break. And then he's coming back and saying, my mentor said that I need to be able to help Naivea, so I need to get my life together so I can help her. And we can walk down the aisle and all this other stuff.

After all of the flipping back and forth about the breakup, he calls himself giving full disclosure, but the way this long-winded bird worded his "entanglements" and the way that he manipulated the conversation, he made himself the victim with all of the women of his past.

His description of the events of the past caused Naivea to say, "Well, I'm not going anywhere. Because it's not like I have anybody else that I want to be with." What he did was a complete 360. He started at one point and came right back to that same point and then made Naivea agree to it.

His actions border on criminally insane. Because there are people that are locked behind bars that have that same type of mentality that is freaking disgusting.

CHAPTER THIRTEEN
THE CALL THAT ENDED IT ALL!

January 28th was a particularly cold and dreary day in Denver, so Naivea stayed inside and worked on creating training modules for one of her new clients. At 7:30 p.m. the phone rang and it was Darla Staples, Charles' administrative assistant. Darla was clearly very agitated, in a way that Naivea had never noticed during their semi-cold relationship over the past four years.

Here is the actual transcription of that conversation:

Darla: "Can I have a confidential conversation with you? I need you to promise me that you won't tell Charles. Can I trust you not to tell Charles?"

Naivea: "Yes, I won't say a word. This conversation never existed once we hang up the phone."

Darla: "Are you willing to have a conversation that's built on truth?"

Naivea: "Of course, I'm all about truth because there's no time for games and lies."

Darla: "Okay. For years you have been a pain in my life. For years I have regretted that I ever met you."

Naivea: "Okay."

Darla: "In spite of that I was kind and helpful to you, and I supported you whenever I was called upon. Yet the agony was tremendous."

Naivea's heart was racing as Darla talked. She was confused as to how she had caused Darla any pain because they only interacted when it was time to schedule Charles' employees for training.

Darla: "You're a persistent pain in the ass for me and my marriage was horrific."

There was total silence as Naivea was really mystified at this woman's vitriol for her. Naivea thought to herself, "I don't know her well enough to be a pain to her marriage. I didn't even know she was married."

Darla: "I'm not even really sure what I want to say to you. I have thought about this moment for so long, and yet I'm lost for words. There's a part of me that wants to curse you out with words that I don't even know, and there's another part of me that doesn't even want to talk to you at all. I thought you were a woman of integrity and decency and truth and of God. I chose to think of you along those lines, and repeatedly you proved me wrong and still I kept those good thoughts about you."

At that point, Naivea was getting upset at Darla for insinuating that she was a bad person, but she needed to get to the bottom of Darla's issue, so she continued to listen.

Darla: "The deceit all around is enough to make me vomit. I regret the day I ever met you and introduced you."

Naivea was in total shock at this point and very angry.

Darla: "What if anything do you know about what's going on right now?"

Naivea: "I have no clue about what you're talking about Darla. We don't have that much interaction for you to be so angry at me." I know we had a few issues with scheduling some of the employees for training, but other than that, I don't even know you."

Darla started asking questions about Charles LaDron and although Naivea was reluctant to answer, she answered a few of them concerning their business relationship and the fact that their personal relationship ended a short time ago.

Finally, Naivea stopped answering questions, "Darla, What's this about. I'm not used to being interrogated so you need to tell me what's going on!"

Darla: "Who do you think I am to Charles LaDron?"

Naivea: "He told me that you are his administrative assistant and that you help keep the business running, and I've witnessed that as being the truth."

Darla: "Have you ever wondered if I was more than that?"

Naivea: "Yes."

Darla: "Have you ever asked him."

Naivea: "Yes."

Darla: "What was his response?"

Naivea: "When I asked him if he was ever romantically involved with you, he said no, and that he didn't choose you, and that you just worked for him."

Darla: "You didn't ask me who I was to him and you fucked my husband!"

Naivea almost fell out of her chair. Her entire world was spinning as she absorbed what Darla just said. She was angry because Darla hadn't said anything for four years, and that she had been lied to by Charles.

Darla: "I've been married to this man for almost five years. This is what this is about. Forgive me for interrogating your ass right now. Do you know the pain I have gone through with you, yet I smiled in your face and did what I had to do? It's critical that you don't have this conversation with him right now, he may physically harm me."

Naivea's mind was all over the place. "How could they be married when he lives in Raleigh, and she lives in Seattle? Why didn't she say something when she started feeling uncomfortable with the relationship between me and Charles?'

Naivea: "I'm blocking him from my phone, and I'll never talk to him again!"

Darla: "Don't do that, he'll know I talked to you and all these other women he has, and he could kill me! Don't do anything differently because my life is at stake. I am no longer with him but we're still in connection because of the business."

Naivea agreed to not make any changes. She didn't want to be the cause of any physical altercations, but she had some questions of her own.

Naivea: "Darla, why haven't you mentioned this to me before since you say I've caused all this pain? The whole thing would have been over long ago if you would have let me know that he was your husband. He lied to me, but you could have let me know the truth."

Darla: "Where do you think he was for a year and a half in Seattle?

Naivea: "He told me that he was with his ailing mother in Portland and sometimes he would visit his aunt in Seattle. He also said he bought a house in Olympia for his mom but she didn't want to move so he has been fixing it up for rental."

Naivea noticed that Darla didn't answer the question she had just asked.

Darla: "He hasn't seen his mother in years! He was here with me and my kids in Seattle. There is no aunt in Seattle, it's me! There is no rental house in Olympia, he's been fixing up our house! Every package that you sent him here I had to go and pick up at the post office because he opened a special box just so you could send stuff there."

Naivea was on high alert. She was listening to a woman that should have known that something was going on – the man opened a post office box for her to send him gifts and Darla knew it.

Naivea asked the question again, this time in a stern voice: "Is there a reason that you didn't bring up any of this stuff to me earlier? Is there a reason why you didn't say, 'Hey, what are you doing – this is my husband?'"

Darla: "That is not my place. You know the man."

Naivea: "As a wife, I would have asked, Darla. I had no idea!"

Darla: "As I wife I dealt with my husband."

Naivea: "Well as someone who was told that he wasn't married and that you were his administrative assistant I agreed to a relationship with him, and although we didn't have formal vows and a ceremony we were married too."

Darla: "Well, you can have him because I'm done. You can have him because at the end of the day he's still a good man. He still has a lot of good qualities."

Naivea couldn't believe that Darla thought this lying cheater was a good man.

Naivea: "No, no, no. I'm done! I was married for over 20 years to a blasted liar and cheater, and I'll be darned if I'm going to deal with this. I have PTSD, right now I am shaking, I'm shaking, because I have been lied to like this again! I can't! So, I'm going to try to do like you asked and not close down communications with Charles so you won't be physically hurt, but it's not going to be easy."

Darla: "I thank you very much."

Naivea: "Does he have a psychological problem? How can somebody lie like this? After all I've been through with my marriage and some other traumas that I shared with him, he still lied and used me."

Darla: "I can't tell you that pain that I've gone through but I won't leave you alone, we can process through this together, but he cannot know that I told you these things. When I found out that he had all these women, including you, he showed up here in Seattle and it was all I could do to keep myself safe.

What you had with him can't compare to what we had, he lived here; you two just had a phone thing and met up a few times and fucked; sorry but you have to understand what I'm going through. All you dealt with was lies, imagine what I've been going through. Down the road you need to find a way to disconnect, but not now. He is divisive and he's a thinker, so if you try to come up with a reason now and it doesn't make sense, he will punch holes in it. So please be strategic with how you do that. It's me and my grown children at stake. You won't have to deal with how we dismantle this relationship.

He came here earlier this week trying to plead for his family back and I asked him was he in a relationship with you, and to my face he said no. He repeatedly denied having a relationship with you until I was able to get it out of him today. But that's not something he was ever planning to tell me.

All this is going to do is create some horrific things. He is very deflective; he is very defensive. There's so much involvement you've had in our life and I was going to talk through that with him but I can't because the only way he can handle it and process it is to blame me for not covering him from you and all the others, and to question my love for him.

I was doing everything for him, everything, and for the people that he was fucking around with! I don't make a dime from this business. Every dollar that's made goes straight to his account; I'm that wife, I'm destitute, I have nothing. I have built this business to where it is ridiculously successful, and I have nothing. I'll figure it out though."

Naivea now thought about the fact that there were others, and they were probably the women that she was concerned about throughout the relationship. She decided to ask Darla more questions, "What about Pamela? Was she one of the women? She flew out to Raleigh last year and I felt that she was gunning for him."

Darla: "It's interesting that you phrased it as she was gunning for him. Listen to me carefully, this is an alpha male, nobody does anything that he doesn't want to have happen. She could have been gunning for him all she wanted, but nothing was going to happen unless he wanted it to. He has to make people feel like he's the victim, so he acts like these women are coming for him."

Naivea: "There was a time when I thought to myself either this thing is real or he is telling a boatload of lies, and now I know."

Darla: "What made you wonder about that?"

Naivea: "There were some things that have happened over the years, and I did ask about them, but he always had a valid excuse for every one of them. Like why is he having to go to Portland to stay with his mom every winter. He told me that his brothers needed a break, and because business was slow at the end of the year because the students were on Christmas break, that was the time he did his part to take care of her."

Darla: "He's been here with me every Thanksgiving and Christmas!"

Naivea: "You said you got married five years ago, did you get married the regular way?"

Darla: "No, the fucking non-state-sanctioned way, which I will never do again. But I had a ring, and I had a certificate. We live together, we have children who, although they are not his biological children, they call him dad." Do you have powder blue walls in your house?

Naivea: "I do not have any blue walls in my house. Why do you ask?"

Darla: "Because there's a video that one of these women made for him and he looks at it when I'm sucking his dick!

Naivea was jolted again. Darla was okay with Charles looking at videos with other women while she was giving him head. "Wow!" she thought to herself.

Darla: "When he left Seattle to go back to Raleigh in the Spring of last year, all hell broke loose because all the women that he had been putting off while he was here for a year and a half started coming out of the woodwork."

Naivea: "And I believe that Freda is one of them."

Darla: "This whole thing blew open because I got a phone call, and that's why he showed up here on Monday, and left Monday night because I couldn't have him here. All day Monday from 7 a.m. to 10 p.m. I felt like I was in a hostage situation. I was praying to come out of the situation in one piece, and it's still tense. He found out that I knew about the women, and he didn't want me to leave him. I had to be nice and calm and talk him down all day because he was like a raging bull. At the end of the day, I was able to get him a plane ticket to go back to Raleigh and an Uber to a hotel to spend the night before his morning flight.

He acted like he wanted to have a civil conversation but once I started talking, he started arguing and screaming and shutting me down and putting me down and questioning my love for him. But it was because of my love that I put up with all of his shit, and he has all the money in his account, and I have nothing. It's because I loved him that I dealt with all his bitches!"

Naivea remembered the shutdowns and putdowns happening to her over the last four years, and she realized that this was normal behavior for Charles. She also realized that Darla knew that Charles was dealing with multiple women but did nothing about it. She began to look at Darla as a weak, desperate woman. Naivea thought of another question that she wanted to ask Darla, "How long ago did you get that phone call from the person that broke this saga open?"

Darla: "At the beginning of the year. That's when all hell started breaking loose, and this has been a world wind of a month."

Naivea: "Based on the things that he has done to me and the things that you've told me, he has phycological issues. This is not normal. This is not normal. And I know part if it is me being naïve, but I asked questions, and they were always justified."

Darla: "So when were ya'll going to get married?"

Naivea laughed, "Charles said when I get myself together because I am not a wife yet and I need to be a wife before we get into one household."

Darla: "Charles would get up out of our bed in the middle of the night to go downstairs to call you! One time he even went into the closet. I would leave our bedroom and couldn't come back in for hours because he was on the phone with you. I asked him was there an emergency for you two to have to talk to Naivea every night late into the night?"

Naivea: "OMG! That's why when we were talking, he said he had to be quiet. He would say that his mom was sleep!"

Darla: "I got really sick in last year and I came home from the hospital just barely making it. Even though I was still sick, he wanted me to make him breakfast. I came upstairs with the breakfast because he didn't want to come downstairs and be disturbed by me or the children because he was on the phone talking to you. I had to ask for permission to enter my own bedroom, I put the food down and waited. He gets off the phone with you and says to me, 'I love you but you can go to hell for disturbing my call with Naivea!'"

Naivea was shocked that Charles would say that and shocked that Darla would take such abuse. But she quickly remembered that, although it wasn't to that degree, she had accepted verbal abuse from Charles as well.

Darla continued, "So, he's this big important CEO and he says I'm acting like he's not a CEO. He had all of this free time because I'm capable. I'm capable of running this household and the entire business, so he was freed up for all that time to be fucking around with everybody and trying to marry everybody.

It was abundantly clear that it was supposed to be me and him – those were the grounds of our marriage. He writes me repeatedly in text messages and voicemails saying he has one wife, and that I am the only Mrs. LaDron. And of course, I am because I take care of him in every way."

Naivea started to see that Darla was second guessing her decision to leave Charles. She was using terms that indicated she still wanted to be with him. Naivea didn't care, she was done, but she found it quite interesting that Darla was defending a marriage that was obviously a sham.

Darla continued, "I try to bring him peace, but he brings me war, and I still manage to circumvent that and bring the peace, but I'm dying on the inside."

It was then that Naivea remembered the conversation she had several days ago with La'Nita, and she looked up at the prayer that she wrote down, "*Lord, please remove anything and anybody from my life that is hindering your call on my life and what you have for me.*" God had just answered her prayers. It wasn't the way she thought it would be, but that prayer was answered just the same. Naivea told Darla about the prayer, and that she and Charles were married based on their vows and terms.

Darla had more to reveal. "He placed camera's all over this house. We were supposed to drive to my cousin's wedding in Las Vegas last May, but at the last minute he decided to leave us uncovered and stay here in Seattle, and he was distant the last few days before we left. Later, I realized that he just wanted to take advantage of that time while me and the kids were gone to freely communicate with all these women. While we were gone, I couldn't reach him often, and when we talked it was two minutes. So, I did something that I'm not proud of. On the way back home, I pulled up the cameras on my phone, and listened in. I heard him tell you, 'In our marriage, I want you to open up to me. I want you to feel like you can say whatever you want, and I want to listen to you.' And I'm shaking at this point. When I got home and confronted him about it, he told me, 'Naivea just wanted to know what it would take to marry me and I told her, this is what it will take.'"

Now Naivea realized that Darla knew a lot more than she was first led to believe, and that Darla was actually complicit in Charles' dealings with her and other women. Naivea felt that it was her that Darla was most angry with though, because of the conversation that was taking place about the extensive amount of time Charles spent with her.

Darla started to question her life, "He was the love of my life. I don't doubt that he loved me. We had a real life together, but he had all this other stuff going on. I served my husband

WELL! I was the ultimate wife. I was feminine, anything my husband wanted, sex, any which way, he got it. If he wanted food, I cooked all day every day, and all the time, gourmet meals all the time. I even ironed his underwear!"

Naivea stopped Darla, "But why? Why did he do this? He had everything!" Darla didn't answer, probably because she didn't know the answer.

Darla continued with the rest of the story about when she listened in on the cameras while she was on the road home from Las Vegas. "So, when I was listening to his conversation with you over the camera, I heard him tell you that marriage is the highest honor that a woman can get. I said to him, 'You gave Naivea the highest honor, so you're telling me she meant nothing?' And Charles told me that it was nothing, that it was not a marriage, and that he was talking hypothetically because you had been coming on to him. After that, he removed me from the cameras, and I could no longer see to protect the house. But I unplugged all the cameras last week; all this bullshit needs to stop."

Naivea was sick at the stomach and mentally exhausted because this conversation had been going on for over an hour, but she wanted to find out all that she could in case Darla decided to shut down at a later date.

Naivea asked again, "Darla, why is he doing this?"

Darla said, "Whatever his issues are, they revolve around how he feels he has to be with women, and there's a part of him that genuinely feels that he is doing good. I was his cash cow. I was his lover, his servant, his everything, and that's major to him that I'm not going to be those things anymore. That's why he's fighting for daylight in every way. I have to be careful."

Then the bombshell came from Darla, "In addition to this madness, there is also a state-sanctioned legal wife! That is why I only have a ring and a certificate and not a state-sanctioned marriage because he couldn't marry me the regular way without become an illegal bigamist."

Naivea was about to pass out at this point. "Who is this state-sanctioned wife," she yelled out in shock.

Darla responded, "You think back into the relationship, and you'll be able to figure it out." Naivea thought for a while, and each name she mentioned, Darla said that was not the person. Then, the person that was in the picture that Naivea never worried about from a romantic relationship standpoint popped up in her mind. "I know you're not talking about his Aunt Ida," Naivea said to Darla sheepishly. "Yes, Ida is not his aunt, as he has told everyone. Even though she is seven years older than Charles, she is his wife. All of the property is in her name and so are the bank accounts!"

Naivea put her head down on her desk. She couldn't believe it. Darla continued, "When I found out, he said there was no relationship there, he said they were getting a divorce, and that he had just never done the paperwork. Naivea angrily asked, "So, is there a relationship or is there not a relationship? If there is still a relationship then Charles could have gotten us killed, us showing up and staying at the Raleigh house and she has it in her name. He must have had me stay at the hotel last November because she was at the house. He lied and said his son and his friends were staying there."

Darla started again, "There are a lot of people that were hurt by this man. He will find out about their past and then find an angle to get close to them to take advantage of them once they let their guard down. He has done this to many women."

Naivea chimed in, "Based on what you've said, he looks for women that don't have a lot of street sense and don't have a high body count."

The conversation ended with Darla's summary, "I know this is a lot, but you prayed for the Lord to get things out of your life, and He did. Know that although I meant this call to be a nasty one and for me to blast you, it turned out differently because of the revelations that we both made. Be well and call me whenever you feel the need."

Naivea, now in tears, responded in the affirmative and they both hung up. It was only a little after 9 p.m. but Naivea was numb and drained. She drank some water and laid across the bed as tears streamed down her face onto the pillow. After an hour, she got up and showered because she felt nauseous. When she put on her pajamas, she felt anger coming on, and she immediately thought of throwing out all of the gifts that Charles had given her over the years. However, she realized that if she did that, one quarter of the items in her house would be gone to the dumpster. She began to think about how Charles used to call her his Moon, his everything, and she threw up.

As she cleaned up her toilet bowl, she thought to herself, "How could a human being do this to anyone?" She remembered a story that she heard on a Christian radio show. It was a woman telling of her childhood when she was in foster care being abused by the man in the house. She didn't tell the teachers because the man threatened to kill her little brother if she told anyone what was going on. The woman said that as she rode the bus to and from school every day, she noticed that the bus driver was kind to all of the children. He seemed like a good father-figure and all the children liked him. One day after a very hard day at the foster home she decided that she would tell the bus driver what was happening.

She waited till after school, and she hid in the back of the bus until all of the other children had gotten off the bus. She envisioned herself telling the bus driver about the abuse, and him calling the police to come and get her. She went to the front of the bus and told him everything. He listened very intently, shaking his head to signify that he understood. After she finished telling him what had been happening to her, he took her to the back of the bus and raped her! Naivea felt like that little girl, violated by someone that knew she had already been through hell and back.

It took her a long time to get to sleep, but Naivea finally drifted off. She woke up several times during the night thinking of the devastation that had occurred. "How am I going to be able to function?" she asked herself.

Chapter 13 Commentary
The Tea on NPD and Relationships
Telsha Edenburgh

I thought Chapter Twelve was bad. But then when I got to Chapter Thirteen, I was just like, I'm just really done. The call from Darla comes in, and you get to see the carnage that Charles has caused with all these women. The carnage. And then further along, when the timelines start happening, you can see the lies that he told Naivea, like, about his. mother, this child, his Aunt Ida. Aunt Ida was the woman that had all of the business bank accounts, the older woman. He said that was his aunt, his father's youngest sister. And in reality, that's his wife. His state licensed wife!

I was trying to wrap my mind around Darla. Something had to be wrong with her too, for her to be okay with this, because clearly, it was not normal. I said to myself, "Something is wrong with him, but something is wrong with you, too, boo." There's no way that a normal human being that did not have some type of psychological disorder would put up with that. To see what Charles was doing and to agree with, and go along with it, because people don't just do this. This is crazy. And then she asked Naivea did she have powder blue walls in her house? And said that he would be watching this video of him having sex in some house with blue walls while she was giving him oral sex! I sat here, I was like, you can't make this stuff up.

Clearly, this man is a straight up sociopath. But I think he also borders on psychopathic, because no one can keep up with all these different women like that. In my opinion, he has to have multiple personalities going on simultaneously to interact with all these different women like that. He was running the same game on all of them.

When he talked, he probably had to remember who he was with, because he likely said the same things to everyone. I doubt that he ever changed his playbook. It was just a matter of, "I got to remember not to say the name." I recall that he would say girl or baby when he and Naivea were in the sex act. I'm sure now that he trained himself to say those two endearments so that he wouldn't call out the wrong name in bed.

Based on the conversations in Chapter 13, Charles didn't change who he was, what he did, and what he liked. The rotation of the women was the part that is sociopathic I don't know how the other women felt about Charles, but it's fair to say that they were just as much in love with him as Naivea was, and for him to crush multiple women in that manner was purely disgusting!

In my opinion, Darla has borderline personality disorder; she has abandonment issues. Something is psychopathically wrong with her, too. What she was doing and the conversation she was having with Naivea, and how she felt about what had happened was not normal. Yes, her anger was normal. But the fact that she stayed and put up with that for five years! She put her total life in Charles' hands, and he smashed her like a bug. Darla was a quintessential Main Supply because she came in and supported that business with this man; helping him build a profitable business, and because narcissists are stingy and greedy, she likely didn't get any of the money that Charles got from the bank accounts that were in Ida's name.

I want you all to understand the type of female that it takes to go through this thing, like what she was doing. Darla wasn't in tune with reality; she was delusional. Narcissists have delusions of grandeur, you know; narcissists are delusional. Both Charles and Darla are delusional. You've got to realize too spiritually, when they start to mix with that narcissist, then they take on those spiritually transmitted demons as well. That's why they are delusional together.

Borderlines love narcissists, and narcissists love people with borderline personality disorder. Borderlines are close to being narcissists themselves, but they still have the empathy piece. They do have all of the narcissistic tendencies, but borderlines will do anything to not be abandoned. Now, they get mad with the narcissist. It takes them a long time to get upset with the narcissist, but they won't leave them, and they will agree to some heinous things for fear of abandonment.

Narcissists and borderlines are totally attracted to each other, and they go like a hand in a glove. Why? Because the narcissist wants a fool. And a borderline doesn't want to be discarded or abandoned. A narcissist wants a person that is always going to be there. And guess what? A borderline will always be there.

This situationship was like a cesspool of a mess. But Darla just fell into it, and she gelled with it until she got upset. But based on what I see in Chapter 13, she is likely still dealing with this bird on one level or another. You're not going to be able to survive with a narcissist without making them your god. You have to idolize them, they may even demand that you worship them.

When I look at the scenario with Charles and Darla, this is what I see: Darla, with her borderline personality disorder, interacts with Charles, a cerebral, somatic narcissist. This is a recipe for disaster and even death, as so many other women are in this web that Charles spun, and Darla cultivated. Charles is, mostly cerebral. He does the sex piece because he has to. But he's mostly cerebral because in his mind there is a depth of manipulation like that of a pimp.

When you look at this whole situation, this man was beyond toxic. He was like, straight manipulating, playing mind games with all of those women. Most narcissists are jealous and insecure. However, Charles was beyond being jealous and insecure. No, his narcissism was on another level. Like, he had built a web around all of those women. It was a web that was closed. Each one of the women had their own bubble and that was wrapped up by the web, and Charles was the nucleus that had a line into everybody's life. But none of the women were allowed to connect with each other except for business; other than that, they had no relation to each other until his scheme was exposed in Chapter 13.

When the dust settled, Darla stayed there through it, likely because of her abandonment issues. More than likely, somebody abandoned her at some point in her life, and what she did was develop what they call an anxious attachment disposition. People with anxious attachment disposition are very clingy. They tend to hold on to people, no matter how bad they are treated or how horrible the people are.

Narcissists, more so, have an avoidant attachment style because they really don't want to attach. They just want to suck from you. They want to drain you, but they don't want the deep commitment needed to form a lasting relationship.

Naivea asked Darla why she didn't mention that she was married to Charles. Darla didn't say anything to Naivea for four whole years because that would have gotten her abandoned. Charles would probably have told Darla, "You gotta go." A borderline will do anything to not have to experience the pain of abandonment, the feeling of being abandoned. So whatever Charles asked her to do, she was going to do it. Based on the things Darla told Naivea in Chapter 13, I believe that Darla has Stockholm syndrome.

To sum up Chapter 13, my feelings about both Charles and Darla are sheer utter disgust.

CHAPTER FOURTEEN
THE ROLLER COASTER IS BOTOMLESS!

The next morning when Naivea woke up, she realized that her world had been turned upside down. There was no smile when thinking of Charles, only hatred. She kept thinking to herself, "How could he have done this to me? How could anybody do this to anybody? There never could have been a marriage!" She said out loud as she took the purse that Charles gave her and threw it up against the wall.

Naivea got up and got some water, and took some Kava to calm her nerves, but she couldn't function. "There's no way I'm going to church today," she thought as tears began to flow down her face. She laid in the bed half the day, only getting up to go to the bathroom. She wasn't interested in eating, and she only drank water because when she was upset her body dried out.

Then the phone rang. It was Darla calling. Naivea didn't want to talk to Darla, but she decided to answer just to see if something Darla would say could ease the pain that she was experiencing. Naivea didn't do much talking at the beginning. It was Darla that had some confessions to make.

Darla could tell that she was crying. "How are you, Naivea? I can tell that you're crying. I still break down and cry in the middle of a sentence sometimes. This situation makes you crazy. "I'm numb," was Nivea's answer as she sat up on the bed and put the phone on speaker. "I have some things that I want to let you know," Darla said, as if she had sat down and made a list of things to tell Naivea.

"Charles and I were spiritually married because he said he didn't believe in state-sanctioned marriages. We did vows and I have a ring, and a certificate, signed by a minister friend of his. But now I totally understand that we couldn't have had a state-sanctioned marriage because he is still on the books as being married to Ida in North Carolina.

I first discovered that Ida was his wife about three years ago, although I didn't know if they were still married. I was in the upstairs office at his house in Raleigh, and I found a prayer book. When I opened it, I saw a written note to the Lord asking the Lord for help and for prayer for 'my husband.' I immediately dropped the books and ran out. Then I went back into the office and placed the book back on the shelf, never to reach for it again.

The next time Ida came up was last year when Charles was here in Seattle with me and my boys. He got sick, and after a few days, the police showed up at the door to do a wellness check. When my oldest son asked the police who was inquiring about Charles, the police said his wife. My boys thought that was strange because I am his wife, and I had just left to go to the grocery store. They showed the police his driver's license and said he was sick. They didn't want to come into the house and check because they were afraid to catch anything. When I got home, they told me about the police visit. I went up to the bedroom, woke Charles up, and told him what happened. Reluctantly, he had to tell the boys that he was still married on paper to Ida, but the marriage was over long ago. He said that as soon as he got back to Raleigh, he would go ahead and finalize those divorce papers, but he still hasn't done it."

Darla changed subjects and started talking about the gifts that Charles bought Naivea. "I told you before that Charles and I had our most fierce fights about you, Naivea. For example, most of the time Charles sent you gifts, like those nice bags and shoes. I helped him pack them up. He said that because you and other women helped him a lot in the business, he sent you all gifts to keep you all happy and helpful." Naivea thought about the many gifts that she received from Charles. She remembered feeling special when she received them, but now she felt manipulated. Again, the thought came to mind that she should gather all of those gifts and throw them away. But then she thought that she would be shooting herself in the foot because she would be further devalued. The gifts, especially the Mont Blanc pen and pencil set, and the designer bags and shoes, helped her keep a very professional and upscale image.

Then Darla switched subjects again and started to describe Charles' abuse to her and others. "After the police visit, he started talking bad about Ida, presumably to normalize their lack of relationship. What bothers me most is the way he puts everybody down, and I know he was putting me down when he was around you and other women. His putdowns are very painful and cruel, and he knows enough about women to know that when he says denigrating things about one to another, the one listening is going to be happy and think that he's not interested in the one he is putting down, when in actuality, he probably just slept with that one 72 hours ago."

Naivea thought about the times he downplayed the pictures of Freda that were in his briefcase, and the visit from Pamela Pie. She wondered how long he had been having relationships with them, and if when she had come to Raleigh, either of them had been with him shortly before or after her visit. Then Darla kept the confessions coming. "I literally ran that business from six months after he started it until now. He doesn't do much of anything. I am coming to realize that, as his wife, I thought I was freeing up his time to be creative and build the business, but all I was doing was giving him time to fool around with other women."

Darla was on a roll now, "You above all others were the scourge of our marriage. For the almost two years, while he was here in Seattle with me and the boys, he would call you late at night almost every night. When you all were talking business, he would stay in the bedroom with me. But obviously, when he wanted to talk relationship, he would get up and go downstairs. He would say he had to pull some records from the computer in his downstairs office for the discussion."

Naivea chimed in. She was puzzled that Darla knew so much yet never said anything to her, "So you never felt that something more than business was going on between us? Why didn't you call me years ago about spending so much time with him?" Darla responded, "Every time I asked him about you all's relationship, he would shut me down by saying there is no relationship and that you were just an older colleague that he liked to talk business with at night." Naivea thought to herself that there was no way she would be okay with letting any husband of hers stay up late at night talking to any other woman. She felt the urge to blame Darla for all the time she wasted with this horrible man, because Darla knew or should have known more than business was at hand. Then Naivea thought about all the times she had suspicions but brushed over them with Charles. Sometimes she had voiced them and sometimes she didn't. She remembered telling herself that, "once we are in one household, those concerns will dissipate because I will be with him on a daily basis." "Boy was I a fool!" she said to herself.

Darla continued with her confessional dialog, sensing that Naivea was thinking she should have received yesterday's call long ago. "Any time I would start questioning Charles about his time with you, or any other woman for that matter, he would quickly throw things from my past up in my face and try to shut me down. He uses words as weapons. As a matter of fact, his tongue is a weapon. He makes a person not say something that they were going to say by being very calculating with his words. He's called me insecure, nagger, negative, and even demonic at times, when I was angry that he was spending so much time with you. And the first time he told me you were coming to Raleigh for a conference I just knew he was going to find a way to sleep with you!"

Not only was Naivea shocked to know that Darla knew of her visits to Raleigh, but in her mind everything that Charles ever said to her was now in question; every story about him and his family, every business story and every excuse he ever gave her for not calling, not coming to visit her in Denver and every excuse for not being with her at the hotel when she came to Raleigh. She also started thinking about the times when Charles used to lie to get off the phone when things weren't going his way.

"This man has some serious psychological issues. He obviously has narcissistic personality disorder," Darla blurted out in anger. "And his womanizing is out of control!" Naivea was getting angry, and she wanted to get off the phone. "Darla, I have to get some work done, so I need to get off the phone, but thanks for calling. We can continue this conversation later though." They said their goodbyes and Naivea laid back across the bed. She needed to decompress from all that anger so she wouldn't explode, so she ended up going to sleep.

Several hours later Naivea woke up in a cold sweat. She got up and took a shower and made some eggs because she knew she needed some sustenance but she didn't feel like eating. As she sat at her kitchen table, she thought back over the last four years and asked the Lord why he let this saga occur. There was no answer. After she ate the eggs, she went to her office and sat at her desk, numbly staring at her calendar. She started looking up narcissistic personality disorder because Darla had mentioned that phrase in that morning's conversation. She had heard of the word narcissist before, and she thought it meant someone that was cocky and self-centered. But until her research, she had no idea that there was a whole pathology behind it. Before she knew it, Naivea had spent two hours researching this thing called NPD.

After her research, Naivea laid back down on her bed. Then, an hour later, the phone rang, and it was Darla again. Naivea answered the phone. "Hi Naivea, I have Freda on the line now and we wanted to talk to you together." Naivea sat up straight in her office chair to listen to what these two women had to say. Darla started out the conversation. "I have been crying as much as when my mother died, and I thought about you being there all alone and I wanted to say that we need to support each other.

Freda and I became friends when I came into the business. She had already known Charles from high school and was actually the one that helped Charles start the business. I had no idea that she was having a relationship with him until the first of this year when she felt led to tell me about it. I had asked Charles had he ever had a relationship with Freda and had he had sex with Freda, and he told me no. What an asshole! Turns out they have been married for almost 8 years!"

Darla reiterated that she and Charles were married in December five years ago. "Now I understand that he married me so that he wouldn't have to pay me the $10,000 per month salary to run the T-shirt business," Darla said in hurt and anger. "Truth be told, I did have my suspicions about him over the years, but every time I asked a question, he had a valid answer, and he shamed me for asking. I'll let Freda take over from here," Darla said as she stopped talking to allow Freda to vent. Freda had a soft, sad voice as she started speaking. "Hi Naivea, so I hear that you've been in a relationship with Charles for quite some time. Well, here's what has occurred with me over the past several years:

On January 1st, I told Darla that I was in a relationship with Charles for quite a while. She knows that I thought she was, and now she is confirming that she was, for almost six years." Freda continued, "I also had some suspicions about Charles over the years and especially since he has been in Seattle. He has always used his mother as an excuse, or the fact that he needed to meet with everybody on the team up in the northwest. It never made sense to me, so I did my own research. He sent the same dick pictures to all of us and uses the same playbook on all of us. When he calls one, he calls all of us with whatever story is his next deception. That's how he keeps everything straight, we all get the same story, the same pictures and the same gifts. Do you have any designer purses?" "Yes," Naivea answered Freda, "four of them."

The ladies talked about all of the common gifts they were sent by Charles, and they talked about all of the expensive gifts they gave Charles. Although Darla hadn't given Charles many gifts, the most crucial "gift" she gave was her time. She was working in the company and not receiving any salary, while Ida's name was on the bank accounts. Ida, being the only wife with a state marriage license, was a key factor in this web of lies, but neither of the women knew much about her except that she was seven years older than Charles.

Then Darla chimed in. "Charles uses a lot of people's names to cover for the fact that he wants to be with one of us exclusively for several days or a week." Freda then stated that Charles was in Denver with her in April four years ago. Naivea thought back and realized that week she was speaking at a conference out of town. Naivea realized that this was the first time that Charles was supposed to come to Denver to be with her, but he had to abruptly change his plans. At that time, Naivea didn't know of Freda, but now she understood what happened with that failed liaison. According to Freda, Charles got sick while he was in Denver, and he flew back to Raleigh. Once in Raleigh, it was revealed that he flew Darla there to take care of him while he was ill. "So, he was actually planning to visit me, but he got sick while he was with Freda on the other side of town, and he went home," Naivea deducted.

Darla started in, "He told me that he was flying to Denver back then and he said he was going to stay with a male friend to help this new guy build the business. Come to find out that he actually stayed with Freda, his second wife as far as we all know, and now I realize that he was planning to leave Freda's place and come across town to spend time with you Naivea; that's when his sorry ass got sick."

Freda spoke up again. "Putting the puzzle pieces together, we can see that Charles married Darla in December five years ago, and I left Raleigh earlier the same month! I didn't want to move to Denver. My entire family is in Raleigh, and I was going to decline the move to Denver even though the pay was higher. Charles encouraged me to move here and now I totally understand why. He didn't want me in Raleigh any longer because when I was there, we often spent time together. For two and a half years, I was always at his house, and he was always at my place. It's very clear that he wanted me out of the general area so that he could run his game and get Darla to be his Main Supply. Charles has not been to Denver to see me, his wife, except for that one time in April.

The money that my job paid me for relocation and to buy a house was $15K in total. Charles had me give him my relocation check, and he wrote out all of the things that he needed to do with MY CHECK so that *we* could buy a house for *us* in Denver! Money to pay his attorney $2,000. He carved out money to have me rebuild my credit after having me file for bankruptcy after buying him those two luxury vehicles. He had me get a secured credit card and put $2,500 into it, and the list goes on. But the bottom line is, the last thing he said to me was don't penny pinch him for that money because it has to go for buying a house for 'our family' here in Denver. Every year since I've been here, I've never seen a home. But Charles took that money and the opportunity away from me to get a home here, because he wanted to be in control of my money, so it angers me when I think about it." Freda went quiet.

Naivea decided to tell the ladies her version of the visit Charles made to Denver four years ago. "That April visit to Denver that was cut short has a different twist for me. It is apparent that while he was here in Denver with you Freda I was speaking at a conference, looking forward to rushing home to be with Charles. I had the house professionally cleaned and my truck detailed. Before I left the conference, Charles texted me to let me know that he had to change his plans and fly from his meeting back to Raleigh. I remember all the wind going out of my sails, and for the rest of that conference I was devastated. Charles told me that he had to rush back to Raleigh because an employee had broken her leg in the T-shirt processing area, and he had to go back and see about her.

When he arrived home, he let me know that he had gone to the hospital to see her twice, then he noticed that her story didn't add up. He said he looked at the security cameras and noticed that she got dropped off at the back door of the building that Saturday, and when she went in, he couldn't see everything because of the camera angles, but he eventually saw her on the floor. Turns out that she broke her leg at home, but since she didn't have health insurance, her boyfriend talked her into pretending that she broke her leg at work so that the company would take care of the medical expenses. He told me that the girl apologized, and with the approval of her supervisor, he decided to keep her on staff."

"That's all a damn lie!" Darla said as she groaned deeply. "There is no employee, there is no administrative staff!" "But he told me that he has an administrative staff of 17 employees that he pays every other week, and he even talks about payroll when we talk on Fridays!" Naivea shrieked. "Yes, that's all a pile of crap," Darla grunted, "I AM the administrative staff!" "The sales team gets paid on commission and a payroll company takes care of that!" Freda said in agreement with Darla. Naivea took a deep breath. She again questioned each and every thing that Charles ever told her.

"I'm not surprised that Charles took the relocation money from you Freda," Darla whispered sorrowfully. "Anytime any money came to me as a gift from a relative, he would ask for it all or for a portion of it. He would say, 'You know better than to try not to give me everything as the man of the household, and when you give to me, you never know, I could turn right around and give it back to you, Darla.' That never happened." "And it will never happen, that's not who he is," Freda said as it was apparent that she was weeping.

Charles owes Darla $600,000 for not paying her a salary for the last six years, and I'm claiming that for you, Darla," Naivea stated with righteous indignation. "Thank you for that proclamation, Naivea," Darla said. "That man wouldn't give me $60 – well he may give me $60 but not $600,000 – he would die first!" All three ladies laughed. Darla continued, "Really though, as much as this is painful and upsetting, at the end of the day, there's tomorrow and I have to figure out a path forward. I have to live, and I need some way to produce income for this household."

Freda started to reveal more details about their relationship and how she and Darla discovered that they were both in a marriage to Charles. "Charles and I started the T-shirt business together seven and a half years ago. At that time, the business was a thought in his head, and we both had ideas about packaging. The whole concept was born out of me and Charles talking at length about the products and how to launch these shirts. Keep in mind that I still worked a full-time job, and he needed someone to help him run the business. I knew that I wasn't going to be able to work with him full-time. Charles had me research to see if I could find someone that could run the business. There were quite a few people that I ran across that I thought were going to be capable of helping run that business. Eventually, Charles and I were referred to Darla through a high school friend that was a recruiter. That friend had been in communication with Darla, discovering that she was a possible candidate to run the business. The friend contacted Darla, and she had not responded via email, so I called and talked to Darla and asked if she could meet with Charles and I on a conference call.

Their story began a week after I first communicated with Darla. The three of us had a couple of group calls, and after that, Charles reached out to Darla to foster a relationship with her." Naivea was in shock! "This is EXACTLY how my relationship with Charles started," she thought to herself. Freda continued. "Charles brought Darla to Raleigh to meet the manufacturer and for the three of us to meet as a team to see if she was the right person for the business. Unbeknownst to me though, he was already in a relationship with her. He had cultivated the relationship over several months over the phone, and she succumbed to his charm, so that when they did meet, it was like they had already been together.

After the meeting with the manufacturer in October, I switched cars with Charles because I was moving out of my apartment and moving in with my mom short term. I knew I would be leaving soon for Denver in December, and I didn't want to renew my lease. After we had our meeting and switched cars, as I was leaving to finish packing, I asked Charles not to take Darla to the house or back to her hotel. I already knew there could probably be some attraction there, but I had no idea that he had already cultivated a full-blown relationship; and they did go to the house, and they had sex. Later, he yelled at me for asking him not to take her back to the house or her hotel, claiming that he didn't when he actually did. I just asked him to please not take her to the house – basically covering him, like he always wants to be covered from 'these women.'

So, my relocation to Denver went like this: I was offered a position here and Charles encouraged me to take the position and relocate from Raleigh to Denver. He named all of these great reasons for me to relocate. By this time, he was focusing on building the T-shirt business. He even told me that I would be the head of the Colorado division of the business. But I was so homesick. My children, my mom and most of my family members are in Raleigh. I don't have any family here in Denver. But I said to myself that he is my husband, and he is encouraging me to leave and stating all these great benefits. As I said before, he took my $15,000 moving allowance and said he was going to find us a nice house to buy in Denver. He never returned my money. Then I had to file for bankruptcy because of this nut. His theft of those relocation funds, along with the other items that I purchased, 'for my husband' have virtually wrecked me financially," Freda squeaked as she again started to cry. Naivea was shocked to hear Freda's story. She wanted to hear more about how Charles drove Freda into bankruptcy, but she didn't ask. Then Freda continued.

"That's how this all got started; and hearing about how Darla is married to Charles was devastating for me. The whole idea of me living alone in Denver is surreal now. Mind you, we spent a lot of time, money, and effort fixing up his Raleigh house, so when you all were there, most of what you saw was what I purchased, and those decorations were my doing." Naivea remembered thinking that Charles' home looked like a woman decorated it. "Now I know why I had that thought," she said to herself.

Freda started to explain her reason for contacting Darla the first of the year. "When Charles spent the year and a half during the countrywide lockdown in Seattle, that time allowed me to sit down and really begin to be silent and hear the Lord. I asked God to please let me know if this is the relationship I need to be in and remove it if it's not because there were so many gaps in the relationship that didn't make sense. I doubted myself during that entire relationship after moving to Denver. I reflected on him being in Seattle, him calling me while he was there doing FaceTime and saying he is there on business; saying that he was building the business for our family and telling me that Darla is building the T-shirt business for me and him. I also reflected on him talking very little about the rental property that he was fixing up to rent out because his mom didn't want to live in it and remembering that he said the tenants that are in the investment property were trying to run off without paying the cable bill. It was just so far-fetched. It didn't make sense to me, and he was trying to make sense out of it. That year and a half that he was in Seattle allowed me to sort things out in my mind, and I was being led by God to pay attention to my relationship. It took everything out of me not to go to Seattle and knock on the door. That's where I was at."

Naivea remembered, on more than one occasion, wanting to get on a plane and go to Seattle to see Charles and find out why he couldn't come to Denver. Freda went on. "There were times when I wanted to call Darla and ask her were they in a relationship, but I told myself that it wasn't the right time. In actuality, I may have been afraid to hear her answer. I held on to that fear until January 1st of this year. I got up early and called Darla, I literally felt that I was standing on the edge of something, and I was pushed to ask the question. I told Darla that Charles and I are in a relationship, and it caught her off guard. Darla then said to me, 'Wait a minute - are you talking about today?' and I said yes. I told her that we have been in a spiritual marriage for eight years. After that, there were several questions that Darla asked me; questions to confirm that I was not some random woman calling to say, 'I want your husband.'

The questions Darla was asking me were meant to determine how familiar I was with the house and about places in the house and rooms in the house where we may have had sex. Darla was trying to get confirmation that I actually do know that house very well, I bought most of everything that's in it. Based on the questions that Darla was asking me, I was almost sure that she was also in a relationship with Charles. But Darla wouldn't immediately admit it. It took Darla about seven hours of talking with me before she revealed that she was not only in a relationship with Charles, but that she possessed a certificate of marriage and a ring. 'We are married,' Darla said to me.

That revelation caught me off guard and I immediately felt he was having sex with multiple women; making them believe that having sex with them constitutes marriage. To hear that they are married threw me for a loop and it was tough, but I had that year and a half while he was in Seattle to process what

I always believed. I had wanted to break up with him but I couldn't just say I'm breaking up just because he wasn't coming to Denver or because he wouldn't make arrangements for us to be together, because it's the same as having a husband in the military that's gone for six months at a time, or like a business man traveling for work. I've seen those relationships and I know what those are like, so I didn't want to say I'm breaking up with this man because he's physically not here with me.

I needed to get proof of what I was thinking inside – that this is not a man traveling for work, there is something else going on. At that moment, when I said okay I'm done and I told Darla, we agreed to call him that same day and let him know that we both knew about one another. Once we revealed our discovery to Charles, he had the gall to say that he wanted to continue the relationship with me, Darla and two others! He started pleading with us to continue the relationships as they are! In his mind, it had been going on with me for eight years and with Darla for five going on six years, so it's been working. He asked us to continue to make it work in our respective locations.

Charles had brought up wanting to have relationships with multiple women before, but as I told him then, that's not something I'm interested in being a part of, because his idea of a relationship with multiple women includes sex and that's not what I'm about. I want a monogamous relationship, not a polygamous relationship. After that initial conversation, if I ever hinted around that he appeared to be getting close to other women, he would always cut the conversation short, and he never circled back around to it. But in the meantime, he has been having sexual relationships with hundreds of women. Now it makes perfect sense why he presents himself as a single man and why he never publicly says anything about being married. He keeps all of these women in the dark, including the women he calls his wife."

Darla chimed in. "I was devastated with the news that Freda was married to him all this time. During that three-way conversation, he mentioned that he was with all these women to try to see who really loved him. I said to him, 'I've dedicated my entire life to you! Are you trying to say that you don't know if I love you?' He said, 'No, that's not what I'm saying, I know you love me, but you know women come at me and throw themselves on me. I still wanted to see if they loved me or not.' Naivea remembered Charles repeatedly asking her if she loved him, and she realized that he must have felt unloved as a child.

Darla continued, "I was furious! I told Charles he had everything he needs right here with me; there wasn't anything I don't do for you, I told him. I wake up, I work, I breathe, I sleep Charles LaDron – that's all I do. I've worked in our family business for you, and you are questioning whether other people love you and are dedicated to you, and you have everything here? The thing about him that's DANGEROUS is how he creates this narrative to support his behavior. He has only one playbook, and he has been running the same plays on all of us for years. I also happen to know that he keeps notes on all of us in his phone, so that he can go back and review what he told us about different things – so we can't catch him in a lie. I figured this out earlier this month that these folders that he says contain business notes actually contain a list of the lies he has told us."

Naivea felt her anger rise as she thought about all the time she wasted with Charles over the years. She started to vent. "I had an idea, Freda, that you had been in a relationship with Charles, although I didn't know it was current. But I didn't know he was in a relationship with Darla, let alone married to her, because he told me that when he was up in the Northwest, he was with his mother and his aunt. He said that his mother had dementia, and he had to put her in a home, and then his brothers dropped the ball, and she got put out of the home. He said that eventually they had to go find another home so that he could properly serve his mother – all these lies." "He told me the same thing," Freda proclaimed.

"His mother doesn't have dementia," Darla said with a grunt. "She is traveling around and living her life. This man is psychological! What Charles does is he serves with his dick, and he serves EVERYONE that he comes across with his dick. And he exchanges that for your femininity, commitment to him, and your loyalty. He also wants cameras set up in your house so he can see you and make sure you're alone. Both Freda and I discovered that we have the same brand security system, suggested by Charles, through which he could see us and even talk to us through the speakers. I have 14 cameras inside and outside. We've both turned the cameras off and are in the process of dismantling the systems.

He also wants your phone location services turned on so he can know where you are at all times. He wants these things so that nobody else has access to you." Freda chimed in, "And, he needs to know where we are so that we can't just show up unannounced at his house in Raleigh while another one of us is there with him!" Naivea thought about the fact that Charles also had her turn on location share on her phone. She also remembered that there had been a heated discussion about her setting up a certain brand of security cameras in her home, but since she already had a different brand and resisted changing due to the investment that she would have to make, Charles got upset. But when she mentioned not having the money because she gave it to him, he left the subject alone. "I am so glad I didn't get those cameras," Naivea thought to herself.

Naivea had a thought, and she didn't want to lose it in the midst of this heavy conversation, "Has anybody talked to Ida?" "No," answered Freda, "there's been a desire to talk to her because that woman has the answers to all of these unanswered questions. We don't know what she knows or if she even plays a role in this sick saga, but eventually it will all reveal itself" Just as Naivea was thinking of why Darla stayed married to him when it was revealed two years ago that he had a state-sanctioned wife, Darla started to explain.

"Charles told me that there is no love in their relationship, that this was Ida's third marriage, and she just wanted financial security. He says there is no marriage and that he just didn't do the paperwork to get the divorce because Ida was safe; meaning that, it was easy to tell people who would accost him all the time that he was married and it was a protection from all the women that he didn't want to pursue, as he kept it from those of us that he wanted a relationship with. He told me that he didn't know that he would meet someone like me, the love of his life, and fall in love with me and have a family, otherwise he would have done the divorce papers a long time ago." Naivea thought to herself that she wouldn't have stayed with him after finding out he was married, no matter what excuse he gave for not filing for divorce. But she remembered that she also tolerated a lot of abuse in this marriage to Charles.

Darla continued, "Just yesterday, he called me and I didn't feel like talking so he asked me to just listen. The reason he wanted to talk through this was because he knows I'm done, but he doesn't understand how we had a whole life and family, and I could be done with him that quickly. He said he needs to process through this and bring closure, but when I would ask questions, he would just shut me down. I threatened to hang up because he was shutting me down, then he apologized because he still thinks there is hope. What he was really doing was trying to manipulate me into continuing to be his little cash cow and submissive wife – serving him to the hilt!" Darla was getting loud and angry, and she started to talk to the ladies as if she was talking to Charles. "You want to get your family back? It's too late for your family, it's too late for your family!"

Freda started talking as if to calm Darla down. "Yea, that's the response of a narcissist, as we now know narcissistic behavior, and because you recognize that, he's not going to be able to wiggle his way back." Darla didn't calm down, "Charles told me that I need to create a narrative about who he is and make him out to be a villain and see all this stuff without recognizing his humanity and without giving him grace and mercy. I'm not Jesus Christ, nor am I Job!

He has drained me. I worked for this asshole for almost six years, and he's never paid me a dime. Thousands of dollars come in every day, and I don't see a dime of it. All the money goes into his account, and that account has Ida's name on it! Last year I told him that we are making over $1,000,000 that Ida has access to, but I don't, and you don't pay me a salary for all this work. He told me that Ida doesn't have access to that money and that I do have access to the money. I asked him how I can access the money, and he said that when he is here in Seattle, I can use the company debit card to pay bills and buy groceries. But that's not access, that's akin to a child's allowance! This man makes me wanna spew a bunch of curse words!" Darla started to cry.

Freda was sounding frustrated with their situation also, "I think we've only scratched the surface on this whole ordeal with Charles. I think there's so much more that we don't know, and I don't care to know. I just want to get out, but there are just so many more unknowns that people like Ida would be able to answer." It seemed that on the one hand Freda was ready to run away, but on the other she wanted to stay and see the rest of the saga play out.

Darla needed to vent more. "So, this is his scheme now – letting me know that he is getting rid of all these women. Yesterday, he was naming the ones he got rid of, trying to let me know that he messed up and failed, but he is human. He had the nerve to say that all these women set him up, and that I wasn't seeing his side of things. He kept claiming that these women wanted him, and that they didn't want to be alone. He said all of you wanted sex, and that all of you harassed him about why he wasn't coming to see you or have you all come out to Raleigh.

He said he finally gave in, and had you come out, Naivea, but he didn't tell me it was three times last year. Now he's claiming that everybody is out of the picture, and he just wants his family back. He had no idea that I'd talked to most of the women within the last three weeks and he has no idea that I've spoken to you, Naivea. You can't tell him because he may literally kill me for ruining his thing with you.

You seemed to be his secondary source based on the amount of time you all spent on the phone and the agony your relationship put me through. I know you didn't have anything to do with it; you didn't know, but for years and years and too many instances to recall, you came between us. That's why I had such animosity towards you. I had to try not to hate you because I know I can't get into the Kingdom if I hated you, but it was bad, it was a lot, and I prayed you away for years, and I said to the Lord, 'Why aren't you answering my prayers? Looks like this woman will never be out of our lives, she's tied him up with projects, she's always wanting something, she's very skilled at taking up his time, one, two, three, four o'clock in the morning my husband is talking to this woman on the phone. He's addicted to her, what is it? I hear him talking about marriage to her, what is this? I've prayed this woman away daily, Lord.' Finally, the Lord revealed a couple of weeks ago. He said, 'You're praying for one woman to go away, meanwhile I'm in the background working on getting all the women to go away!'"

Naivea was a bit taken aback by Darla's rant. She understood that Charles spent a lot of phone and FaceTime with her, but she had come to realize that Darla was there most of that time, perhaps in the same room with Charles and perhaps in another room, but she knew. Darla knew that Charles was spending a great deal of time with her, but said nothing to her, and she started to resent Darla. "If Darla had mentioned early on that she was married to Charles, I wouldn't have had to go through all of this pain," Naivea lamented. Naivea sat there with the phone on speaker trying to absorb the fact that Darla must have been afraid that if she confronted any of the women, Charles would leave her. From that point on, Naivea thought of Darla as having Stockholm Syndrome.

Naivea spoke up. "I was literally shocked when he wanted to pursue a relationship because I felt like, okay, I'm older and I didn't feel like I was his type, but with those smooth words I said okay I guess he really does want me." Darla interjected, "You're not his type. Just up until recently he says to me, 'You know Naivea's not my type, but I wanted to help her.' But here's the spin: forget who you are, age, looks, height – forget all of that and think about his type as somebody that can do something for him. In that case, those people become his type. He will deal with you with disgust because, as you said, you're not his type. But he will override that fact to get at what his type is, which is a woman who could do something for him, and who he can gain something from. If he can't gain, he's not going to be there.

Again, Naivea felt a way about what Darla said. Evidently Darla thought she was Charles' type but that Naivea wasn't, and that it could be that Charles was dealing with her with disgust. "He wasn't disgusted when he had me going from the bed to the sink to the table to the wall. I was surely his type," Naivea thought to herself as Darla tried to make herself out to be someone that was indisputably Charles' type. It was evident to Naivea that Darla was so wrapped up in what Charles was feeding her over the last five years that she actually didn't see that she was little more than the Main Supply of a cerebral narcissist; someone that had grown this man's T-shirt company over the last five years with zero pay and no access to any of the bank accounts. As a matter of fact, Darla was destitute at that moment because she didn't have money for the next month's mortgage payment on that Seattle house.

Freda had a few more words to add to the conversation. "He had me borrow money from my dad when we first started dating, so six or seven years ago, we went together, and I bought the Range Rover. I was paying for it not knowing that he was married to Ida and then Darla. Then shortly after that he wanted the BMW, so he put money down on it, but I carried the note. He used me to get the things that he wanted – his toys. I bought him suits, luxury bands for his Apple watches, and clothes. When you walk through the front door of his house there are expensive paintings, all paid for by me during the years I was still living in Raleigh. I bought him iPads, laptops, and watches. You name it. In the kitchen, he wanted this special coffee maker, an expensive knife block, and so many other things that I bought. He uses people for what they can provide for him and when the money stops coming in, he moves on to the next person. His mind associates love to money. He is a greedy man, first off, and if someone stops giving to him, he equates that to them taking their love away because he equates love to money." Naivea thought about all of the expensive gifts that she bought Charles and wondered if he had given those gifts to other women. She also thought about all the times he wanted expensive items and she didn't have the money, so she purchased many items with a credit card because she loved him. She started to feel sick to her stomach.

Darla then screamed out, "Yes, he loves money! I listened to him. I wake up, work all day and night for him, and all he does is help you and Pamela Pie. He never helps me with the business." Naivea chimed in, "I didn't know he wasn't actively running the business. When he told me that he had an administrative staff, I thought he was supervising them." "As I said before, I'm his whole fucking staff!" Darla howled even louder, blowing her top. "I do ALL of it, and he said to me, 'I need you to tell these people that you have an administrative staff, because when you think about it, the stuff that you do, it should take about 12 people to do what you're doing.'"

Freda spoke up with a soft, calming voice. "He's not done with you yet, Darla. You're his income, his cash cow. You drive the income coming into his bank account every single day, and he's probably scared to death that you're just going to drop the business in his lap. He has to walk a very fine line and be apologetic about everything he has done, that is, until he finds someone else to run this blasted business – a new primary source. Even though this is what's going on, don't change who you are, Darla. Charles was the wrong person to be such a great wife to. He saw your willingness to love, honor and respect him and he took complete advantage of it. Based on our conversations, he carefully vetted all of us in that same way; saw that we were smart, loyal, and willing to help him make money, and he pulled us into his wicked wife web so that we could do his work. He will change you—he does have a way of changing people—the fabric of who they are, in order to meet his criteria; fulfilling his financial and sexual desires. He would use assets and benefits from each one of us to build his life up because it's all about him. This horrible ordeal has helped me understand who he is as a person. NARCISSIM IS REAL!" All three women agreed in unison.

"You're right!" Darla groaned. He is a true narcissist. After he found out that Freda and I talked, he showed up on my doorstep all the way from Raleigh! He came unannounced, and he's never done that before. I always buy his tickets to get here, and I pick him up from the airport. Charles rarely goes anywhere, but when his wife web fell apart, he got himself on a plane, arrived in Seattle, took an Uber to the house and called me saying he was on the front porch. And he was in a different state of mind, he looked different. I knew I needed to keep him calm and reassured and that it needed to end amicably, because that day was not the last day that I would have to deal with this fool. I knew there would be more days to come where there would be an interaction of some kind because I run this business."

Naivea had a thought, "It's diabolical to have all of us working together like this, that's the way I look at it. It's like all these women crossing each other's paths and working together, talking on the phone and in meetings sometimes, knowing that he claimed all of us to be his wives, and taking the risk that we wouldn't say anything to each other about the marriage, until you did Freda." Freda spoke up. "What I see as diabolical is that he had us at that house like a revolving door. According to what Darla told me yesterday, there were several times that you flew into Raleigh the day after she left to go back to Seattle. And the fact that both you and I live in Denver is a trip. I came here shortly before he started the relationship with you, so it seems that he was very careful not to come here while we were both here at the same time. This man has only been here to visit me once, and now we see that that was a time that you were out of town for a long stint. This man's game is strong!" All three ladies took a long breath and a roaring grunt.

Darla shrieked, "How does he sleep at night?" Freda and Naivea chimed in with agreement. Naivea's thoughts trailed off, and she started thinking again about the last four years. "All this time, the things that I was thinking; the times I felt that something was wrong, and I was wondering if I was crazy and why my mind always went to the negative when Charles would make up excuses for not coming to Denver…all this time I was right! My spirit was trying to tell me, but I wouldn't listen.

Now I have to forget about all this and move on because I have to do the things I need to do to get my life back together. I have to build this training business back up, and make enough money to take care of myself and my parents in their later years because I don't have any retirement funds and Charles' lies have me way off track when it comes to my finances."

Freda agreed. "I also felt the confirmation that I'm not crazy, and that he really is a demon, and he is not anywhere near normal. Now I need to be at peace and get my life back together. I don't have any retirement either because Charles took that too! He literally had me draw money out of my retirement account to give to him. It wasn't much but it was all I had, and now I too have to totally rebuild. We are going to rebuild, and at the very least, he will no longer be able to manipulate us and run his game and impose his narcissistic behavior on us anymore, and that's what's most important."

Naivea had a thought, "Yes, he'll have to find somebody else to start over at ground zero with." Darla and Freda both agreed. Freda lamented, "He'll find other people that will fall right into his arms because he's a charming man; a handsome, debonair, charming man, and he uses that." Darla chimed in, "With a nine-inch dick and a Maybach S." The ladies chuckled. Freda continued. "But he's getting old and he's not going to be able to sustain that lifestyle for much longer. All darkness comes to light and I'm glad that the light is shining on us because we've been in the dark for so long. Now we can move on and start our lives over."

Naivea's protective nature kicked in. "I'll pray for us, but also that nobody else gets trapped in his web. I want to come up with a way to expose him so that others will see who he is and avoid dealing with him." "No woman should be left to the wiles of the enemy in Charles' hands. If there is a woman, then she should not be left to his devices. I know there are other women that he's been dealing with, but some women are so deeply entangled in his web that no matter what you say, before you hang up the phone with them, they're going to go straight back to him and tell him what you said, and he will find a way to deny it and call you crazy." Darla sounded like she was definitely speaking from experience, and Naivea again wondered how long she had known Charles was this way and how many women were involved.

Naivea had a question. "Thinking of women, I have thought for a long time that Charles was also dealing with Pamela Pie. She said on air a few months ago that she was in a relationship with someone in Washington, D.C. but my gut said it was really Charles. Then a few weeks ago when she was on air you can tell that she was obviously distressed, and she had been crying. I know that because although you can't see her, she kept sniffling like someone that has been crying. When Charles finally went back to Raleigh early last year, I thought he was going to come to Denver on his way back from Portland, which I now know was really Seattle. But he insisted that he had to rush back to Raleigh. Next thing you know he's telling me he has to meet with Pamela Pie. I was pissed and I felt sick but since she's been helping grow the business as a radio personality, and I didn't want to sound like a nagging wife, I kept my mouth closed."

Darla started speaking. "You are correct in your thinking. Pamela is one of the last women that he began a relationship with and told her that he would marry her. For months I was hostile towards her, and she didn't understand why. Once this wife thing blew up, I called her on the phone and she verified that when she went to Raleigh, the time you were talking about, they did spend that time together. That was early last year. She was also there last October and again in December. When Freda and I talked to Pamela on the phone she told us everything. The story is basically the same for all of us, except neither of us brought Pamela to the table; Charles found out about her from his friend, and he contacted her directly. I didn't ask Charles if he was having a relationship with Pamela. I had already asked him about you, Naivea. I told him that I brought you to the table and that I suspected that the two of you were having a relationship. He shut me down and denied it every time I brought it up. He asked me how I thought he would be with that older woman, and he said disparaging things about you. He was always calling somebody something derogatory." "He wasn't doing any derogatory talking when we were dancing between the sheets," Naivea thought to herself.

Darla continued, "When we talked to Pamela, she revealed a lot of the same things that he was doing with us. He wasn't paying me; he was taking money from Freda, you, and Pamela. I suspect he would take that money stolen from you all and buy all of us gifts, so he would never have to use the money that I made him in the business. Charles asked Pamela to give him part of her radio show commissions because he had helped her increase them. He also treated her poorly when they were together. Although their relationship only lasted a few months before he was exposed, she is devastated and angry. When Pamela confronted Charles and asked him probing questions, he admitted to having relationships with others including you, Naivea. He would never admit that to me and that is why I never called you until yesterday."

Freda had more to add. "Naivea, your name came up on the call Monday when all three of us confronted him, but what he said was that he never had a sexual relationship with you, even though he'd told Pamela differently." Darla explained, "That's because I was on the line. It was very important for him to deny that to me, He told others that he had sex with you, but he couldn't say it to me, until last night when he had to admit it. At first, he denied it again, but I told him that I believed Pamela when she said she was recently told that it was true, so I pressed him more and I probed him for details. He said he denied it all this time because he was embarrassed, and because we had gone through so much turmoil for the last several years concerning the time that he was spending with you, Naivea. He gave me hell over the last four years as I would watch him spend hours and hours on the phone with you, send you gifts and even take things from my house and his house and send them to you.

For example, I had two very nice LED desk lamps. One day Charles told me to pack them up and send them to you, and he would buy me new lamps. I did send those lamps to you, and he never got me any new lamps! When he mentioned a couple of times that you had come to Raleigh for work or for conferences, I knew in my heart that you were with him. At the end of the day, he just didn't want to admit that all my suspicions were right. So, once he started talking and giving details, I kept probing, and when I couldn't take any more, I got off the phone with him. I waited about ten minutes and then I called you. That's why I had so much venom when we started talking yesterday. I didn't just not like you; I hated you! Charles would ask me to get on the calls with you at first, saying that I was covering my husband and business partner. Then, it got to where he didn't want my covering, even though he claimed last night that the reason he stopped having me on the calls was because you said I didn't like you, and that you were uncomfortable, and you just wanted to be on a call with him."

That's total BS," Naivea blurted out. "I did notice in the beginning that we were on three-way calls a few times, and I did notice that he started calling me alone, but I never thought you didn't like me until much later when I started noticing a change in your attitude towards me. Now I thoroughly understand why." Darla had a thought. "Even after he stopped me from being on the calls, sometimes when he was on the phone with you and I was there in Raleigh, he would come upstairs in our bedroom from his office and put the phone on speaker and say to me, 'can you believe this woman?' That only happened when you were talking business deals and plans. Every time the conversation would change to romance, he would take the phone off speaker and head down to his office. DEVIL!"

Now Naivea knew that Charles was crazy. She was a little embarrassed and off-put to know that Darla had overheard some of their conversations. She felt their talks were private and sometimes intimate, but she needed to stay focused on the fact that this man was a monster and that it appeared that he had no conscience. Darla told the others that she would be off the call for a second. Freda and Naivea continued to talk. Freda wanted to update Naivea on the research that her, Darla, and Pamela had recently done. "We have been studying narcissistic behavior for a few weeks, and a lot of things, including him popping up at Darla's house on Monday, are a part of that behavior. When we started talking earlier this month, we realized we were dealing with a narcissist, and this one is skilled at it, very skilled. There's a video that Pamela sent to me and Darla a few weeks ago when we first started researching narcissism, and it was spot on. It had Darla in tears because the video explained that there are different levels of victims to a narcissist. Darla is the primary source – the one that makes the money for him and is treated the worst – and he does that to her because she's very docile."

Chapter 14 Commentary
The Tea on NPD and Relationships
Telsha Edenburgh

Chapter Fourteen. I don't know what to say about it. I really don't, because the fact that when he was confronted, he still asked for everybody to remain in their respective places was beyond bizarre, and I was so done. I had to literally put the book down and I had to go to the kitchen. I had a bottle of wine in there. I said, I don't drink, but this is too much. Seriously! I really could not. I mean that really disturbed my spirit. I said, I'm gonna not read this for about an hour. I'm gonna put it down and I'm just gonna really let this sink in, because I just couldn't believe it.

Now Darla, the one in Seattle, was giving up all of this information, and she was telling Naivea, "You destroyed our marriage." I was like, really? I said, this woman might have narcissistic personality disorder, too. Darla was trying to fit a square peg into a round hole, and she made it fit in her mind, because if you know that you've heard him on the phone telling another woman that he's given her the highest honor, which is marriage, how can you make that fit into that hole? She seemed to totally ignore the fact that Charles had a state-sanctioned wife that he had plenty of time to divorce if he wanted to, and this woman had the purse strings to all of his money – her money that she worked to earn by building that business.

But then she was talking about the size of his penis. You know what, I was like really? It's evident that sex is a big motivator for a lot of people, and it's no different in this case. I've seen people do things that they never would have done before. These ladies sat and talked about that whole sexual prowess thing concerning Charles, and that it was something he prided himself in. That's part of that spirit latching on to these women. They like to really get you really good and messed up in the head in the bedroom.

So, in this chapter, I'm doubling down on my belief that Darla had Stockholm Syndrome, because she'd been shown the truth. She saw the truth. She knew the truth was true, but she still couldn't believe it. She still couldn't come out of that caged mindset. Something is wrong with her, and it's because she's been conditioned to that so long that she can't come out of it.

It's really sad to see it happen, because you don't want to see a person really lose themselves like that. And it was apparent that the girl had worked really hard because the business was thriving.

Naivea definitely seems the most level headed of everybody because once she realized what was going on, she didn't have any second thoughts about immediately severing the relationship for good. When Naivea realized that Charles was laying pipe on Pamela Pie, she was dumbfounded. The lesson here is, and one of the things I say on my channel is, that with the narcissist, it doesn't matter what the people look like as long as they got a hole. There's no such thing as my type or not my type with them. They go after what they can have sex with, male or female.

Now, Freda, the one that he went to high school with and had the eight-year spiritual marriage with, she decorated Charles' house and paid for all the decorations, but he told Naivea that he decorated the house. I think Freda was a codependent, and I know that Darla was. Darla was messed up in the head. With Freda, he took her money. He took $15,000. She also paid for two of his luxury vehicles to the point that she had to file for bankruptcy. It appears this happened before Darla grew the business. But we can see that even after the business grew, he didn't bother to help Freda with her finances.

Also, I'm trying to figure out how Freda didn't ever run up on Ida in eight years of dealing with Charles. He must have really had tabs on both of them to avoid any interaction. Charles loves to lie. The lies. You have to have a demon for the lies to roll off your tongue like that. He cut Naivea off at every pass whenever she asked questions that would have exposed him. He was quick with his tongue, and a quick thinker. That's how he kept all this mess going for so long. The man is just full of dark, black holes in his soul. No one can keep up a demonic façade like that, except they'd be full of demons. He was full of them. He has a maggot brain. Seriously.

When narcissists have multiple supplies like that—as mentioned in this chapter—they build a web. With the female narcissist, we call them the black widow. The black widow builds a web, and she traps the guys in her web. And you know how black widow spiders are – they kill and eat the male spider.

In Charles' case, he paralyzes the victims and continues to drain them of their life force, until he is ready to discard them. This man is so egotistical though, that he somehow thought he could keep all of the supplies, and continuously drain them all at one time. This behavior is unprecedented, and it took a lot of mental energy to pull this off for as long as he did. By the end of this chapter, I wondered where things would have gone if Freda had not confessed to Darla that she was having a relationship with Charles. I wonder how long all of these women would have been trapped in that web having the life sucked out of them.

My entire perspective on Charles changed in this chapter. He showed psychopathic features, and I see him vacillating between cerebral and somatic narcissism along with being a histrionic as well. Histrionics are narcissists that can create these elaborate, grand stories and lies, and make them seem so real. That's what he did because Darla mentioned that she'd found a folder in his phone where he had written down all of the lies that he had told to the women. I was like, this fool is a histrionic, too. They are very good at creating narratives and telling big lies, and they really believe these lies themselves.

Charles doesn't have ASPD, which is the anti-social personality disorder, because he does understand how to socialize, and he wants to socialize to gain Supplies, but the man is absolutely sick. He's a psychopath. At this point, the way that he was treating Darla, was almost like she was a slave. Based on her conversations, she was in a position where she had no income when he met her, and she was in a position where she had no income when all this stuff blew up.

When you look at the situation, Charles is actually like a pimp. He had all these women, and he was literally making money off of them through their businesses or his business, and he was taking their money and sexing them up too!

For somebody to be so sadistic as to know that there's no way that you're marrying all these people, and they're not coming to your house to live, but to continue to use them like this, mind boggling.

It was as if Charles had cast a spell on all the women he was with. It was almost like he was a sorcerer. He may have even been blatantly practicing witchcraft. His mouthpiece and the level of manipulation that he could do with that forked tongue was nothing less than high level sorcery. Because when you can get into a person's mind like that and make them like puppets and make them believe and run with you, when you know you ain't right. Come on. That right there is a whole other level up.

CHAPTER FIFTEEN
PAMELA'S STORY

Darla came back on the line. "Pamela called while we were talking, so I just updated her on where we are and now, I've patched her in."

"Hi Ladies!" Pamela said as she joined the conversation. "We may as well have a conference about Mr. Charles and all of his dick adventures." Everyone laughed. "Pamela keeps us smiling for sure," said Freda. "Pamela, you're free to tell your own story; we didn't tell Naivea much."

Pamela began, "Our relationship started two years ago in June when he approached me about sponsorship on my radio show. At first it was about business, we weren't talking about a relationship. I had just gotten out of a situationship, so I wasn't into dealing with a relationship at that time. Then, our communication became more friendly and casual, not sexual yet though. The progression was quick, and by the end of that year, we weren't quite in a relationship, but we had already gotten super familiar with each other – to the point where we were phone sexting, because I'm hot to trot!" The group laughed again.

"The next year, when he was gone from Raleigh, his lie to me, and probably everybody else, was that he was going to his mother's to take care of his investment property in Washington. At the time, I didn't have a reason not to believe that. During the year while, as we know now, he was in Seattle with Darla, he continued to cultivate a relationship with me. The first time I saw him was in May of last year when he returned to Raleigh, but before that, we were cultivating an EMOTIONALLY DRIVEN ROMANTIC RELATIONSHIP where marriage was supposedly the goal. My stipulation on it was that he needed to move to Miami, which he pretended was something he wanted to do and was going to do.

He introduced Darla as his trusty assistant, not his wife or anything else. The way he talked about Darla let me know that they were friends, but he never gave me anything to think they were married. So in the beginning I started to reach out to Darla for friendship, and at first, everything was fine. Charles was supposed to be coming to see me in March of last year, and stay with me a month, but that never happened." Naivea thought to herself, "Charles doesn't change his pattern at all. He did the same thing to me on more than one occasion."

Pamela continued. "Getting back to our first encounter, it was May of last year and he flew me up to his house in Raleigh, and I'll tell you, it was one of the most stressful three days that I ever spent with a man that's supposed to be your man." Everyone laughed. "All he wanted was his dick sucked. He gave me a song and dance about not having vaginal sex and that meant marriage and he wasn't ready for it because I'm the problem. He would say I have all these problems, and that's the reason we can't get married, and our relationship can't go any further.

Now that I think about it, after all that I've learned, although he still tried to push that people were married once they had sex and consummated the marriage, he didn't hesitate to try to have sex with me because he knew I was already recently sexually active; whereas you Darla and Naivea, from what Darla told me, you two weren't sexually active. So, he had to immediately proclaim you two were his wives in order to get what he wanted."

Darla spoke up. "I didn't know you told him he had to move to Miami." Pamela answered, "Yes, that was my stipulation, but once he got me to the house in Raleigh and sexually abused me, he stopped talking about it and thought he could get around it, but it was a hard stopping point. He thought that if he could wrap me up emotionally, professionally, and all around, that I would be too wrapped up to care that he didn't come to Miami. But because I have a disabled brother that I have to take care of and all of his doctors and medical care is here, there's no way I was going to abandon him. Back to that second year, after Charles' sponsorship and the T-shirt sales began, my radio station ratings started skyrocketing and I started getting requests to interview pretty important people, and requests to travel to L.A. and different places as a guest MC.

For the first time I actually started making money. Immediately his hand went into my pocket. He claimed that as his future wife, he had to teach me about money. He found an event in the summer of last year in Detroit that he wanted the T-shirt business to sponsor, so he wanted $10,000 from me to help sponsor that event and for me to go as a radio show personality and push the shirts. When that fell through, he told me that I should pay him because he could write off certain things on his corporate tax returns that I couldn't write off, so, I gave him $5,000 then $10,000, then at another point, it was $3,000.

I went back to Raleigh at the end of October of last year and I was at his house broadcasting the show from there." Darla interjected, "I knew, based on the sound and the fact that you said you were out of the studio, that you were there in Raleigh; I shared that with Freda even before you told us earlier this month." Pamela's admission also confirmed Naivea's suspicion that she was with Charles in October.

Pamela continued. "On that October trip, he sexually abused me, and it was painful. I don't want to get into detail, but it was certainly not normal. I left after two or three days. The last time I went to Raleigh was in mid-December, but that time sadly for only a day, and this time he put me up in a hotel. At this time, we were working on a project to promote the T-shirts nationwide, and Darla was being asked to be heavily involved with this endeavor. Knowing full well that Darla is his wife, Charles was positioning me as the sidepiece that was trying to ruin and break up their family. As he was having a relationship with me, Darla felt something was going on because he was way too involved with me." Again, Naivea saw that all of this was a pattern – a playbook that Charles never changed.

"When the nationwide project started, there began contention between me and Darla," Pamela continued. "I was carrying wife energy in front of Darla when we spoke on the phone, and I noticed this whole new energy built up between us, and it wasn't good. In early December we had an unpleasant conversation. Darla called me and said that she wasn't feeling the way I was addressing her, as if I was getting too familiar with her. Underneath all that was the fact that Darla was angry on a deep level, and I was trying to figure out why. I didn't like that phone call because what needed to be said was not said. There was a storm brewing, and I felt that Charles and I were going to break up. I told Charles about that phone call with Darla and told him what happened on the surface. He played it off and said we should hash it out between the two of us.

After I came back home from Raleigh in December, where there was more sexually deviant activity, something didn't sit right with me. The vibe between me and Charles was a little better, but the time was nagging me. He didn't know that I was going to break up with him by Spring of this year if he didn't move to Miami. I wasn't going to tell him that, but that was my plan. On December 31st, I sent him a sentimental voicemail and text and he did not answer; that's how he is when he's trying to be with someone else, he was pulling away. I started praying, '*Lord, show me what I don't see, because there's something very important that I'm not seeing. If he's not for me, remove him!*' He was quiet Saturday and Sunday. Around 6 p.m. Sunday evening, January 1st, I called him, and he answered the phone in the shower. He thinks that's tantalizing but it's annoying." Naivea giggled under her breath because she knew that talking to Charles while he was in the shower was tantalizing to her, so he must have thought all women thought that was sexy.

"When he started talking, he said, 'Pamela, you either have good timing or bad timing, I don't know which one yet.' He said he had a real tough day, and he would gather himself together and call me back and tell me about it. Around 9 p.m. I got a call from Darla, which asked me to be honest and if I feel obligated to tell Charles about her calling. Then Darla said she needed to know that I won't tell Charles about the call and to text her a statement swearing that I wouldn't tell Charles about the call. After I texted her a statement swearing that I wouldn't tell Charles about the call, Darla asked me was I interested in truth or was I interested in having a relationship with Charles. I told Darla I was interested in truth.

From that point, Darla asked me if I had a sexual relationship with Charles and I said yes; then Darla asked me details about the sex. But me, being from Miami, felt like Darla was getting all up in my business and I wanted to know where all these questions were coming from. Darla told me that she was his wife for going on six years! I was standing up and I had to sit down. I then realized where the animosity was coming from. Darla broke it down for me and then she got Freda on the phone, and they told me that earlier that evening, they had confronted Charles about what he was doing. They told me that he had been married to Freda for eight years. I was not super surprised, and I believed them 100%."

Then Darla had to try and protect herself. "Naivea, just understand that Pamela has covered me to this day, and I am grateful, because Charles doesn't know that I called Pamela. The spirit told me to call Pamela and tell her what was going on. As far as Charles knows, Pamela called me. But because I would have been in grave danger, Pamela covered me." Pamela started again. "The three of us talked for three hours. At first, I said I needed to talk to Charles because I was mad and confused, and I wanted to kill him; I felt like he needed to go missing. That's when Darla reminded me this is the reason that she had me text that promise that I wouldn't tell Charles.

The next morning he called, and I tried my best to act normal. Every morning, I used to start our conversations with my sexy voice and a special radio shout out to him from me because 'that's my man.' I couldn't quite fake it because my emotional energy was off the charts. I faked my way through the conversation, but he still picked up that something wasn't right, and he was probably scared the ladies called me. I knew that I was going to break up with him on my own merit because he wasn't going to move to Miami. I didn't have to reveal anything that went on with the conversation with me, Darla, and Freda. So, on January 3rd, I broke up with him. I told him that I knew he wasn't really serious about me because he hadn't mentioned moving to Miami and that he knew that was a requirement for us being married. I told him that he was wasting my time, that he withholds dick, and that I haven't been sexually satisfied yet. After I went on that rant, can you believe he actually said he was going to marry me? I told him that I felt like I was a project to him – a Miami hood rat that he was trying to build up for his personal use – and that I was done.

Then he said he needed to come clean about a few things. He said he really loves me, and then he said, 'I have had sex with all of them.' I asked him who he was talking about, and he started naming names: Darla, Freda and you, Naivea, were the names I recognized. I was in shock! He didn't say anything about the fact that he had married you all, just that there was a sexual relationship."

Darla chimed in, "See, even on January 3rd he was still denying to me that he had a relationship with you, Naivea, but he told Pamela that he had." Pamela continued, "After he told me about all these women, I started crying and telling him that he lied to me, so I could get off the phone and get on the show. After the show I called him back and that is when I broke up with him. He did not realize that I had talked to Darla and Freda.

During my next conversation with Charles, which was the next day, I told him that I called Darla to talk to her because he namedropped everyone, and I said, 'and so this is your wife? You got me playing in this woman's face, thinking that she's the help, but I'm the help! Got this woman mad at me because she knows I'm on my knees sucking your dick in Raleigh – that's why she's mad!' Immediately, he went into his manipulative spill. He had also told me that he was up in Portland with his mother, or at his rental property in Olympia, Washington. All that time he was in Seattle living with Darla and her boys – that's another thing I found out on January 1st. I cut him off from his game and told him that I knew he wasn't with his mother, and he was stunned that I knew."

Darla interjected, "This man was here one and a half years, only two and a half hours from his mother, and he never went to see about her once! He has this picture that he circulates to you all when he wants to make excuses about having to take care of her. But that picture was taken several years ago when he was here in Seattle, and I drove him down to Portland to see her. He told me to wait outside the restaurant in the car while he met with his mother. He does not love his mother, and he does not want to see her. Whatever the situation was, it pertains to his childhood, and it was obviously very bad.

He told me not to go far if I wanted to get something to eat because he wasn't going to stay long. He didn't even want me to come into the restaurant where they were to get something to eat. That was the only time in all these years that he's seen his mother, yet he is quick to lie and tell you all that he is taking care of a sick mother to throw you off from insisting that he come to see you all. This is a damn shame. All of us have been played like a fiddle. "

Naivea started to get hot. She had a thought to share. "He seems to get great pleasure and even demonic energy from manipulating us. I remember a few times that I was in Raleigh in bed with him and he would be on the computer listening to Pamela's radio show, knowing that he was playing us both." Darla spoke up, "Yes, that was normal. There were times that I was on my knees sucking his dick, and he had the radio on agreeing with what Pamela was saying, not at all being intimate with me. It's like he gets a lot of energy from knowing that he has all of us in check – one here, and one on the phone, while this one is on her knees." Now Naivea was certain that it wasn't just money that Charles was thinking of when they were together as he had Pamela's show playing – it was the fact that he had control over all these women.

Naivea spoke up. "I really need to pray because I can't talk to anyone in my environment about this. My family is hovering around me like vultures on dead meat asking what's going on. It's been four years! One of my friends actually told me to tell Charles it's time to piss on the pot or get up! And my church members—because I didn't know any better—I'm talking to people at the church about my relationship and my elders are my brothers; and they're coming saying what's going on with you and this guy, he ought to know by now if you are the one for him. You just need to go ahead and cut this." Freda agreed, "Exactly! I've had that same thing from my family, only my family knew about it early on."

Freda then changed the subject, "When Charles was back home from Darla's house, he got back to Raleigh and reengaged all the women he was having close phone relationships with." Darla added, "Yes, he went back home and went crazy." Naivea was puzzled, "The whole thing is crazy to me. He got the ultimate woman in you, Darla. You do everything for him. You even iron his pajamas, and he did this. The whole thing is just crazy." Naivea's brain was on overload trying to understand what was happening; not only to her, but to all of the women.

Freda wanted to console Darla, "He's not going to find another Darla at all." Pamela agreed, "No, not in a million years. He can search far and wide." Freda continued, "He's getting too old to get out there and attempt to find someone to put up with his crap. He is slipping and he's going to slip up with these modern younger women if he tries to go after them. I don't think he'll go after the younger ones because they'll only be after him for his money and he wants people to fall in love with him and worship him." Everyone agreed with Freda.

Darla had a thought. "I remember how we would do these dinners and breakfasts – very healthy, very gourmet-like, and the table was always set, and Charles got to where he thought he was a king. If he came out of the office after I said we were ready, but I had gotten up again to do something, and things weren't in perfect order with everyone sitting at the table, he would fuss and say, 'Why isn't everybody sitting? The kids and you need to be sitting, waiting until I come!' So, we would just sit and wait until he came out. Sometimes he was on the phone with you, Naivea, or Pamela, and I'd be steaming mad because the food was getting cold, and I would have to heat it up again." Everyone laughed, but Naivea was thinking, "This man is a megalomaniac! How did I get bamboozled by him?"

Freda made a calculation. "When you got into that courtship with him it was only one and a half months from start to marriage, Darla. You didn't get a chance to learn who he really is and that's what a narcissist does. They get you entangled within the first 60 to 90 days of knowing them, so you don't have a chance to know the real person until you're entrenched; and once you're entrenched, they don't have time to keep up the act. They're going to go back to who they truly are, and that's what you recognize. You didn't get a chance to know Charles long enough to say okay, this is genuine or not genuine."

Darla got a little angry at her decision to rush into marriage. "He keeps calling me and saying that he did wrong and made mistakes and I need to have grace and mercy and he's changing his ways and that he learned, he didn't know that would upset his wife, and once he knew it upset me, he would never do it again. That's a lie too!" Naivea agreed. "Not only is that a lie, but what he did to us was no mistake. These were not mistakes." Freda agreed, "That's right, mistakes are leaving the pot on the stove too long and burning the rice. This was not a mistake." Naivea continued, "You don't mistakenly fly people out." Freda chuckled, "Ya'll got flewed out!" The four of them laughed loudly. Freda proclaimed, "That's okay ladies. This is just going to make us wiser and stronger."

The four ladies then started to discuss the first, real, state-sanctioned wife, Ida. Freda asked Naivea if she was going to Raleigh to find out what Ida knows and Naivea said no. It appeared that all four ladies had a desire to know if Ida was involved in this scheme, because she was obviously not living with Charles during all of the years that he had these four women thinking they were wives, or a potential wife in the case of Pamela. Freda commented, "That would be an interesting meeting. It would be a chance for us to understand her pain because she's probably gone through a lot, and she may even be open to a conversation." Naivea interjected, "I don't want to know any more details, it won't be helpful for me to know any more details about any of this." Freda agreed, "Yes, you're probably right, it won't help with the healing."

The ladies agreed and said good night.

Chapter 15 Commentary
The Tea on NPD and Relationships
Telsha Edenburgh

Pamela's story was quite interesting. One thing I wanted to say about Pamela is that when Pamela was talking, and she said that the first time I saw him was in May of last year when he returned to Raleigh, but before that, they were cultivating an emotionally driven romantic relationship, that's how the snake charmer charms you. He was charming. Her situation went a little faster than Naivea's I think, because she said herself that she was hot to trot, meaning that she was a sexually driven person.

Charles sodomized Pamela twice. I can understand why she didn't want to get into it. In my life, that's what narcissist number 1 – the one that I was engaged to – that's what he wanted to do. And I said, why do you have such a fascination with that? But I wanted to go on record and say that this is indicative of the spiritual stronghold in their souls. And that's very important for people to know, because this is how people's destinies are stolen, is through their rectum. Sodomy is high level sorcery.

In high level sorcery, if they want to steal the destiny of a particular person, they sodomize the person. And that's how the destiny is stolen – it's through that act of sodomy. It's high-level witchcraft and sorcery. That just goes to show you why most narcissists have a fascination with that part of the body. Also, in that world, the rectum is considered the mouth of Satan. So, when they insert the penis into the rectum, it's like they're inserting it into Satan's mouth. And that's the gruesomeness of that world, because everything is supposed to be gruesome, and opposite of what God wants. And it's also the act of depositing life in a place where waste is.

These narcissists are stealing destinies from unsuspecting people. And those destinies become, what the Bible calls "the treasures of darkness" because these destinies didn't belong to the enemy. People need to understand that being with a narcissist is spiritual warfare. It's not just that you're with a person that's evil, you're with a person that is literally being controlled by demons, and they're doing everything under a demonic agenda, whether they know it or not. It's their actions that are being perpetuated by the spirit that's inside of them.

The only way that they can go back and reclaim that destiny is they would have to destroy that covenant and destroy the stronghold. That person would have to repent and uproot that whole action and that act. Even though they didn't mean to do it and they didn't know what was happening with it. Their bodies and their souls were still involved in it.

They need to repent for that. And they need to ask God to cleanse them from that. And then they have to go back and destroy that covenant and the altar that was created to pull that destiny from them. What I mean by stolen destiny is their ability to have children, that could be sacrificed; their ability to maintain and sustain happiness and have a husband or a wife or be married, that could be sacrificed. So, it doesn't have to just be the person's life that is sacrificed and they die, it could be different parts of their lives that could be wagered on a demonic altar.

But I saw some things in Darla that was just really concerning. Something's truly wrong with her. Darla wanted to paint Naivea out to be the toy, but she wasn't the toy. Pamela Pie was actually the toy, because he didn't want commitment with her. He promised and lied to her and said that's what he wanted, but she was a tertiary Supply. So, you have main Supply, you have secondary Supply, and she would be considered like a tertiary Supply. Tertiary Supplies are ones that they engage with, but they don't engage with them as often or as frequent and as intimately as they do with the main or secondary Supply. Although she was on the radio show, and he was showing interest in that as a money-making vehicle, he had plenty more intimate engagements and interactions with the main and secondary Supplies.

During the main portions of the book, Darla was the main Supply. It used to be Freda, but it went from Freda to Darla when Charles found that he could use Darla to grow the business because Freda didn't have the time to do so. At that time, Freda and Naivea became secondary Supplies, with Pamela Pie rounding it out as the tertiary Supply.

And all of Charles' other women were right along in that same place with Pamela Pie, because there were others that he tinkered with, but they didn't have positioning like the top tier Supplies. The top four Supplies were working in Charles' business in one capacity or another, thus, he was engaging with them on a more frequent basis, according to what Darla was saying. And Darla knew about Naivea and everyone else named in the book. She knew about the other people too. That's why it was so crazy.

CHAPTER SIXTEEN
A WIFELY TUG-OF-WAR

When Naivea woke up the next morning and looked at her phone, she realized that Darla had called her after midnight when her phone was on silent, so she called back. Darla had stayed up half the night mulling over in her mind how and when Naivea and Charles were together. Naivea told Darla the times she was at his house and the times she was at a hotel instead. Darla proclaimed, "This fills in a huge gap for me because I wondered for years, how is it that Naivea is in town, but Charles didn't go see her? I knew the two of you would have sex. He would talk about your breasts a lot. He said it didn't mean anything, that it's just a body part. I know him and his pattern. He gets close and the closeness brings connection and the connection brings intimacy. That was the pattern in my head, and I could see him doing that with you and with others, and it scared me because I know what happened with us. The moment I connected the two of you I knew I'd made a huge mistake! It was instant on that first call. Something hit me in my gut. I told Charles everything that I'd heard about you and the research that I did about your training success, and I knew he was going to be pleased with me for finding such a good person to train the sales team.

We had several types of team calls, and the interesting thing is that I didn't connect him to everybody before the call. I also introduced you to Charles because your fee for the teleconference was a bit high. Little did I know the following year he was going to be fucking you. This man is something else! When I got both of you on the phone and he got excited about your bio and experience, I said to myself, 'I don't know what trouble I have on my hands but I'm in some trouble.' We were only five months into the marriage and it felt weird, so I stayed close to you. You were the first red flag in our marriage."

Naivea started wondering how many red flags appeared from that time to now. She started wondering again why Darla never told her about the marriage, especially now that this woman has revealed all of the grief that she endured due to Charles and Naivea's relationship. "If it were me, I would have confronted him long ago," Naivea thought. Darla continued, "After you did the teleconference, we got off the phone and I felt the excitement in him. He was intrigued with you, and I even felt a type of physical energy between the two of you. To this day, I have not introduced him to another person, and I told him that I never will.

He called me right back after the teleconference. I was here in Seattle, and he was in Raleigh. He started asking me did I think we could collaborate with you, and as the dutiful wife I said 'absolutely,' even though in my heart I wanted you to disappear right then. He then said we would figure out what we can do with you. We talked about events, meetings, and sales trainings all over the country. Then he said let's get her on a call, and at first, he would never call you without me on the phone. I felt secure in that. And then one day he told me that you called him, and that was my first beef with you, the first time I got upset with you, and that remained for a long time."

Naivea spoke up. "I never called him; he always called me." Darla responded, "That actually makes sense, I didn't know he lied. The next time I flew out to Raleigh, I was determined to get his attention off you, so I made sure that I was extra freaky in bed. I didn't say this before, but he liked anal sex with me. He used to bend me over from the back and fuck me in the butt until I squirted, so I made sure on that next trip I gave him what he wanted so I could get his focus back on me. By the way, did you all have anal sex?" It was as if Darla was holding back on asking Naivea that question for the longest, hoping that she said no, so that she would at least have one thing that was hers alone. "Heck No!" Naivea was disgusted. Charles had mentioned anal sex to her before, saying that he used to date a girl that liked anal sex. Naivea had given Charles such an emphatic NO that he never asked her about it again. Now she realized that he wasn't talking about someone that he dated in the past, he was talking about Darla, and all she could think about in the moment was her putting Charles' penis in her mouth after he had rammed it down Darla's rectum!

Aside from being disgusted, Naivea was a little upset now. She realized that Darla had a beef with her from the beginning, but she wondered how she was supposed to know that Charles and Darla were married. Charles certainly wasn't revealing that fact. "Darla knew what kind of man she had from the beginning, and she let this masquerade go on for years." Naivea said to herself.

Darla went on. "I thought I was protecting our marriage by keeping close tabs on you, but it's evident that I wasn't achieving that goal because even though you two were miles apart you still managed to form an emotional and spiritual bond and even a physical bond. He used to always talk about keeping his private life private. But what he was doing didn't need protecting. It was way past time to stop the secrecy, which I always hated. I always said to him, there's a difference between private and secret, and we have to protect our private married life from all these women coming after you but keeping our marriage a secret is not good. He tried to placate me by introducing me to a few people in his life, but not many. He would say, 'If I tell these women that we're married, they'll take it out on you, Darla. They will be angry towards you, and they'll stop doing business with me.' To me that didn't make sense. When I pressed him, he said he was the leader and that I needed to follow his leadership, so I let it be. He promised me an announcement and a big ceremony, so for years I held on to that. Now I know that all he was doing was keeping me and the rest of you a secret so he could have multiple women."

Naivea noticed that Darla refused to refer to any of the other women as wives, only herself. "She talks as though I was only a sex toy to Charles. I wonder why, since Freda was a wife before her and Ida is still Charles' state-sanctioned wife." She started focusing back on Charles and what he had done to her. "Nobody can be this evil," Naivea began to rant. "Several times he got mean and disrespectful to me and I would tell him I was done, but he would reel me back in with talk of a ring, a marriage ceremony for my family and friends, a visit, or some sad story. Is this a human being? I also noticed a lot of similarities in why he picked us. I was sheltered, and you mentioned being sheltered. Also, Charles told me the reasons he picked me, and the first was that I grew up with a dad in the home, meaning that I knew how to respect a man. Another big similarity was that we both were cheated on, and he always wanted to know so much detail about that!" "Same here," Darla shrieked.

Naivea continued, "I felt that he thought that I was used to being cheated on so I wouldn't kill him if I found out what was going on. He always complained about my guns and knives, and I wonder if he was scared that I would blow his head off if I found out anything." Darla was quiet after those comments by Naivea. Naivea figured it was time to get off the phone, so she told Darla she had to go to the bank, and Darla mentioned that she had to go to the doctor. They ended the call.

The next day, Darla called Naivea to see how she was doing. She mentioned that she had talked to Pamela. "Pamela's radio show ratings are down," she started. "It's because her countenance on the show is in the dumps. Pamela says she has to do something quick because she doesn't want to lose her show. She has decided not to promote the T-shirts anymore; she wants to cut all ties with Charles, but she's having a hard time trying to find a way to explain the departure to her audience. Pamela is at a very low point right now, just like us. She thought she was going to be Charles' wife. There were some listeners on her show that she felt wanted a relationship with her, but she blew them off because she thought she was going to be Mrs. Charles LaDron.

Remember when she revealed that she had been at his house in October doing the broadcast from there? Well, I told her that when she got to Raleigh, I had literally just left the day before. Then I remembered that you said you were there in early July. Well I came to Raleigh right after you left. To him, this revolving door of women made him feel like he was a god, or king or something. I thought about all those cameras he had put up here in Seattle and in Raleigh, and even the cameras he had Freda put up in her place – all so he could see us and make sure we weren't with any other man, and to make sure that none of the women ran up on his house surprising him when he has another one of us in there. That got my blood boiling this morning as I woke up, and I really had to get it off my chest, so thanks for answering the phone."

Naivea could tell that Darla was extremely agitated, and she wondered if Darla was going to have a nervous breakdown because she seemed to feel trapped with no other source of income. Naivea's heart also went out for Pamela. "He set all of us up!" she said in anger. "He's like a non-human entity that feeds off of our worship of him." Darla expounded, "Not only that, but he also gets off on playing us against each other. For example, you have a picture of Charles on your dresser facing your bed." Naivea, answered, "I HAD a picture of Charles on my dresser, but how did you know? Darla explained. "I have the same picture of him that you had on your dresser, and he showed me yours. Evidently you enlarged the picture that he texted you and placed it near your bed. My disgust with you was growing when I realized that you had a picture of my husband on your dresser so you could see him from your bed. He had to set up this animosity between us. It's the same thing he did with me and Freda. He wanted me, his wife, to hate all these women."

Naivea was fed up with Darla acting as if she was the only wife and the rest of the women were just flings. "Did he show you the picture right next to his picture? The one with me and him at a restaurant in Raleigh right after he had just ran me up one wall, through the bed, and down the other wall?" Naivea wanted to show Darla that she was the main Supply of many Supplies, but that she was just a Supply. "I don't think she understands what's going on here. All of us have been devastated, yet she still finds room to put herself above us, not understanding that she is the one that is worse off in this sick saga," Naivea thought.

"No, he didn't show me that one," Darla admitted. She changed the subject, "Ida has been at the house many times, and I believe she stays there sometimes. When Charles was in Seattle with me, I know that Ida received the packages that came to Raleigh. I didn't have the heart to tell Charles that I knew he was lying in my face when he said that Charles, Jr. would go and get the packages. I'd confronted him so many times before on different subjects, and it always blew up in my face and ended in a fight because he would shame me, insult me, guilt trip me, and always say he was right, and I was wrong. I believe they call that S.I.G.N. language. I got sick of hearing all his excuses and stories and I just stopped saying anything.

Ida would also send things there to Seattle for him. I think she thinks this is a rental property, just like he told you and all the others. He would say Charles Jr. sent it, but I could see that it was Ida's writing because I've seen her writing in the house before. I just kept quiet because I didn't feel like being gaslighted." Naivea, thinking that Darla was crazy to have known all of these things and stayed with Charles, started talking about the danger that Darla placed her and the other women in by not revealing what she knew. "It scares me that I've been laying up in that house and Ida could have showed up at any time and shot me. What if I was there in my lingerie or even naked and Ida walked in?"

Darla tried to dispel Naivea's concerns. "From day one of our marriage, I was over in Raleigh with him every month, sometimes for the whole month, until he came to Seattle to spend time here. But, after a year or so, I didn't go as much." Darla's comment didn't dispel the thought of being exposed by Ida's appearance at the house; nevertheless, Naivea's mind went in a different direction. "What did he think was the end goal of this?" Naivea said as if questioning herself out loud. "He should have known that all this would eventually go south. How come he didn't see that?"

Darla came back with a swift answer, "Because he let his dick rule him, and he let his greed for money and manipulation take over, and when you're juggling four, five, six …," Darla stopped and took a deep breath, "When we spoke at the beginning of last week, I said to him, 'Do you realize that you just told me SEVEN WOMEN?!' He then said to me, 'I got rid of Angela Baker, Naivea Hope, even Ida, and Tabitha. Freda and Pamela broke up with me before I broke up with them.' So that's six women and there was another one he mentioned in passing, and then your wife!"

She continued, "I failed to mention to you that there is a much younger woman that worked with him to get his consulting business up and running when he first moved to Raleigh – before the T-shirt business got started. She was an accountant and knew how to start businesses. He had this girl wrapped around his finger, and when we married and I came to Raleigh for that first Christmas, she had sent him gifts and a card. The card wasn't sealed, so I peeked in and almost passed out. The card referenced their two children that were in heaven! It was apparent to me that during their relationship she had had not one, but two abortions! Lately I've seen her face on his phone, indicating to me that he is still messaging her and vice versa. This is a nightmare!"

"What's her name?" Naivea asked, wondering if it was one of the women he'd showed her text messages from. "Her name is Joy, and she is still texting him. They broke up long ago but now it appears that she wants him back. He recently showed me a text from her where she is literally saying that she is ready to bend the knee to him!" "He showed me that blasted text too!" Naivea squealed. "He also showed me other text messages from her, and he said he left out the naked pictures that she sent. Seems like he was always trying to convince me that hundreds of women were after him, so I'd better be happy that I was his everything – his Moon."

Naivea wanted to counter punch Darla's constant insinuations that, just because he spent more time with her, she was the only real wife. She wondered where Darla got off with referring to herself as the only wife despite the existence of Ida and Freda. She thought to herself, "So, he admitted to Darla that there were at least seven women, including his first child's mother, Tabitha! And even Angela Baker, who he was with, supposedly at a party, on New Year's Eve! This monster must think he's King Solomon – four wives and four concubines." Naivea started to get sick at the stomach.

Then Darla went in, "Charles specifically told me that he didn't love you, but I said to him, 'if you don't love Naivea, how is she at our home in our bed spending days with my husband, cooking for my husband?' He said, 'She can't cook!' Then he tried to call you disparaging names to make me understand that it wasn't love." Naivea laughed, partly because it was true that she couldn't cook well, and partly because he evaded the question all together and Darla let him get away with it. She felt that Charles, in his sick way, was able to show her some semblance of love when they were together, and on the phone and FaceTime, and although she now knew that he was mentally ill, she knew that their relationship, whatever it could be called, was much more than just sex.

Naivea spoke up, "Again, I think back on the beginning of our relationship before our marriage [stressing to Darla that she too was married to Charles] when Charles told me, 'You will never be able to say that Charles LaDron betrayed you.' He is the best actor and liar that I've ever met in my life. Except for Satan, I haven't even heard of anyone that told lies so smoothly and eloquently." Darla agreed, "He is so dangerous. This is where he gets his energy from. It's like he's an entity outside of humanity that thrives on this chaos. That is why when I approached you, I wanted to emphasize the danger, because it is so easy to underestimate him, thinking he won't do this or that. Charles LaDron, if he thought that I spoke to one of the women and it interrupted his money flow, he would take me out – he would kill me. I don't have any doubt believing that!" Naivea felt that, without knowing it, Darla just admitted that it wasn't about him wanting his family back, but it was about making sure his money doesn't stop flowing from the business.

Darla continued, "If you and Charles didn't still have business together, then I would get on the phone with you and call him, but because he renewed your contract to train the team, I feel that he would kill me for telling you about our marriage. Last week when me, Freda, and Pamela were on the phone with him together, it was because all of us were done with him and there were no more business ties. Even after that call, Charles had the nerve to tell me not to talk to any other women that he was in business with, and I thought to myself, 'You mean in bed with?' He thought he had us all played, telling me that he didn't love Freda and Pamela, and that he was done with them, then immediately hanging up and calling Pamela and begging her to come back. He didn't know that the three of us were talking until last week when he was carrying on about not loving Pamela, and all that other foolishness. All three of us jumped on the phone at the same time and he just about crapped his pants! Once he realized that we had been talking for a while, and he thought back on the things he had told us individually and he got very defensive."

Darla was on a roll. "Earlier in our marriage, I told my boys that I planned to die in this marriage, and truth be told, the marriage was killing me slowly, but I was committed to stay in it for the sake of the family and the children." Naivea got the strange feeling that Darla was now talking herself into going back to Charles, even though he was still legally married to Ida. The way she had been calling him her husband, low-key denying that any of the other women were wives, and now talking about staying committed for the sake of the family, even though the boys weren't his and they were both grown men in their twenties. "I don't care if she does go back to him," Naivea thought. "I just want my money back, all that money he took from me talking about it being for our family and our union." Naivea needed to get off the phone, but she had a few things to relay to Darla before doing so. "My family had such high hopes for me finding love again, and he screwed it up."

Darla interrupted, "It's embarrassing, and he looks for people that he can manipulate. He likes that you have a relationship with your father, Naivea, and he likes that you are uncovered, that you've had some trauma in your life, and that you have strong earning capability. He tests you early on to see how much he has your loyalty. All of the women are scarily loyal to him, he creates this loyalty by being the knight in shining armor and making you feel that you need to depend on him in every aspect of your life. IT'S A CULT FOLLOWING!"

Naivea recognized that Darla left herself out of this cult framework. "But we don't know we're in a cult!" Naivea said loudly, partially blaming Darla for not revealing the parts of this horror movie that she saw earlier on. "When he broke me down was when he had me take a naked picture, and it was a really high high for him because I told him that I'd never done that before. The part that pisses me off is that, as you revealed, he immediately came and showed you, Darla, and proclaimed to you that I was after him – as if I had voluntarily come up with the idea to send him that picture. That's when he knew he'd broken me."

"Right," said Darla. "He did show me right away. And when he told me about the picture of him on your dresser and I said it makes no sense, he said that he'd talked to you and told you to remove it, but that you weren't listening to him." Naivea wanted to reiterate the reason she wasn't concerned about him being in what she thought was Portland and Olympia for such long periods of time. She wanted to leave Darla with the knowledge that her relationship with Charles was real, even thought they were not together much.

"Before we get off the phone Darla, I want to remind you that Charles, lying wonder that he is, told me that the reason he had to spend so much time in Portland during the end of the year, was that his brothers took care of his mom all year, and that it was his turn while business was a little show. Then he said he bought the house in Olympia and had to fix it up for rental. I thought that was very noble, and I encouraged it, not knowing that it was a lie and that he had a whole family not too far away in Seattle, and that he didn't spend any time in Portland with his mom, and the Olympia house was actually your house in Seattle.

Like I said, he's a lying wonder. Because I didn't have much experience with men at all, I didn't know how NOT NORMAL this was. In addition to the criteria that you mentioned earlier, I think he picks women that don't have a lot of experience in relationships with men, nor a lot of street sense. It's like in the Bible when the prophet Nathan told David about the rich man that had lots of lambs, but he went next door to the poor man's house and took and cooked his pet lamb.

Charles could have picked any of these women out there that are looking for a man, but he defiled me, someone that had been chaste for over four years waiting on the Lord to send me a husband. He took that from me and wasted four more years of my life lying to me. Charles will pay for it, by God." Naivea was now angry and weeping. Darla was disgusted. "He's such a dumb fuck, he knows nothing about how to run this T-shirt business except how much money I'm over here making for him and this family while he's going around the world getting women and breaking their hearts. Now my friends and relatives look at me sideways, but they don't understand the web we got into."

Naivea continued with her closing statements. "Know that he will continue to try to get back with you, Darla, because you are the goose that lays the golden eggs. You ultimately hold the key to his purse strings. And if they are truly still in a relationship like I suspect they are, Ida can't even get any money if you're not working the T-shirt business. So mark my words – he will continue to try and lure you back in for the sake of his income." With that said, I have to go, but keep yourself safe and stay away from this monster!"

The two women got off the phone.

CHAPTER SEVENTEEN
THE SISTERHOOD CRUMBLES

Throughout the next 30 days there were more phone calls, more texts and more revelations. Once Charles found out that Naivea knew about all of the other women, he bashed Darla, and called her unthinkable names for calling Naivea and some other women; but he still tried to convince her to get back with him.

Darla and Freda wanted to know what Ida knew. Naivea and Pamela did also. Darla found out where Ida worked, and they all cooked up a plan for Darla, Freda and Naivea to show up at Ida's job on a Friday afternoon around closing time and confront Ida in the parking lot. They figured they would all converge in Raleigh on a Thursday, stay overnight in a hotel, and drive to Ida's job Friday afternoon and wait for her to come outside. They knew what she looked like because Darla and Freda had found her on Facebook. Naieva wondered why she didn't find Ida way back when she was looking to find out more about "Charles' aunt that had the purse strings."

After planning for about a week, Darla decided that she wouldn't be able to fly to Raleigh because of her finances. Freda also backed out, claiming that she had a serious project going on at work. That left Naivea to fly out there and confront Ida on her own. Naivea didn't want to go out there on her own. It was a very risky plan to begin with. Ida could have had a weapon, she could have called security on her job, or she could have called the police on them. If all three of them, or even two of them were there, they would have a better chance to defuse the situation, but having only one there, Naivea, it would have been her word against Ida's.

By the time the plan started falling apart, Pamela had stopped joining in on the conversations. She told the women, "I'm moving on, ladies. I think that Ida is in charge and that she has Charles under her thumb. In all his past dealings I believe that somewhere he messed up big time, and she knows about it. Call it blackmail or whatever you want, but whatever it is that she knows, she's making him give her money, making him keep her on the bank accounts, and making him stay married to her to keep that secret." Naivea was surprised that Pamela had the perspective that Ida was in charge. Pamela had even called Charles a gigolo for Ida during the conversation, which Naivea thought would totally be poetic justice because of his perceived sexual prowess.

Darla and Freda still wanted to find out what Ida knew. The women stressed the importance of getting out to Raleigh soon before Charles figured out that they may approach Ida. Naivea really wanted to know, and she wasn't afraid to go, but she wasn't going alone. "I'll pay for your flight, Darla, and a separate hotel room near Ida's job," she said while the three of them were on the phone. "I still won't be able to go," Darla said sheepishly. "I have to stay here and finish packing up all of Charles' clothes to ship them back to Raleigh. This room has all these big boxes in it, and it looks like a graveyard." Naivea got the feeling that the two of them were trying to goad her into going alone, so she told them that she wasn't going alone and that she would just have to be okay with not knowing Ida's roll in this sick drama.

Then, in the second month, Darla started to turn back towards Charles – claiming that it wasn't just about her, but it was about her boys also. "He's their daddy," she said. She also started talking about marriage was for life, and that forgiveness is of God. Freda didn't have a problem with it, claiming that Darla had to keep working with Charles for now because she had no other source of income and Charles proclaimed that he wasn't paying the mortgage or any of the other bills at the Seattle home unless and until Darla continued to work the business. Naivea and Pamela were both stunned. Naivea considered a lawsuit against Charles for theft and breach of contract, and she told the ladies her thoughts. Freda and Darla, which had formed a very close bond, tried to talk Naivea out of exposing Charles and themselves, by filing a lawsuit.

Darla and Freda started calling Naivea daily to convince her to try and get her money back from Charles, instead of filing a lawsuit. Naivea never wanted to speak to Charles again, so she wrote one of her famous letters to try and get her money back. Here is the actual letter she wrote Charles:

Accountability – Consequences – Restitution

Charles LaDron,

You left my life in broken pieces. YOU KNEW that I had been through severe trauma in my younger years. YOU KNEW that I had been through a marriage with an adulterer, yet you still chose to further break me by telling me I was your wife and that we would be together in one household, knowing that you already had at least three wives including one that has a state-sanctioned marriage license and although she lives separately, she is still primary on your bank accounts and real estate.

You told me you were paying a staff of seventeen people and paid payroll every two weeks, but there was none. You were a river of lies while you continuously accused me of being a liar.

You told me that I needed to be held accountable for my mistakes and undesirable actions. You told me that there had to be consequences for my bad behavior. I hold myself 100% accountable for falling for someone that was not even a real person. The consequences for me being a woman willing to believe that "I am not Harold" and willing to trust you at your word, willing to forgive you for letting me down so many times when all that was a lie, of daring to believe in love one more time… the Consequences are DEVASTATING all the way around! At my age, I have just been set back a decade by the things that should have happened over the last four years that didn't happen because of your lies and deception.

Although some good lessons came in this time, these years that I could have been properly planning for my retirement years and to take care of my parents instead of preparing to be your housewife will never be given back, and because YOU KNEW I could never really be your wife you have stolen my time, money, energy and love! This whole saga is surreal and makes for a blockbuster movie!

Restitution – the restoration of something lost or stolen to its proper owner.

I am not able to get my time, energy and love back, but I would like you to partially restore me by giving me $100,000

USD. Much of that is for the money that I gave you on behalf of "our family," money that I borrowed from refinancing my home, and from the lawsuit from my old job, and from investing wisely. You have left me way behind and starting over financially.

I am an individual. My healing from this trauma is going to be different from the other women because of my age, and it must include restitution so that I can move on in a place that will help me be ready for retirement since I will not be a housewife.

There is no verbal conversation necessary. There is no negotiation to be made. The $100,000 USD does NOT include the exchange of personal gifts over the years. Nor does it include all of the work that I put into perfecting your projects for you as "your wife." Nor does this restitution include all of the pain and suffering from the constant gaslighting and S. I. G. N. language that I endured over the last four years as you continued to weave your web of lies. These damages are being balanced out with the good things that occurred during the last four years. In other words, there is a "wash" – the mental abuse factor goes to balance against the few positive outcomes there were.

Today is [Month, Date, Year]. Please respond by wiring the funds to:

Naivea Hope
[Bank]
[Routing number]
[Account number]

Either in a lump sum of $100,000 or $20,000 increments over the next five months, or in another payment plan that you spell out and I accept, that will be equally spread out and paid off no later than [Month, Date, Year]. You have cash at home and the T-shirt business brings in $50K or more per week.

If this is done, no legal or other actions will be taken against you, and I will consider the matter closed and you and everyone else involved will be in the process of being erased from my life.

Naivea Hope

Charles refused to return the money that she had invested in various projects for their marriage. Here is his actual response:

Naivea, you know I'm not reading this document. I can't even open it but I'm pretty sure of its tone and purpose. Please know that I never meant to hurt you, I apologize for my actions. I pray that you heal and forgive me. Please. Vetting, trying not to get played or hurt, and dealing with my own trauma, I wound up hurting many people, including you – it wasn't malicious or intentional. I am getting the help that I need. I poured into you, and I did love you. Everything I ever gave you or your family was from my heart.

Whether you send a message via document, text, email, fax or certified letter, I don't care to read about your contempt for me or go back-and-forth with you. You know I never cared for your long letters. I just want to move on with my life and I was hoping you'd do the same. If you absolutely have to get closure (I do think it's important), then please call me Monday evening (or a time fitting your schedule – I am away this weekend) and I will make time to hear you, and we can discuss our relationship like adults.

Naivea did not want to ever hear Charles' lying voice again. She totally cut ties with Charles after receiving his response and giving a short rebuttal, making sure he knew that his "pouring into her" could never offset the carnage that he left behind in her life.

Darla and Freda found out that Charles refused to give Naivea her money back, and they started to press her even harder to forego filing a lawsuit against Charles. Naivea knew that the two of them would talk on the phone, then call her on a three-way call to ask her not to file. Freda proclaimed her forgiveness of Charles. She said she had a three-hour conversation with him and told him how he had hurt her emotionally and financially, and that she got closure from just that conversation. Naivea thought to herself, "Good for her, but that's not cutting it for me, and I'm never speaking to him again."

Naivea tried once again to make the women understand why she wanted to move forward with the lawsuit. "Listen ladies. If a drunk man gets into a car and starts driving around hitting multiple cars and running from the cops, when he is caught, after leaving several crashed cars behind, there are consequences. The owners of those cars don't just proclaim forgiveness, get in their wrecked cars and drive off. There is restitution to pay for the damage. Charles has damaged several cars. If you two want to forgive him and drive off with wrecked cars, knock yourself out. I am not driving away with a car that is old and now irreparably damaged because he doesn't want to pay for the repairs!" Darla got upset with Naivea for not backing down off the lawsuit idea, and she said a few things that totally set

Naivea off. "You claim to have three Bibles on your bed, Naivea, but they don't seem to be doing any good." Naivea was outdone.

The day after Darla pissed off Naivea, Pamela called Naivea, and she told Pamela what the ladies were doing, what had transpired the night before, and that Darla seemed to want Charles back. Pamela went ballistic. "She just wants to get rid of all of us so that she can have him for herself!" Pamela blurted out. Naivea was surprised. She thought Pamela was over Charles, but evidently that wasn't the case.

Later that night, Pamela called Freda, then Darla, and cursed both of them out for their devious plan to stop Naivea from filing a lawsuit. She called Darla everything but a child of God for going back to Charles. Darla called Naivea after that tongue lashing and blamed her for telling Pamela about their conversation the night before. "Why did you tell her I am back with Charles? I'm back working with him but that has nothing to do with the marriage!" "I didn't tell her you were back with Charles. I told her what happened last night, and she went off. She accused you of trying to get rid of all of us so that you can have Charles for yourself!"

The next day, Pamela called all three women and told them to never contact her again. Pamela had found a man and, after exposing the saga to him, he told her to cut all ties with everyone involved. She had already cut ties with Freda and Darla. Pamela called Naivea and expressed her appreciation for her and the way she handled the whole saga. She said that this would be their last conversation and that she was deleting all their phone numbers and blocking Charles from all of her social media. Naivea wished Pamela well, and they said their goodbyes.

"It's funny how the sisterhood fell apart when Darla decided that she would go back to Charles," Naivea thought.

CHAPTER EIGHTEEN
THE LONG LONELY ROAD BACK TO NORMAL

April was a cold month for Naivea – physically, spiritually and emotionally. As she waited in line at the bank, while transferring money to make ends meet because of her financial state after Charles, she peered into the office of the branch manager. He wasn't there, but she noticed a framed quote on his wall, "Time is infinitely more valuable than money." She thought about the four years that she had spent with someone that wasn't real and had profusely lied to her every step of the way in the relationship. She thought about all the mental abuse, the shaming, the guilt trips and the insults. But the most hurtful thought that came into her mind was the fact that Charles had taken money from her, knowing that she could never really be his wife, and he could never really bring her into his household. Now she had to find a way to reignite her business so that she could make sure her parents were taken care of, because he had lied and said he would take care of them. Naivea began to weep in the bank. She swiftly turned and went to her car so that the people in the bank wouldn't see her. The tellers all knew her, and she didn't want any gossip to get started.

After she dried her tears, she went back into the bank to make the transfer. When she got home, she sat at her desk. She felt lonely and alone. She went from hating Charles to thinking about the good times they had. Then she said to herself. "I can't honestly look at those as good times because they were never real! It was all imaginary and I was trapped in a fairy tale with the story being made up by Charles daily. He is not real – he is imaginary. But I miss him.

Naivea sat at her desk thinking about the last four years, until it was dark. She then wrote a poem before going up to her room for bed. She placed the poem in a special drawer in her desk, where she kept other reminders to never again be seduced by Satan.

Missing The Imaginary You

I'm missing the imaginary you
The one that was telling me the truth
The one that said he'd revive my youth
The one that said he'd love me to the end
The one that had me on the mend

I'm missing the imaginary you
The one that told me I was hot
The one that said, "You're all I've got"
The one that accepted me – faults and all
The one that didn't care about "the wall"

I'm missing the imaginary you
The one who said he'd take care of me the rest of my life
The one that said I was his beautiful wife
The one that stood with me through pain and strife
Not the one that stabbed me in the heart with a knife

I'm missing the imaginary you
The one who said I was your queen, your muse, your Moon
The one that said we'd be in one household soon

But after four years it turned out to be a scam
I got punked, I got jilted, I got flimflammed!
And I'm left here picking up the pieces
Mournfully missing the imaginary you.

Epilogue

Naivea was devastated. She couldn't wrap her brain around the fact that this demon, this man with spiritual leprosy, knowing about her serial cheating ex-husband, and knowing about the life-devastating event that happened to her immediately before her divorce, still came into her life and sucked the love, time, energy, and money out of her for four years.

A year after the saga was exposed:

Naivea has had no contact with Charles, Freda, Darla, Pamela, nor any of the others involved. After expressing her love and devotion to Charles just months earlier, Pamela was soon married to another man. Naivea knew this because Pamela announced it on her radio show. Pamela went on to grow her audience and become the best radio show host in Miami, and Naivea was happy for her.

Naivea struggled to build her business after scaling back so that she could be a good housewife for Charles. She started therapy three months after the revelation that Charles had multiple wives. Five months after starting therapy, she retained an attorney to explore the possibilities of getting her money back from Charles, via a mental abuse, breach of contract, or theft by deception lawsuit. She goes back and forth as to whether to expose him and his business so that other women won't get caught in this trap.

Naivea doesn't care if Charles ever remembers her name. She just wants to save other women from his clutches and inform other women and men that people like Charles exist. Naivea sometimes thinks about the other vulnerable women that were caught in this web, and that maybe some very vulnerable woman in the future may commit suicide after finding out what Charles is doing to her and others.

It's unknown whether Darla is back with Charles in the marriage relationship, but she is still listed on the T-shirt business website as a key contact. It's also unknown whether Charles is still married to Ida.

This book is the final step in closure for Naivea. It was also written to make as many men and women aware that yes, there are people out there that will, despite your past hurts and tragedies, still use you, abuse you, and devastate your life.

Ladies and gentlemen both. Please be careful and get to know people before jumping into relationships that you desire will lead to marriage. If the relationship is a long distance one, please wait even longer and make sure you spend sufficient time in the presence of the person before committing to them.

If you got caught up with a narcissist, you cannot get into a self-destructive pattern. Here are some ways I learned to heal and give myself closure:

- Acknowledge that it was literal abuse, and it was not your fault.

- Allow yourself space to grieve and to feel sadness, anger, and confusion.

- Seek support through friends, family, support groups, or

informed therapists or coaches.

- Set a boundary and go NO CONTACT with the narcissist.

- Journal – write down your experience, like I did.

- Focus on the present by letting go of the potential of the relationship and who you thought the narcissist was.

- Forgive yourself for your perceived mistakes and realize that you didn't know then what you know now.

- Find the closure within yourself. Focus on your own healing, your self-care, setting goals for the future and creating a fulfilling life.

- Healing takes time, so seek support whenever you need it.

And finally, if you've been seduced by Satan, don't get lost in your pain. Know that one day your pain will become your cure. Let go, and let God turn your pain into powerful purpose!

Naivea Hope

Chapters 16 - 18 and Epilogue Commentary
The Tea on NPD and Relationships
Telsha Edenburgh

In Chapter Sixteen, Darla was outwardly comparing her relationship with Charles to what she perceived to be his relationships with Naivea and the other women, especially since Charles had proclaimed to Naivea on the overheard phone conversation, that he had given her the highest honor in marriage. Darla appeared to be elevating herself high above the other women in status because she had a ring and a certificate, and Charles had stayed with her during the lockdowns. In actuality, she, being the main Supply, was earning Charles thousands of dollars a day through the business, without him having to pay her for it, so instead of having a privileged status, she was more along the lines of being a servant.

Darla is fact-finding, trying to find out a timeline of when Charles and Naivea had been together during the entire four-year saga. It appears that her thought pattern centered around mitigating the importance of Naivea's relationship with Charles based on the limited time they spent together physically. Darla had put Charles in the place of God, and now she was trying to trick her mind into justifying that move by making herself the queen of the harem of women in Charles' life.

She was trying to show in these conversations that she had more experience with Charles than all the other women, and the others were just little side pieces. It was some type of solace that she wanted to give to herself because she knew she was being a fool for him. She basically covenanted herself spiritually to this man. She let him do everything, including have anal sex with her, which we already talked about as being the gateway to hell when we discussed it in Pamela Pie's case. You gotta remember, when you're dealing with a narcissist, you're dealing with a person that has a spirit of perversion. So anything that's perverted, they want. When it came to Naivea, which Darla said was the scourge of her marriage, it's just as sick for her to look at the anal sex as an exclusive between her and Charles once she found out that Naivea wasn't down for that.

This woman also sacrificed herself for that wealth that he has—that he didn't give her none of—because she's already committed herself to him. And on that altar, she can't leave. She ain't gonna leave him; she ain't going nowhere. She in that with him. For life. I kept thinking to myself, how she making that type of money like that, and he's not giving her anything. Like he owed her all of that money. But she had sacrificed herself. That's why she kept giving him her rectum. Like most people that are spiritually bound to a narcissist, she knew it was bad. They know that they need to go. They know that this person is not being honest, but they can't leave because it's a spiritual thing that they've done.

A lot of times, there are similarities in the way a narcissist will pick his or her Supplies; they have certain "check marks" that they like the Supplies to adhere to. Even though Darla and Naivea didn't like each other, they had some traits in common, and these are probably the traits that Charles selected them for.

Both women grew up with a father in the home, presumably they learned how to obey a man. Another trait mentioned was that both of them had husbands that were serial adulterers. Charles likely picked that trait because he thought they would put up with him having other Supplies. Darla obviously did, but Naivea didn't. One other trait that all four of the women shared is that they were older and probably lonely. Bad people in general, and Charles specifically, prey on older single women, playing on their emotions and their desire for companionship. It looks as if, at least in the case of Darla, Naivea, and Pamela, Charles did this. Freda and Charles went to high school together, so that situation may have been a little different, but Freda was older and single when they reconnected.

One more trait these women had is either they had money, access to money, or the ability to make lots of money. Charles had a thriving business because of Darla, but he was a greedy man and wanted more. Naivea and Pamela supplied him with thousands more. His relationship with Freda had cooled down by the time these other women came on the scene, but prior to that, she had purchased him two luxury vehicles and given him her relocation funds.

Charles was a greedy cerebral sociopathic narcissist, and because if this, I can honestly say that Charles didn't choose his Supplies at all. The demons inside of him told him who to choose. The demons told him which ones he could lock in on and manipulate. So, how he chooses each Supply is spiritual. It has nothing to do with how you look naturally. These demons tell him, "This is what you need," according to what they want to get done and what their agenda is. When he's going through the interviewing process, the demons are telling him what to ask. He doesn't know that because it's just questions in his conscious mind, but it's coming from a subconscious place. They tell the narcissist which man or woman to choose, or else the narcissist wouldn't be able to get it right and have such power over the Supplies.

This is how it works. When narcissists are interviewing you, they're not just carnally interviewing you. Those spirits are actually gathering information too, because they're trying to see how they're actually going to manipulate you in the scope of things. The information that they're gathering develops into how he's going to use that information carnally. But the spirits are telling him how to manipulate the Supply, because people can't just manipulate a person like this on their own. It's too deep, it's too vast. It's too entangled and entwined for a normal person to just naturally do that.

Another point that I want to make about these last few chapters of the book is that when the narcissist is being used by the enemy, the thing the demons have to do is make them fearless in their sin, because the demons need the narcissists to keep sinning. That's the way the enemy is keeping the narcissist's soul bound and working for him.

A good example is how Charles appeared to have no fear of the women finding out about each other. At one point Darla was trying to get a timeline for when Naivea was at the Raleigh home, or in Raleigh at all. Once the ladies started putting the puzzle together, they realized that Charles had a revolving door going, except for during the lockdowns. As soon as one woman left, another one was in town within 48 hours. He didn't even seem afraid that one was going to show up while another one was there. Part of that confidence was the fact that he had cameras all around and inside the house. But beyond that he didn't fret when it came to planning to have each Supply at his side.

I noted that Charles fed off of the women being upset at, jealous of, or in competition with each other. In her conversation, Darla said that Charles showed her a nude picture of Naivea at the beginning of the relationship, and again showed her a picture of Charles on Naivea's dresser. He may have also talked to Freda and the others about their counterparts just to get a rise out of them – a touch of jealousy from them so that they would never contact each other. The fact that Darla and Freda became friends probably didn't bother Charles because he knew that Darla would never say anything about their marriage, as he had told her not to. We see that it was Freda that ended up confessing to Darla about their relationship. We know that Darla wasn't going to tell anyone anything. She even knew a lot about Ida – way before her hospital stay.

Speaking of Ida, in Chapter Seventeen, the conversation starts out trying to determine just who this Ida is. We don't find out much about Ida in the book. However, since she and Charles were still married, and it was clear they didn't live in the same house, my guess is that she may have agreed to a polyamorous relationship with Charles. Darla told Naivea that during her last visit, when she was stuck at the hotel, it was probably Ida that was taking pictures of the purse that Charles gave Naivea. It may have been another woman, too.

Another theory is that since Ida had sent packages to Darla's house, not knowing it was another wife; and she sent the police to Darla's house for a wellness check on her husband, she didn't know what Charles was doing, and maybe they were just estranged. Ida is the biggest mystery in this book. On the one hand she lives in a nearby city instead of living with Charles, but on the other hand all of the property and bank accounts are in her name. Ida and Charles must have worked out some serious kind of deal!

I think he probably told Ida that even though he may go and take on other wives, that she would be the only one that he was on paper with. And that every investment and all the money that he made, because she was the wife on paper, she would be the only one that had access to those assets, as long as she agreed to his scheme.

This is how manipulative he was. See, he needed to get somebody that would be weak enough to agree to it so he could play other women, because there was no way he was going to be able to get on paper with another woman, because he was already on paper with Ida. So, all he was going to do was manipulate the other women, and tell them about a spiritual marriage.

Now, Pamela Pie thinks that Ida is in charge and that she has Charles under her thumb and that whatever it is that she knows, she's making him give her money, keep her on the bank accounts, and stay married to her.

Let me just say something about Ida. Pamela Pie may have been right in her assessment that Ida was in charge in the marriage to Charles. Ida had him on the hook by default, because she's his "real" wife. They've been married over ten years on paper. So, he's got to answer to her, whether he wants to or not. He can't divorce her without her consent, and she may not want a divorce; so as Pamela says, Ida may be the true kingpin of the group.

Another observation is that in this book Charles is in his mid-fifties. Although he's tall and appears to have been handsome, he won't be able to keep this up for much longer. He won't be able to pull the young or older pretty women in his old age. Those demons wear on you physically as well as mentally. His memory is going to start to slip. It's almost over for him. It's like an old dog strutting around, biting people; now, he's losing his teeth and his eyesight.

Also in Chapter Seventeen, Naivea threatened a lawsuit against Charles for theft and breach of contract. Darla was originally being nice to Naivea, but the lawsuit brought out her true colors; and in her defense of herself and Charles, she severely offended Naivea and set her off, showing that they were never in a sisterhood. This is what I have to always remind myself of – that when I'm dealing with people, especially when dealing with contrary people, I have to remember that people will do and say and behave out of what's rooted and grounded in their hearts. Out of the abundance of the heart, the mouth speaks; and Darla still had an inner hatred for Naivea, even after all of the revelations of what Charles had done.

Darla and Freda were not only against the lawsuit because they would be exposed and their secret would be revealed, but they wanted to protect Charles. I also think that they were afraid that Charles would find out all the things they told Naivea about him, and about their relationships during the initial fallout of revealing his web. Yes, I believe they were desperate to keep everything quiet – especially Darla – because everyone, and I mean everyone, would have been questioning her as to why she stayed in that relationship knowing that Charles was married to Ida, and that he had all these other women. Now, Freda was a defender of both Charles and Darla. She seemed to want to stay in the shadows also, and she didn't want Charles to know that she too, had also been running her mouth to Naivea and Pamela. What stands out to me in this section is my belief that Darla and Freda had developed Stockholm Syndrome. They were in an abusive relationship, and once it was revealed that Charles had all these woman, normal women would have done what Naivea did, and cut ties. These two women began to defend their abuser. That's classic Stockholm Syndrome. When you can sit there and know all of this information and still be able to rock with an individual, you have Stockholm Syndrome. You have bonded with your abuser, and you're okay with that. We're looking at Freda, who was eight years into the relationship with Charles, and Darla who was five years into it. You've got that Syndrome because you don't have anything else that's holding you and binding you to that individual other than manipulation.

Naivea's letter to Charles asking for her money back summarized all of the tactics narcissists use on their Supplies; calling them liars when they are the ones that habitually lie, shaming them, putting them on guilt trips and extracting money from them. Charles showed his true colors with his response. He said he was getting help, but in the end, we can see that he was non-repentant, and he doubled down on his idea that he had helped Naivea's life improve somehow, amidst all of the damage that he caused.

In Chapter Eighteen, we begin to see the aftermath of the whole episode. Naivea is no longer tied to Charles or any of the women, and she had to start putting her life back together.

When Supplies get to this point, there is a long road ahead. The best thing to do is start self-reflection and self-care. Reading, meditating, going to a good therapist, and maybe even some deliverance sessions will be of great benefit to get on the road to recovery.

The two worst things a Supply can do after the ultimate discard are (1) to isolate yourself, because when a Supply isolates themselves, it's easy for the devil to pick them off mentally – like a lioness picks off an isolated gazelle in the wilderness; and (2) to jump into another relationship.

A lot of times when people go through this, they just want to forget about it. They don't want to talk about it. You can see how painful it was for Naivea and all of the women. Imagine going through this and telling someone what you've gone through, and having people looking at you like you've lost your mind. Because they're trying to figure out how you got yourself into that situation, and at the same time their looking at you with pity, because let's be real – most people are gonna say, "How could you be this stupid?"

I don't like it when people say stuff like that because they don't understand the level of manipulation that victims endured. Victims aren't responsible for another person's actions and the way that they live their lives. We didn't know. Now, once you find out about it, now it's your decision. It's your job to do something about it. But I didn't know that these people lied like that, nor did Naivea.

If this happens to you, please tell somebody. An isolated Supply can get into their own mind games, blaming themselves totally for the situation, and this could lead to serious mental and physical problems. It may even lead to suicide.

Now, the absolute worst thing a Supply can do after the end of a relationship with a narcissist is jump into another relationship – with a narcissist or otherwise. When this is done, all of the baggage from the abusive relationship is carried right into the next. There was no self-reflection, no therapy and no deliverance. This appears to be what Pamela Pie did, and we will never know the outcome of that new relationship that she entered just months after the breakup with Charles. However, the typical outcome when a Supply "rebounds" into another relationship turns out much worse when a normal relationship ends, and the person jumps straight into another one. Both of the individuals usually suffer in multiple ways, which would be a whole other book, so I will leave it at that.

Finally, in Chapter Eighteen, the poem that Naivea wrote reflects the fact that she realizes that she had been living in a fantasy world under demonic influence for four years. It usually takes people two or more years to get back to some semblance of normalcy. Although it will be rough for her, eventually she will be able to smile again, and hopefully to love again.

In the epilogue, the thing that jumped out at me was the use of the term spiritual leprosy. Charles, and other narcissists do have spiritual leprosy – that's an excellent term to use for them. They don't have feelings, and their useful parts fall off as time goes by while they live in their sin, until they are no more.

In conclusion, this book is a summary of a narcissistic relationship that takes place over four years with a narcissist with multiple Supplies. It's not even a relationship – it's a constant transaction. Some people call it a transactionship. I call it an addictionship. But I'll say this: it's a powerful summation of what people literally go through in these relationship endings. And it's unfortunate that their story sometimes never gets told. I'm glad that Naivea had the courage to stand up and be heard!

Telsha Edenburgh